T0369366

HE THAT OVERCOMES

A Study In The Book Of Revelation

H. A. "Buster" Dobbs

WESTBOW
PRESS
A DIVISION OF THOMAS NELSON

ISBN: 978-1-4497-3061-1 (e)
ISBN: 978-1-4497-3062-8 (sc)
ISBN: 978-1-4497-3063-5 (hc)
Library of Congress Control Number: 2011960105

WestBow Press books may be ordered through booksellers or by contacting:

WestBow Press
A Division of Thomas Nelson
1663 Liberty Drive
Bloomington, IN 47403
www.westbowpress.com
1-(866) 928-1240

Printed in the United States of America

WestBow Press rev. date: 11/15/2011

To the incomparable Martha

Foreword

The book of Revelation is an often misunderstood and largely neglected part of the New Testament. The ordinary reader is many times confused by the imagery and highly-spiritual nature of the book. And yet, a blessing attends the reading and respectful keeping of the admonitions it contains (Rev. 1:3). If the book is not important to the Christian faith, if it can be ignored as we pursue scriptural knowledge, then the Holy Spirit gave it to the apostle John in vain.

Surely, there are things of great value for us in the book of Revelation. Even though it has suffered from interpretive mistakes and biased applications, it is still a part of the word of God and deserves our careful attention. It is not as difficult as some have imagined it to be.

H. A. Dobbs has brought long years of study to this inspirational examination of the book of Revelation. It is not written as an aloof academic exercise, nor is it filled with theological jargon. The author believes that the Bible can interpret itself, and uses scripture to explain scripture. Things that seem difficult are best understood in light of clearer, plainer passages of holy writ.

This work is intense. It is personal. It directly involves the reader with many confrontational challenges and questions. He often addresses the reader. He pleads for the modern believer to take a stand on the word of God, to be a good soldier in the ranks of God. It is this personal aspect of the work that makes it a valuable and spiritually profitable study.

Dobbs sees the overriding theme of Revelation as an immense struggle between good and evil, truth and error, God and Satan. Throughout Revelation and this study there is the great concept of spiritual warfare, with its demands for courage and faithfulness, and with its promise of great reward to those who overcome. Victory for the Lord and for his faithful followers is the key to its appeal. Dobbs emphasizes that idea. He gives us instructions about becoming a Christian and encouragement in pursuing the battle for the glory of God and His Christ.

This is a good study of Revelation. It will clarify some of the more difficult passages. It will demonstrate the relationship of some of the Old Testament prophecy with the imagery in John's language. It will urge the serious student of God's word to be an overcomer, to look forward to receiving the white stone inscribed with a new name, and to eat of the tree of life.

I have enjoyed reading this inspirational and challenging study of the last book of the New Testament. I am happy to be the author's brother in the flesh and his brother in Christ.

---James 0. Dobbs

The Magnificent Christ

Chapter 1

The book of Revelation chronicles the most devastating of all wars. More souls (lives) have been lost in this mother of all wars than in all other wars combined. It is the greatest tragedy ever to befall mankind.

The closing book of the Bible describes a non-carnal, spiritual fight between the forces of evil and the forces of good. It is stated in colorful, prophetic, poetic imagery, designed to command our attention.

It opens with a description of those who fight on the side of truth. They are arrayed against the forces of evil.

The army of Satan is described and his technique of using material things and godless leaders to attempt to defeat the army of the Lord is faithfully reported and the army marches under the captaincy of a vicious murderer and the "father of lies" (John 8:44).

The battle rages over thousands of years and ends in the final skirmish, called in Hebrew Har-Mageden.

The army of the Prince of this world, also called the Prince of darkness, is utterly defeated by the army of the Prince of Peace, also called the Prince of Life.

The war delineated in the book of Revelation is not a temporal battle, seeing that the kingdom of Christ is not of this world (John 8:23; 18:36). No "rockets red glare ... no bombs bursting in air."

The Devil may employ godless governments in an attempt to ruin the blessed Redeemer, but the gigantic contest is for human hearts and continues until ages are no more. It is not fully visible to mortal eyes, but it is real.

The fiery climax of the fight between right and wrong concludes when Satan and his minions are captured and punished, and the universe passes into oblivion.

The fight is on, the trumpet sound is ringing out,
The cry "To arms" is heard afar and near;
The Lord of hosts is marching on to victory,
The triumph of the right will soon appear.[1]

CHAPTER ONE OF THE BOOK OF REVELATION

The timeless history of the hostile conflict between the Devil and Jesus begins with a description of the Captain of Salvation. It is told us by an old man who was on a rocky island where prisoners were forced to work at hard labor in the mines.

The island was named Patmos and it was the place where the government of Rome once exiled prisoners.

It was a short but impassible distance from the mainland. Escape was impossible, especially by one weakened by the ravages of time.

Verse 1
The Revelation of Jesus Christ,
which God gave him to show unto his servants,
even the things which must shortly come to pass:
and he sent and signified it by his angel unto his servant John;

The old man was named John and he was an apostle of the Christ. He began his prophetic history, a history that continues to record the fortunes and misfortunes of earthlings, by saying that what he was about to write was "The Revelation of Jesus Christ, which God gave to him to show unto his servants" (Rev 1:1). Prophecy is history told in advance and that is what John does in this astounding book. It is an adventure, an exciting experience.

---

1   *Words & Music:* Leila N. Morris, 1905

The disclosure was sent by an angel to the servant/apostle of Jesus, and concerned things that might take very long time to unfold, but described by the prophet John as "things that will shortly come to pass." Man's little stay on the planet earth is like a breath or a sigh when compared to eternity (Rev 1:1). "Shortly come to pass" does not mean the things written in the book will all soon occur, for even a casual reading of this revelation describes a long period whose duration is not known by man. John is saying that the things he describes would begin to happen soon and would be repeated in every generation for as long as the world continues. These things happened and kept on happening. History repeats itself. It started in the first century and continues in every century and will still be happening at the last century of earth and time.

Verse 2
who bare witness of the word of God,
and of the testimony of Jesus Christ,
even of all things that he saw.

John, who was a brother of James and a son of Zebedee, taught the Word of God, which is the testimony of Jesus. This was his crime. This made him an enemy of the ruling power.[2] This earned him a hard seat on a despised and lonely island. All who would live godly in Christ Jesus can expect and will receive similar rejection and punishment.[3]

Verse 3
Blessed is he that readeth,
and they that hear the words of the prophecy,
and keep the things that are written therein:
for the time is at hand.

John, wrote what an angel of God signified to him, and part of that included these words, "Blessed is he that readeth, and they that hear the prophecy, and keep the words that are written therein: for the time is at hand" (Rev 1:3). It is unfortunate that many rob themselves of the promised blessing because they have been duped into believing that the book of Revelation is written in unintelligible language that tends to overwhelm or intimidate. They are cowed by the book's undeserved reputation of not

---

2   Rev 1:2, 9
3   2 Tim 3:12

being understandable and consequently they neither read nor listen to its stimulating message and deprive themselves of utmost bliss.

There are things written in the book of Revelation that need to be kept; things that encourage and strengthen and things that need to be understood, believed and obeyed.

The time, says John, is at hand. He is about to describe an awful war between the devil and his underlings and the Lord and his slaves. He is warning believers about dismal days of stress and disappointment, which can be turned to the virtue of consecration and victory. Such days are "at hand" for every generation and will be until he who made time brings it to a sudden end.

Verse 4
John to the seven churches that are in Asia:
Grace to you and peace,
from him who is and who was and who is to come;
and from the seven Spirits that are before his throne;

We learn more about the seven churches in the following two chapters. In anticipation of what he is to say to the people of God who made up the seven churches, John commends them to God and asks for the Lord God to endow them with his rich gifts and with a lovely inner calm; it is the "peace of God which passes understanding."[4] In the midst of the raging storms of life the pious are blessed with an inner quiet that enables them to keep their eyes on the goal, and even stubborn conflict between truth and error cannot reach nor disturb that confidence of faith.

The apostle John was the conduit through which Jesus communicated to the seven churches in Asia.[5]

The communication is from Jehovah, "who is and who was and who is to come, that is, is eternal. The letter also comes from "the seven Spirits that

---

4   Phil 4:7
5   Seven is said to be a perfect number and signifies completeness or perfection. The seven churches of Asia represent all of the churches for all time. The seven letters sent to the seven churches of Asia can be construed as instructions to the church of Christ in all generations.

are before his throne," signifying the Holy Spirit (seven being completeness or perfection) who reveals and confirms divine wisdom.[6]

Verse 5
and from Jesus Christ,
who is the faithful witness,
the firstborn of the dead,
and the ruler of the kings of the earth.
Unto him that loveth us,
and loosed us from our sins by his blood;

The communication is also from Jesus Christ, who is (1) the faithful witness, (2) the firstborn of the dead, (3) ruler of the kings of the earth and (4) the redeemer of mankind[7]. This letter is therefore from God the Father, God the Son, and God the Holy Spirit. It is the wisdom of an infinite three-in-one Being perfectly united in the one Godhead. A priest is one who offers sacrifices and a king is one who rules; the two offices are united in Jesus. Through Jesus we "offer up a sacrifice of praise to God continually, that is, the fruit of lips which make confession to his name."[8] We rule the world because we rise above the world; it holds no attraction for us because our promised reward is not here but hereafter, though we receive blessing in the here and now.

There is no detergent stronger than the blood of the Lamb of God for it alone has power to make our sinful souls as pure and beautiful as new fallen snow.

Verse 6
and he made us to be a kingdom,
to be priests unto his God and Father;
to him be the glory and the dominion forever and ever. Amen.

Jesus made the saved of earth to be a kingdom of priests. The new covenant teaches the universal royalty and priesthood of every believer. All those

---

6   John 16:13
7   Redemption is the constant theme of the saving gospel and is therefore prominent in the book of Revelation. No one can properly appreciate Jesus who does not understand him to be the one-and-only Savior from sin, wreck, and ruin. Expressing any other view of Jesus is blasphemy.
8   Heb 13:15

who are loosed from their sins by the cleansing blood of Jesus are kings and priests. Every saved person is, in the eyes of God, a monarch of righteousness and a priest by the power of an endless life (the endless life of Jesus).[9]

Verse 7
Behold, he cometh with the clouds;
and every eye shall see him,
and they that pierced him;
and all the tribes of the earth shall mourn over him.
Even so, Amen.

Jesus is coming again with the clouds. Coming with the clouds is to come with irresistible power.[10] When he comes again (1) every eye shall see him, (2) they that crucified him shall see him, and (3) the tribes of the earth shall mourn over him. What will happen when Jesus comes a second time is vividly reported in this closing book of the Bible and those things are so manifest and conclusive that no one, on earth or in the heaven of heavens, will be able to miss it or deny it. Up until this moment, it has not happened. "So Christ also, having been once offered to bear the sins of many, shall appear a second time, apart from sin, to them that wait for him, unto salvation."[11]

Verse 8
I am the Alpha and the Omega,
saith the Lord God,
who is and who was and who is to come,
the Almighty.

The Lord God is the Alpha and the Omega, as we might say in English He is everything from A to Z. . He is the almighty, eternal One Godhead. From first to last, He is God. There is none other. The reference here is to Jesus who came, lived, died, and lived again —"is … was … is to come." The unity between the three members of the Godhead is riveted so firmly that it cannot be broken. They are three separate and distinct Beings but their perfect unity make them one God. These three are one. They are one

---

9   Heb 7:15-16
10   Isa 19:1; Deut 33:26; Psa 18:10-12; Matt 26:64-65
11   Heb 9:28

in purpose, thought, word, work, and substance. No other being possess their essence, which is divine spirit, so they alone are one God and besides them there is none other. Each of the three beings of the one Godhead has a mutually accepted role in the divine economy, yet what one does, they all do. The Godhead is all powerful, all wise, and everywhere present; the three being that make up the one Godhead possess infinite wisdom, power holiness, justice, goodness, and truth. In this verse Jesus speaks but the Comforter and the Father are in profound agreement.

Verse 9

I John, your brother and partaker with you in tribulation
and kingdom and patience which are in Jesus,
was in the isle that is called Patmos,
for the word of God and the testimony of Jesus

The apostle John describes himself as "a partaker with you in tribulation and kingship and patience, which are in Jesus."[12] It may seem strange to link tribulation with royalty and patience. Jesus said, while on trial before Pilate, that he came into the world as a king, but within a few hours he suffered the humility and pain of the cross and endured it all patiently. The kings and queens in the Kingdom of God on earth – the church – are beset with the distress of oppression and are longsuffering. The mix may seem singular but it is realistic.

Disciples of Jesus who reign with Him patiently endure tribulation.[13]

John was in this plight because he held tenaciously to the "Word of God and the testimony of Jesus."[14] The book of Revelation commends those who are faithful and true in holding fast to Bible teaching, come what may. "Word of God" incudes the Old Testament with its rich history and abundant prophecies concerning Jesus. "Testimony of Jesus" refers to the New Testament, which is also the Word of God. The importance of God-breathed scripture is vigorously emphasized in the book of Revelation, which is a serious rebuke to religious liberalism.

---

12 John 16:13; Rom 5:3; 2 Tim 3:12; Rev 1:9; 2:9-10; 2:22; 7:14
13 2 Thess2:14; 2 Tim 2:10, 12: 4:3; Heb 12L7
14 Rev 1:2; 1:9; 6:9; 12:17; 14:12; 20:4

Verse 10-11

I was in the Spirit on the Lord's day,
and I heard behind me a great voice,
as of a trumpet, saying,
What thou seest, write in a book and send it to the seven churches: unto
Ephesus, and unto Smyrna, and unto Pergamum, and unto Thyatira,
and unto Sardis, and unto Philadelphia, and unto Laodicea.

John was "in the spirit on the Lord's day," which may mean that he was in the attitude of worship on Sunday, or that in deepest meditation he was caught up in a prophetic trance. He heard behind him a voice that was loud like the blare of a trumpet.

Throughout the book of Revelation voices emanating from heaven are described as stentorian, like a sudden crash of thunder. This is designed to capture and hold attention. We should honor the Word of God with unbreakable concentration, and never in a trifling manner. Worshipping the great I am is seriously important, and must never be reduced to the frivolity of foolishness.

A booming voice commands John to write[15] what he saw in a book and send it to the seven churches.

Verse 12-13

And I turned to see the voice that spake with me.
And having turned I saw seven golden candlesticks;
and in the midst of the candlesticks one like unto a son of man,
clothed with a garment down to the foot,
and girt about at the breasts with a golden girdle.

John received a vision of the Captain of our salvation. In a revelation from the throne room of God, a long war is about to be described. We are first introduced to the commander-in-chief of the army of righteousness.

---

15 John is told a number of times to write what he saw and heard (Rev 2:1, 8, 12, 18, 19; 13:1, 7, 14; 14:13; 19:9; 21:5). The book may give us an excellent clue as to has how the wisdom of God was transmitted to a human agent. This may be the key to understanding how "every scripture" is "inspired of God." Sometimes John saw the revelation in a vision, other times he was told in words what to write, and still other times he both saw and heard the message.

The army of Jesus is made up of himself as the leader, the saved people of earth who comprise the church, and Jehovah with his heavenly host. This powerful force will be set in array in chapters one through six.

All eyes must now turn to John's vision of the glorified Christ. The loud, trumpet-voice-of-God compels us to focus all our senses on the one who is about to be described.

There is a literary technique by which a non-human is represented as having human characteristics and attributes. John uses that technique as he describes the indescribable and bids us look upon one that would otherwise be invisible. Inspiration wisely presents to us with a few bold strokes the vision of Jesus in his glory. It is awesome.

In a vision John sees the magnificent splendor of Christ. This description abounds in symbols and figures. It stresses the preeminence of him who has been given all "authority in heaven and on earth," and whose name is the "name that is above every name."

John saw seven golden candlesticks. The apostle also saw one like a Son of Man in the midst of seven golden candlesticks "clothed in a garment down to the foot, and girt about at the breasts with a golden girdle" (v 13). The Being John saw wore a long, flowing robe with a golden sash, reminiscent of the robe and sash of the Jewish High Priest of Israel.[16]

Verses 14-16

And his head and his hair were white as white wool,
white as snow;
and his eyes were as a flame of fire;
and his feet like unto burnished brass,
as if it had been refined in a furnace;
and his voice as the voice of many waters.
And he had in his right hand seven stars:
and out of his mouth proceeded a sharp two-edged sword:
and his countenance was as the sun shineth in his strength.

His white hair symbolizes purity; and his eyes were a flame of fire, indicating an ability to look upon the naked, quivering soul and see all things both visible and invisible.

---

16 Lev 8:7

His feet were like burnished brass, suggesting that he would trample with indifference all who regarded him, his church, and his cross with indifference; and his voice was soothing and consoling like the voice of many waters. The voice of God can be as loud as thunder or as soothing as a babbling brook, which it is depends on the circumstances.

In his right hand he clutches seven stars: and out of his mouth proceeds a sharp two-edged sword ("For the word of God is living, and active, and sharper than any two-edged sword, and piercing even to the dividing of soul and spirit, of both joints and marrow, and quick to discern the thoughts and intents of the heart."[17] His gentle, comforting words can turn to reproof and rebuke.

He shines with the brightness of the sun at high noon reminding us of his transfiguration on the mountain, witnessed by Peter, James, John, Moses, and Elijah "… his face did shine as the sun, and his garments became white as the light."[18]

There he stands: White, glistening hair, eyes like flames of fire, a sharp sword coming out of his mouth, his robe reaches to his feet, his sash is pure gold, his feet are like burnished brass that has been refined in a furnace, his voice is soft but can be loud and decisive. About this amazing figure is brilliance too strong to gaze upon.

This is Christ in his glory.

Verse 17-18

And when I saw him,
I fell at his feet as one dead.
And he laid his right hand upon me, saying, Fear not;
I am the first and the last, and the Living one;
and I was dead, and behold, I am alive for evermore,
and I have the keys of death and of Hades.

We should not be surprised to learn that when the apostle John saw this manifestation of a divine being that he "fell at his feet as one dead" (v 17). Jesus and John were especially close while Jesus was in the flesh and on

---

17   Heb 4:12
18   Matt 17:2

earth. John sat next to Jesus in the upper room when the Passover of the Jews was observed and the Lord' Supper instituted; John together with James and Peter were with Jesus on the glory mountain when Jesus was transfigured. Though they had been intimate friends during the four years of Jesus teaching ministry, still, to see him exalted was more than human strength could bear and John fell at his feet "as one dead."

Jesus laid his hand upon John and said, "Fear not; I am the first and the last, and the Living one; and I was dead, and behold, I am alive for evermore, and I have the keys of death and of Hades." Jesus overcame sin and destroyed death; he opened the gates of heaven for all who love and obey him. He is the world's redeemer

Verses 19-20

Write therefore the things which thou sawest,
and the things which are,
and the things which shall come to pass hereafter;
the mystery of the seven stars which thou sawest in my right hand,
and the seven golden candlesticks.
The seven stars are the angels of the seven churches:
and the seven candlesticks are seven churches.

This vision of the glorified Jesus was to be written. The information was to be preserved. It was not for John only, but for people of all coming generations. The book that never passes away contains this sublime description of the Holy Being that is to lead in the battle of eternity. He is aided and assisted by His Father and the Comforter, his church, and the heavenly host.

The "mystery" of the seven stars and the seven golden candlesticks is explained. The book of Revelation explains itself and when that is not done an interpreter gives an inspired explanation. We can proceed in confidence that the meaning of the book is given in the book. If we stay with that, we cannot go wrong.

The seven stars in the right hand of Jesus are the angels of the seven churches (of Asia Minor). The seven golden candlesticks are the seven churches, which represent the church of Christ in every period and age.

11

Jesus, holding the messengers of the churches in his right hand, walks in the midst of the congregations of his people. He is with the saved and the saved are, consequently, with him.

The war will shortly begin but will not shortly end. But first John will give us information about the church of Christ and the great, white throne.

This splendid story throbs with excitement and holds the heart in thrall by its powerful attraction.

This is the inspired story of "the good fight of faith."

Letters to the Churches

PART 1
Chapter Two

The Lord told John to write to the church in seven cities the very words he heard from the lips of the glorified Jesus. Let us review the seven letters.

Ephesus
Verses 1-7

Verse 1

To the angel of the church in Ephesus write:
These things saith he that holdeth the seven stars in his right hand,
he that walketh in the midst of the seven golden candlesticks:

The Lord clutches the seven stars in his right hand – that is, his most powerful hand.[19] The stars represent the messengers of the churches, as we are told in the last verse of chapter one. He walks among the seven candlesticks, which represent the churches. These two figures affirm the great love Jesus has for the church and for his messengers who teach his word and encourage others to obey it.

Verse 2

I know thy works, and thy toil and patience,
and that thou canst not bear evil men,
and didst try them that call themselves apostles,
and they are not,
and didst find them false;

19   Ex 15:6; Psa 16:11; 48:10; 63:8; Lk 22:69 – this is, of course, a figure of speech

Jesus does not waste words but is brief and to the point. He knew the works of the saved in Ephesus because he is an all-knowing God; "there is no creature that is not manifest in his sight: but all things are naked and laid open before the eyes of him with whom we have to do."[20]

Jesus knew the works of his spiritual brothers and sisters in Ephesus two thousand years ago and he knows the works of "every creature" today. He is a silent witness of all we do and say and we can never escape his penetrating gaze. We cannot impose on him because he sees all we do, say, or think, and "is quick to discern the thoughts and intents of the heart."[21] This does not frighten the true believer because he knows that the look of Jesus sees in each one the things that are noble and good as well as the things that are evil and bad. He assures us that if we come before him with the cry, "unclean, unclean" and confess our sins "he is faithful and righteous to forgive us our sins, and to cleanse us from all unrighteousness."[22] It is the disobedient unbeliever who should tremble in fear to know that Jesus sees us as we really are and will reward us accordingly.

To the members of the church in Ephesus Jesus said, "I know thy works, toil, and patience." He understood their long, strenuous, fatiguing labor. When in human form and on his earthly mission, Jesus was often bone-tired and drooping in weariness. Picture him sitting exhausted by a well and begging a drink of water from a Samaritan woman.[23]

Even today, with flaming eyes, he looks upon and sympathizes with his hard-pressed, and often worn out disciples. He knows about road-worn, strained muscles and loss of vigor and freshness.

His heart goes out to soldiers in the foxholes as his words ring out like pistol shots, "Watch ye, stand fast in the faith, quit you like men, be strong."[24]

Jesus commends his valiant ones for finding evil men unbearable. He does not expect us to be unreasonably radical and unbalanced in rooting out false teachers, but he does expect us to in all civility identify and reject

---

20 Heb 4:13
21 Heb 4:12
22 1 John 1:9
23 John 4:8
24 1 Cor 16:13

those who falsely claim apostolic power. It is moral to find lying prophets untrue and treacherous.

Jesus knows how betrayal feels!

When those who "were once enlightened" turn "back from the holy commandment delivered to them,"[25] they jeopardize their souls and cause the great heart of Jesus to bleed. They are dastardly traitors to the highest and holiest cause mortals can know.

Their end is perdition.

The Lord's army must find them false, and first entreat, and then rebuke them. If they will not repent, their fate is sure and sealed. We take no pleasure in it, but we would be fools not to recognize it. Jesus takes note of it and so must we. It seems incredible that they would claim to be an apostle of Jesus when they are not. Christ commends the believers at Ephesus for examining the false claims of false teachers and finding them corrupt. He expects no less of us.

The Captain of our salvation does not ask us to endure what he has never known but speaks from experience when he encourages us to be "not weary in well doing."[26] To the Ephesians he gives these soul-cheering words:

Verse 3
and thou hast patience and didst bear for my name's sake, and hast not grown weary.

Do not give up, no matter how heavy the load or rough the road, take his "yoke upon you" and do not allow pain and hardship to cause you to stumble. He gives you strength for the day's labor and rest to your soul. Even when the stormy "billows are tossing high," he gives you a ray of hope and it shines brighter and brighter until the coming of a perfect day.

The vineyard of the Lord is a place of unceasing toil under a brazen and burning sun. We wordlessly bear "the burden of the day and the scorching heat." The work is wearisome, but the joy is as constant as the sun's rays. It is a mixture of labor and happiness. It is, after all, the vineyard of the

---

25　Heb 6:4-6
26　Gal 6:9; 2 Thess 3:13; Heb 12:3

Lord and there is an anticipation of reward at the end of the day. We, like Jesus, "endure" because of "the joy that is set before us."[27]

Discipline is necessary for soldiers. An undisciplined soldier is a disaster in waiting. Infantrymen must learn unquestioning obedience. In the heat of battle, we cannot disregard an officer's command. That would generate chaos. Anarchy has no place in the military and is intolerable.

Verse 4-5

But I have this against thee,
that thou didst leave thy first love.

Remember therefore whence thou art fallen,
and repent and do the first works;
or else I come to thee,
and will move thy candlestick out of its place,
except thou repent.

Jesus admonishes the saints in Ephesus to recapture their ardor. He said, "But I have this against thee, that thou didst leave thy first love."[28]

That is followed by these words, "Remember therefore whence thou art fallen, and repent and do the first works."[29]

He recalls them to the intensity, zeal, and loyalty of earlier days. Paul called on Timothy to "remember the good confession," which he made "in the sight of many witnesses." The aged apostle calls on the young man to recollect the joy, determination, and eagerness he knew when he first confessed Jesus as Lord.[30]

Unbridled enthusiasm rides with the soldier of the cross.

The apostles later adds the powerful plea, "O Timothy, guard that which is committed unto thee, turning away from the profane babblings and oppositions of the knowledge which is falsely so called; which some professing have erred concerning the faith. Grace be with you."[31]

---

27 Heb 12:2
28 Rev 2:4
29 Rev 2:5
30 1 Tim 6:12
31 1 Tim 6:20-21

16

Take careful note of the line of reasoning:

- Fight the good fight of faith; remember the good confession; be possessed of an informed zeal.[32]

- Guard that which is committed to you; turn away from knowledge which is falsely so called; do not be taken in by irreverent babble and contradictions."[33]

- Some professing knowledge have swerved from the faith; God's grace sustains the loyal soldier.[34]

Apathy is displeasing to Jesus. He expects his followers – his soldiers – to be fervent.[35] Service in heaven's army demands being excited about the gospel, salvation, and teaching.

At the first temple cleansing Jesus' disciples remembered the prophecy, "Zeal for thy house hath eaten me up."[36] Upon returning to the well at Sychar with food to refresh their exhausted Master and seeing him animated in anticipation of preaching salvation to a multitude, the followers of the Son of God were amazed, and supposed that someone had given him food. His answer was, "My meat is to do the will of him who sent me, and to accomplish his work."[37]

Half-hearted, sporadic, hesitant service will win no battles. An Army filled with soldiers who understand and love their cause so much that they are willing to die for it often defeats a larger enemy force.

Believe what you believe … and believe it with all your heart. Otherwise, you are not an asset but a distraction.

Jesus calls you to selfless, exuberant service.

He gives this warning: "or else I come to thee, and will move thy candlestick out of its place, except thou repent."[38]

---

32 1 Tim 6:12
33 1 Tim 6:20
34 1 Tim 6:21
35 Synonyms for "fervent" are: "avid, ardent, eager, enthusiastic, passionate, zealous, fanatical, impassioned, burning, intense, vehement, heated"
36 John 2:17
37 John 4:34
38 Rev 2:5

It is an "or else" proposition. You do it, "or else."

Jesus will remove a candlestick for faithlessness. Jesus knows his own and calls them by their name; his own know him and follow him.[39]

Those who do not follow the instructions of the good shepherd are not his sheep. Even those who think they are his sheep are rejected because they fail to "trust and obey."[40]

Verse 6

But this thou hast,
that thou hatest the works of the Nicolaitans,
which I also hate.

"Hate" seems to be a harsh word and we impulsively shrink from it. Most of the time hate is not good, but there is a time and place when it is good for hate to be on display. The sweet singer of Israel knew when and what to hate.[41]

Do not be hypocritical, hate the evil and hold to the good.[42] Those who are on the Lord's side never fly false colors. Love is not deceptive and misleading, but is open and frank. Straightforwardness is virtuous.

The saved in Ephesus hated the work of the Nicolaitans (notice, they hated the Nicolatians' work – not the Nicolaitans). Jesus joined them in hating the wickedness of the Nicolaitans. We will discuss the Nicolaitans in more detail when we review the letter to the church in Pergamum.

Verse 7

He that hath an ear,
let him hear what the Spirit saith to the churches.
To him that overcometh,
to him will I give to eat of the tree of life,
which is in the Paradise of God.

---

39 John 10:3, 14
40 Matt 7:22-23
41 Psa 26:5; 31:6; 97:10; 101:3; 110:104; 139:21
42 Rom 12:9

"He that hath an ear, let him hear what the Spirit saith to the churches. To him that overcometh, to him will I give to eat of the tree of life, which is in the Paradise of God."[43]

Jesus speaks in a royal fashion when he says, "I will give …"

He, too, fought and overcame. He seems to call to his valiant soldiers, "Hold the fort, for I am coming."

The promise is to "him that overcometh." Fighting is always hard; wining is always joyful.

Saints are to "fight the good fight of faith." Those who battle the devil and conquer him are promised the reward of victory.

Life is a battle between good and evil, between truth and error. We may win the battle; and the winning is glorious.

Each of the seven letters ends with a promise. The righteous receive "the recompense of reward."[44] Jesus richly rewards hard work and sacrifice. The blood, sweat, and tears of the war we exchange for delicious fruit when we lay our armor down at Jesus' feet.

At the end of each letter, Jesus helps us to understand another brilliant facet of the heavenly prize. When we consider all the promises, the reward is overwhelming.

Eating of the tree of life, which is in the Paradise of God, means satisfaction, unspeakable joy, and total contentment … happiness that cannot be improved. The tree of life was in the Garden of Eden and has been transplanted to heaven of the heavens. This is a figure of speech and means unrelieved happiness. Always happy!

Next the Lord dictated a letter to the church at Smyrna

Smyrna

.

Verse 8

And to the angel of the church in Smyrna write:
These things saith the first and the last, who was dead,
and lived again:

---

43 Rev 2:7
44 Heb 10:35

Jesus identified himself as "the first and the last, who was dead and lived again." It was because of his resurrection from the dead that Jesus was "declared to be the Son of God with power, according to the spirit of holiness, by the resurrection from the dead."[45]

His spirit re-entered his dead body and he lived, breathed, ate, drank and taught. He had up-close association with good friends as they examined the wounds caused by savage beating and crucifixion.

The eyewitnesses of the fact of Jesus' resurrection sealed their testimony with their own blood. No event, past or present, has more sufficient proof of its truthfulness than does the resurrection of Jesus.

The fact that a handful of humble, ordinary people, within the span of a single generation, convinced the majority of the people of earth that his resurrection was *bona fide* also validates the event. It is neither specious nor counterfeit.

Jesus mentions his victory over death in his letter to the church of Christ at Smyrna to confirm that "all authority, in heaven and on earth" was his.

The wise will hear and obey the glory-circled Christ.

Verse 9

I know thy tribulation,
and thy poverty (but thou art rich),
and the blasphemy of them that say they are Jews,
and they art not,
but are a synagogue of Satan.

Jesus wanted the saved at Smyrna to understand that he knew all about their sacrifices in his noble cause.

Christianity travels through cycles of acceptance and rejection. Sometimes the "shadows are deep and rough seems the path to the goal." Sometimes the victory is sweet and cheers the life of the believer. When storm clouds gather it is a comfort to understand that Jesus knows – he knows about it all.

---

45   Rom 1:4

This awareness makes the follower of Jesus the more determined to stay the course and win the prize.

Jesus turns a sympathetic eye to those who suffer for righteousness sake and bids them to "press on toward the mark of the high calling of God"[46] He does not use his power to remove the obstacle, but allows it to sharpen and strengthen his children. "[T]ribulation worketh stedfastness; and stedfastness, approvedness; and approvedness, hope: and hope putteth not to shame; because the love of God hath been shed abroad in our hearts through the Holy Spirit which was given unto us."[47]

The fact that he knows is a balm to the soul. Jesus knew the tribulation and the poverty of the redeemed and sent the message, "Be strong! Say not, The days are evil. Who's to blame? And fold the hands and acquiesce—oh shame! Stand up, speak out, and bravely, in God's name."[48]

An intimidated church that speaks with stammering lips and is afraid to confront error and sin is a disgrace.

If your boldness in service of Jesus causes privation, then continue in your dedicated devotion and eager testimony, and ignore your deprivation.

A child of God will not allow himself to be weak-kneed with hands hanging down. "Be not weary in well-doing." Watch ye, stand fast in the faith, quit you like men, be strong. Let all that ye do be done in love."[49]

Think of Paul's life and of how he refused to be dissuaded.

> For, I think, God hath set forth us the apostles last of all, as men doomed to death: for we are made a spectacle unto the world, both to angels and men. We are fools for Christ's sake, but ye are wise in Christ; we are weak, but ye are strong; ye have glory, but we have dishonor. Even unto this present hour we both hunger, and thirst, and are naked, and are buffeted, and have no certain dwelling-place; and we toil, working with our own hands: being reviled, we bless; being persecuted, we endure; being defamed, we entreat: we are made as the filth of the world, the offscouring

---

46 Phil 3:14
47 Rom 5:3-5
48 "Be Strong" by Maltbie Davenport Babcock, born Aug 3, 1858; died May 18, 1901
49 1 Cor 16:13-14

of all things, even until now. I write not these things to shame you, but to admonish you as my beloved children. For though ye have ten thousand tutors in Christ, yet have ye not many fathers; for in Christ Jesus I begat you through the gospel. I beseech you therefore, be ye imitators of me.[50]

Jesus knew of their distress, suffering, oppression and poverty. Still, he says to them, "You are rich." Poor but rich.

The child of God is a joint heir with Jesus of eternal riches and enjoys in this life, though chastised and persecuted, the true wealth. Every baptized believer receives forgiveness, peace, hope, assurance, brothers, sisters, and the incredible eternal spiritual treasures of God. Jesus said,

Verily I say unto you, There is no man that hath left house, or brethren, or sisters, or mother, or father, or children, or lands, for my sake, and for the gospel's sake, but he shall receive a hundredfold now in this time, houses, and brethren, and sisters, and mothers, and children, and lands, with persecutions; and in the world to come eternal life.[51]

If anyone is alienated from his biological family because of the obedience of faith, he receives in the great family of God, as compensation, spiritual relatives scattered all over the world. He may lose land and house, but doors are open to him in thousands of shelters.

Notice that in listing the support one receives in the body of Christ, Jesus mentions "persecution," which has the power to provoke full consecration.

He also told his disciples, "These things have I spoken unto you, that in me ye may have peace. In the world ye have tribulation: but be of good cheer; I have overcome the world."[52]

Tribulation? Persecution? Do we count these as the coin in which the Lord pays his servants?

The answer is an emphatic yes. Adverse winds lift the believer to greater heights ... "E'en tho' it be a cross that raiseth me."

---

50   1 Cor 4:9-16
51   Mark 10:29-30
52   John 16:33

Like Jesus, each believer, for the "joy that is before him," endures whatever he must endure, despising shame, and one day to sit down with Jesus in the Father's throne. That is true riches.

When painful opposition, sorrow, separation, trouble and heartache come, "rejoice and be exceeding glad in that day, for great is your reward in heaven."[53]

Jesus is preparing the members of the church in Smyrna for the terrible persecution that was about to befall them.

The Son of God praises the saints of Smyrna for refusing to cave in because of the slander of false Jews. They say they are Jews, but they lie. The blood of Abraham may run in their veins, but they are not truly his children.[54]

A synagogue of Satan is a gathering place for the prince of darkness and his mortal dupes. It is amazing that in the church is a synagogue of Satan, but in the Old Testament altars of Baal were found in the temple that was dedicated to the honor of God. The pitiful cries of infants could be heard at times within the walls of the place where God had put his name. That is enough to make us tremble.

It is tough to hear slander heaped upon you and not retaliate with bitter words. It is not easy to offer truth to disbelievers and have them turn to rend you. It is almost insupportable to listen to your words distorted and your meaning misrepresented.

While Jesus was suffering and dying on the cross, his detractors ridiculed him and misrepresented his teaching with blasphemous slander. Only his God-nature and perfect love enabled him not to call for fire to flash forth from the Father and consume them. He looked on them with pity and answered not a word, saying, "Father, forgive them, they know not what they do."[55]

Hateful words intensify the suffering of physical persecution. To bear up under a hailstorm of slander is a hard thing to do, but it imitates the Suffering Servant of Jehovah.

---

53 Matt 5:12
54 John 8:39-45
55 Luke 23:34

Verses 10-11

Fear not the things which thou art about to suffer:
behold, the devil is about to cast some of you into prison,
that ye may be tried;

Jesus knew that brutal persecution was about to break over the disciples at Smyrna. He does not employ his power to prevent it, but offers kind words of comfort.

"Fear not," he says, "the things which thou art about to suffer." Like a mother's hand on a fevered brow, his care is consolation, and his consolation is strength.

"The devil is about to cast some of you into prison, that ye may be tried." The devil is the source of their misery. Suffering is often the trial of faith. Moral agency is tested. The evil in the world can be traced to Satan. God could neutralize the devil and take away all evil, but to do so he would have to take away our freedom. God must think that being free is more important than suffering evil generated by the devil. He counsels us not to use our freedom as a cloak of wickedness.[56] By so doing, you put to shame the ignorance of foolish men.

We have heard of a man who was laughed at contemptuously for being a follower of Jesus, and who "began to curse and swear, I know not the man."

The moral fiber of our being must be strong to support us when we face ridicule and derision for walking in the "footprints of Jesus."

The heavy-handed persecution Jesus foretold was to last "ten days." Of course, the "ten days" symbolize a short, intense period, just as a thousand years will be later used to denote a long, intense period of unknown duration.

Whether the harassment is long or short, we must learn to summons our strength, look to Jesus, and wordlessly submit to the chastening scourge.

and ye shall have tribulation ten days.
Be thou faithful unto death, and I will give thee the crown of life.
He that hath an ear,
let him hear what the Spirit saith to the churches.
He that overcometh shall not be hurt of the second death

---

56 1 Pet 2:15-16

Jesus promises two things to "he that overcometh" – a crown of life and not being hurt of the second death.

The crown of life is not the monarch's diadem, but the wreath of victory. It speaks of joy, exoneration, admittance and honor. It is the reward for overcoming, which again reminds us of the "good fight of faith."

To win the fight one must be faithful. Be faithful in doctrine, in service, and in holiness. Be faithful even if physical death results from your fidelity, which is a small and inconsequential thing if you are unhurt by the second death, which is everlasting separation from God.

Now, the Lord dictates a letter to the church at Pergamos.

Pergamum
Verses 12-17

Verse 12

and to the angel of the church in Pergamum write:
These things saith he that hath the sharp two-edged sword:

Jesus begins his letter to the church at Pergamum by describing himself as the one who has "the sharp two-edged sword." The sword of his mouth symbolizes his word. His word can be as charming as a babbling brook or it can be like the peal of thunder. It is adjusted to the circumstances under which he speaks.

John the forerunner introduced Jesus as "the Word" who is also God.[57]

Jesus said, "He that loveth me not keepeth not my words: and the word which ye hear is not mine, but the Father's who sent me."[58] He casts this in the negative – If you do not love me, you will not keep my word." The converse is, If you love me, you will keep my word."[59]

The acid test of whether anyone loves Jesus or does not love him is keeping or not keeping his word.

John the apostle saw Jesus as having a sharp and pointed sword proceeding from his mouth.[60]

---

57 John 1:1
58 John 14:24
59 John 14:23
60 Rev 1:16; 19:15, 21

"For the word of God is living, and active, and sharper than any two-edged sword …"[61] There is no sword in the entire world, past or present, that is as sharp as the living word of God. That is a powerful statement and points us once again to the fact that the book of Revelation is deeply concerned with the potency of God's word, and the importance of keeping it.

The sharp sword of Jesus is an awesome force. It will accomplish what God intends for it. Still, with all its incisive strength, it can be resisted by those who harden their hearts to reject it.[62]

God does nothing to force an unwilling sinner to come to him. The power of his word is great but not irresistible. He warns, counsels and implores, but he does not use His unlimited power to compel anyone to serve him. Jesus entreats but refuses to overwhelm the free-agency of humans.[63]

Verse 13

I know where thou dwellest,
even where Satan's throne is;
and thou holdest fast my name,
and didst not deny my faith,
even in the days of Antipas my witness,
my faithful one,
who was killed among you,
where Satan dwelleth.

Jesus knows even our most private thoughts and motives. He has the power to know everything, but chooses to limit his knowledge to those things it is necessary for him to know in order to work out his eternal purpose for humankind. Being omnipotent, God has the power to know or not to know; otherwise he is not omnipotent.

Still, he knows when we suffer pain, disappointment, or loneliness. He knows when the battle for truth and the fight seems to go against us. He knows when we hurt and are sad. He knows when separation comes and we feel a profound, blank vacancy in our souls.

---

61 Heb 4:12
62 John 5:39-40; Heb 4:7
63 Matt 5:39; 11:28; 21:37

To say that Jesus knows is to say that Jesus cares. Just to know that he is aware of every loss we suffer and every bump in the road is consolation to us.

At times of sorrow and stress an angel came to Jesus and strengthened him.[64] How did the angel strengthen Jesus? Did he enter the physical body of Jesus and fortify him against temptation and pain? The strength the angel supplied consisted mainly of being there and caring. The empathy of the Almighty is amazingly refreshing.

Jesus knows where we live and what we endure and he cares. He looks upon us with sympathetic eyes and is our friend. To know that Jesus knows is strength and consolation. He may not remove the affliction – just as an angel visitor did not remove the sorrow and burden of Christ – but He is there and is aware. That matters most of all and is our greatest solace.

Jesus may not prevent the hardship but his unseen presence and loving care helps us to bear any burden and overcome any obstacle.

> *"For the eyes of the Lord are upon the righteous, And his ears unto their supplication:*
>
> *But the face of the Lord is upon them that do evil. And who is he that will harm you, if ye be zealous of that which is good? But even if ye should suffer for righteousness' sake, blessed are ye: and fear not their fear, neither be troubled; but sanctify in your hearts Christ as Lord: being ready always to give answer to every man that asketh you a reason concerning the hope that is in you, yet with meekness and fear."*[65]

The throne, of course, represents the seat of power. He who sits on the throne has authority. Satan is spirit and, like the wind, is invisible to mortal eyes. Yet, he is a real being with great influence derived from the consent of his subjects.

Jesus called him "the prince of this world;"[66] and Paul called him "the prince of the air."[67]

---

64 Matt 4:6; Luke 22:43
65 1 Peter 3:12-15
66 John 12:31
67 Eph 2:2

Satan is empowered by people. When people consent to support the regime of the devil, he is vested with convincing force and becomes a prince. Satan rules by the consent of those he governs.

Pergamum was a capital city of Satan. Jesus said that the wily old serpent had a throne there. Vice was rampant.

The church was in the midst of that carnival of corruption and filth. It required vigilance and courage for the saints to "shine forth as lights in the world … holding forth the word of life" in such a vile community. The church was an island of righteousness in a despicable and repulsive society.

Being surrounded by such decadence, saints must "holdfast to the name of Christ," which means a strong grip on saving truth. Abiding in the doctrine of Jesus is how we have God, seeing that those who abide not in Jesus' doctrine have not God.[68]

The emphasis is on revealed truth because it instructs, corrects, admonishes and encourages. Everyone who continues in God-breathed truth is complete, or perfect. Again, it necessarily follows that all who refuse to obey God and conform to the pattern of his word are incomplete, or imperfect.

Holding fast to the "name of Christ" is the key to divine approval. All others are sent away.

Jesus was aware of the pig sty in which the people of Pergamum lived and sympathized with them and admired their attempt to be faithful in the midst of filth.

When we look at the modern world we are impressed with the need for those who serve and worship in spirit and truth to be vigilant and brave. The devil still has some capital cities from which he directs his followers, entices the gullible, and invents new ways to sin.

Pergamum was a hotbed of shameful conduct.

Jesus calls to mind the death of Antipas who Jesus identified as his faithful witness. The word here translated "witness" appears about thirty-five times in the New Testament and is translated "martyr" here and in connection with the death of Stephen. A martyr is a witness though he has not necessarily paid for his testimony with his life, but he is willing to …

---

68 2 John 9

he is not afraid to die for Christ. Antipas as a faithful witness of Jesus no doubt taught truth in a city where the father of lies ruled. Jesus was hated and killed because he spoke truth and the devotees of Satan hate truth and will attempt to arrange the death of anyone who is a champion of truth.[69] That is all we know about Antipas, but Jesus knew all about him and remembered his martyrdom. He died in a stronghold of Satan. Be sure that the evil one would gladly kill all who call on the name of the Lord and serve him. If you are in that number, the devil is looking for an opportunity to kill you.

"Blessed are ye, when men shall hate you, and when they shall separate you from their company, and reproach you, and cast out your name as evil, for the Son of man's sake"[70].

Verse 14

But I have a few things against thee,
because thou hast there some that hold the teaching of Balaam,
who taught Balak to cast a stumblingblock before the children of Israel,
to eat things sacrificed to idols,
and to commit fornication.

The saints at Pergamum lived in treachery because they loved Jesus. The Lord felt sorry for them, but had some things against them..

There were some among them who held to the infamous doctrine of Balaam, who devised a way to entice Israel to a drunken, idolatrous, and sexually impure orgy to turn God against them and caused 24,000 Israelites to die. Balaam's sin was covetousness, which caused him to traffic in deception and filth in a vain attempt to gain fabulous wealth.[71] Balaam died during Israel's conquest of Canaan.[72]

"For the love of money is a root of all kinds of evil: which some reaching after have been led astray from the faith, and have pierced themselves through with many sorrows."[73] An inordinate lust for wealth was

---

69 John 320; 7:7; 15:18; 1714
70 Luke 6:22
71 Num 22; 23; 24; 25:1-9; see also 2 Pet 2:15-16; Jude 1:11 and Mic 6:5
72 Joshua 13"22
73 1 Tim 6:10

characteristic of some members of the church in Pergamum and this offended Jesus, who knew that loving silver and gold is reckless and ruinous.

Verse 15

So hast thou also some that hold the teaching
of the Nicolaitans in like manner.

There was some relationship between the doctrine of Balaam and the teaching of the Nicolaitans. The only thing we know for sure about the Nicolaitans is what is written here. There are some post-apostolic references to the teaching of Nicolaos but they are dubious speculation and of little to no help. All we really know is that the Nicolaitans had the same glaring defect as Balaam, which was to put a premium upon material wealth and consequently lusted after perishing things and that lead into many other sins.

Verse 16

Repent therefore;
or else I come to thee quickly,
and I will make war against them with the sword of my mouth.

The Savior warns, once again, that his second coming will be quick and unannounced – like a thief in the night. He admonishes the saved at Pergamum to repent of their covetousness and related sins or he would administer to them a scathing rebuke. He warns us that some who think of themselves as secure in his service will be sadly disappointed when he says to them, "I never knew you: depart from me, ye that work iniquity."[74] The sure way of avoiding that rebuke and rejection is to repent, which means to "get a new mind" and "bring forth fruit worthy of repentance." His coming will be sudden and his rebuke will be brief but worthy of the sword of his mouth. That sword represents his word and is sharp, piercing, quick in reproof and rebuke and uncompromising in rejection of the self-deceived and unworthy.

---

74   Matt 7:23

Verse 17

He that hath an ear,
let him hear what the Spirit saith to the churches.
To him that overcometh,
to him will I give of the hidden manna,
and I will give him a white stone,
and upon the stone a new name written,
which no one knoweth but he that receiveth it.

"He that hath an ear to hear ..." We have the power to open circumcised ears to the words of Jesus or to be dull of hearing and reject his words. He is loving and kind and so does not strike us dead immediately (like Annanias and Sapphira),[75] but gives us time to repent. His greatest desire is for our eternal salvation for which cause he sent his son into the world.[76] It is astounding that God Almighty will allow us to harden our hearts and refuse to obey his law.

If we keep our eyes open to his wonders and our ears to his words and our hearts pliable in his hand, then he will mold us and make us after his will, but we have to be willing and responsive. If we trust and obey Him, he promises to repay us with the treasures of heaven.

He exercised his divine authority to make it possible for mortals to rebel against his majesty and to love darkness rather than light, but he pleads with us not to do it and warns us of the consequences of defying him.

At the close of his letter to Pergamum, the Lord promises two blessings to all those who follow him in faith and rejoice in his word.

First, he promises to feed them with the hidden manna. This is obviously symbolic and reminds us of the experience of the nation of Israel in the wilderness before entering the Promised Land. The symbol is that for all eternity he will provide abundantly a sweet, satisfying food to those who delight to worship him in adoration and service.

Second, he promises to give each true disciple who does not turn back from walking in his footsteps a white stone. Again, this is a symbol and represents acquittal, election, choice, and entrance. The stone is

---

75   Acts 5:1-10
76   John 3:16

brilliant and glittering (not dead-white) and may remind us of Urim and Thummim (lights and perfection). The stone signifies approval and is somewhat like the Medal of Honor that America gives to her greatest heroes. On the stone is the new name of the recipient, which is unknown until the time it is conferred. If you walk in the light of his word you will not know your new, heavenly, endless name until you hold the glistening stone in your hand and read it for yourself. This is figurative, but oh what profound glory it suggests.

Overcome in the fight for the right and your head will be held high and your eyes will light up and your step will be jubilant. It is more than worth whatever is may cost you. You will carry this lustrous and resplendent symbol of victory eternally.

Thyatira
Verses 18-29

Verse 18

And to the angel of the church in Thyatira write:
These things saith the Son of God,
who hath his eyes like a flame of fire,
and his feet are like unto burnished brass:

In Jesus' famous seven letters to seven of his churches the Lord vets his disciples that they may successfully oppose evil and promote righteousness. They are "marching as to war" and must be disciplined in the art of hostile conflict.

His primary concern is that they be pure in doctrine and in life. That is all ... it is enough.

His soldiers must be ready.

He addresses this letter to "the" church in Thyatira. His use of the definite article tells us something about Jesus' church. It is both universal and one. It is universal in the sense that it embraces all of the saved in heaven, hades and earth. It is one in the sense that it is solitary. All of the saved are in the church; it is "one body."[77]

---

77 Eph 4:5

The unity of the teaching of Jesus means unity in his church, which Jesus purchased at the awful cost of his own blood.[78] If Jesus' teaching is one, his church is one. It is, as Jesus says, "the" church.

Still, the one church is in many communities. This letter is to "the" church "in Thyatira." This does not mean many churches, but one church manifested in many places.

It is somewhat like a giant company with outlets all over the world. The head of the company wants the outlets to be uniform, just as Jesus wants his disciples to be united to the nth degree.[79]

Jesus emphasizes his words, which communicate his doctrine. "These things saith the Son of God."[80]

He calls attention to the fact that he is "the Son of God," declared such by his resurrection from the dead.[81]

Every child of God, in speaking the words of God, uses a sharp sword.[82] It is a sword that can cut and wound, but its surgical use can heal.

Jesus points to his eyes and his feet. He has "eyes like a flame of fire, and feet like burnished brass".[83]

The fire of his gaze suggests the deep penetration of an unshielded view. "All things are naked and laid bare before the eyes of him with whom we have to do".[84]

When God turns his flaming eyes upon you there is no concealment. You are undressed, and your quivering soul is fully exposed to his view.

The feet of Jesus are as "burnished brass."[85] Those are tough boots. Those who trample Jesus with indifference shall themselves feel the fury of his brass feet. He walks on those who walk on him.

---

78 Acts 20:28
79 John 17:20-21
80 V. 18
81 Rom 1:4
82 Eph 6:17
83 v 18
84 Heb 4:13
85 v 18

The lesson is obvious. Be careful of those who can see your soul and tread on you. This is another reason (perhaps the same reason restated) for us to respectfully listen to the sayings of the Son of God.

Verse 19

I know thy works,
and thy love and faith and ministry and patience,
and that thy last works are more than the first.

Jesus reminds his soldiers that he knows. He has said this before; he says it again.

Who sees with equal eye, as God of all,
A hero perish, or a sparrow fall,
Atoms or systems into ruin hurl'd,
And now a bubble burst, and now a world.[86]

His view is unbiased and perfect. He sees things as they really are. You may think you are unobserved in your underground cavern, but Jehovah is standing at the door with his prophet at his side.[87]

"Hast thou seen what the elders of the house of Israel do in the dark, every man in his chambers of imagery? For they say, Jehovah seeth us not; Jehovah hath forsaken the land."[88]

Jesus knows. He knows what you do in the dark; what you think; what you say; what you desire.

If God has the power to know everything, then everything is important and must be guarded – never run pell-mell and willy-nilly, but watch where your feet go.

"Look therefore carefully how you walk, not as unwise, but as wise; redeeming the time, because the days are evil."[89] Make God's word is your lamp and light.

His flaming eyes see and his burnished feet trample. Beware!

---

86 "ESSAY ON MAN" By Alexander Pope (1688-1744).
87 Ezek 8:1-18
88 Ezek 8:12
89 Eph 5:15

Jesus sees the "works" of the Thyatiran saints. He takes note of works and judges each man according to his works.[90]

Jesus commends the godly people of Thyatira for their love, faith, service, patience and growing zeal (their "last works were more than the first"). That covers the obligation of every worshipper of Jesus. What more is required than self-sacrificing love, obedient-living faith, and expanding service? The list includes our duty to God, duty to self, and duty to others.

Verse 20

But I have this against thee,
that thou sufferest the woman Jezebel,
who calleth herself a prophetess;
and she teacheth and seduceth my servants to commit fornication,
and to eat things sacrificed to idols.

Jesus said to the good people of Thyatira, I have this against you ... you suffer (tolerate, permit) that woman Jezebel to work her shame before your very eyes and make no objection.

The devout did not participate in such scandalous conduct, but neither did they protest. They appear to have been afraid of being accused of judgmentalism and therefore politically incorrect.

The righteous must be bold and brave in opposing evil. Jesus does not recommend the unbalanced radicalism that creates an atmosphere of suspicion and distrust. He requires that his people confront and condemn all that is false, but with the courtesy of civility. It is possible to be polite while making a strong and bold objection to sin. A failure to do so is to court spiritual disaster. "A little leaven leavens the whole lump."[91]

To take your place in the frontlines of the good fight of faith and oppose the evil one is required of a good soldier. To let wickedness pass unchallenged and unopposed is traitorous. "They enslave their children's children who make compromise with sin."[92]

---

90 Rom 2:6; 2 Cor 11:15; 2 Tim 4:14; Rev 18:6, 20:12-13
91 Gal 5:9
92 THE PRESENT CRISIS By James Russell Lowell (1819-18910

It was outrageous for the blood-washed saints in Thyatira to cover their eyes and refuse to look upon the rampant wickedness that was all around them. "She teacheth and seduceth my servants to commit fornication, and to eat things sacrificed to idols."

"The Lord is not slack concerning his promise, as some count slackness; but is longsuffering to you-ward, not wishing that any should perish, but that all should come to repentance."[93]

Verse 21

And I gave her time that she should repent;
and she willeth not to repent of her fornication.

"I gave her time ... but she willeth not to repent ..."

Your will is involved in repentance and doing the will of God.[94] You have power over your own will. You can will to do right, or you can will to commit fornication and eat things sacrificed to idols.

God is longsuffering, but he is also holy and just. Peter tells us that a time will come when the patience of God will no longer be extended to a world full of wickedness and he will end the universe in flames of fire. "The earth and the works that are therein shall be burned up."[95] The sun, moon and stars will "fall to the earth as fig tree casteth her unripe figs when she is shaken of a great wind"[96] That day will come.

It may not seem tactful to talk about torment, but it is dishonest to fail to do so. The final judgment and punishment of the rebels to righteousness is inescapable, and they deserve to be forewarned.

The living and the dead shall witness that awful event. There are not enough rocks and mountains to bury one deep enough under their mass for him to be unable to see the pouring out of the wrath of God, the Almighty.

---

93   2 Peter 3:9
94   John 7:17
95   2 Pet 3:10-11
96   Rev 6:12-17

Verse 22

Behold, I cast her into a bed,
and them that commit adultery with her into great tribulation,
except they repent of her works.

Solemn threats of a judgment to come were often heard from the mouth of Christ. It is kindness to warn people of a coming day of reckoning. The bed into which Jesus will cast this evil woman and her cohorts is symbolic of the river flowing with fire and brimstone.

Verse 23

And I will kill her children with death;
and all the churches shall know that I am he
that searcheth the reins and hearts:
and I will give unto each one of you according to your works.

Some in Thyatira were faithful and true and Jesus said to them, keep a strong, tight hold on what you have. To maintain a grip on the unchanging hand of God demands eternal vigilance.

Simple neglect results in drifting.[97] It is not hard to fall away from truth and out of grace and multiplied millions have done it. To stay committed, however, requires earnest effort and strong determination. One cannot be saved accidently.

Verse 24

But to you I say, to the rest that are in Thyatira,
as many as have not this teaching,
who know not the deep things of Satan,
as they are wont to say;
I cast upon you none other burden.

The advice of Jesus is "hold fast that which you have."

Satan is not ignorant. He is a cunning and slippery deceiver. He will fool you, if you are not vigilant. You must hold fast.

---

97   Heb 2:1-3

The devil is not above using the very scripture he is trying to destroy to accomplish his mad purpose of ruining as many lives as possible.

Part of his bait is to say, "Let us taste the deep things of Satan so we can understand his methods and defeat him." He is a skillful wizard. If you bite the bait the hidden hook will be sticking in your bleeding mouth and getting free of it will not be easy. Therefore, hold fast to what you have – love, faith, service and zeal.

Do not foolishly suppose that you can aimlessly win this fight of faith. "For your obedience is come abroad unto all men. I rejoice therefore over you: but I would have you wise unto that which is good, and simple (innocent) unto that which is evil. And the God of peace shall bruise Satan under your feet shortly."[98]

Satan says, "Taste the deep things of Satan so you can successfully defeat him." Jesus says, "I would have you innocent of that which is evil."

Whose counsel will you follow?

Will you dirty your soul in sin in the mistaken belief this will empower you to defeat Satan, or will you maintain the piety of the purity that pleases God? "Be not deceived. God is not mocked"[99] You cannot win by losing.

Jesus casts this solitary burden upon you. Nevertheless, it is a burden, but he will make it tolerable.[100]

Hold that which you have until Jesus comes. The majestic and magnetic appeal to restore first century Christianity to the current century is impeccable. Hold to it!

Do not be ashamed of God and he will never be ashamed of you.

Hold the fort. Jesus is coming. The time of his coming no one on earth can know. They can uselessly speculate, but they cannot know.[101] God fixed that and you cannot change it.

---

98 Rom 16:19-20
99 Gal 6:7
100 Matt 11:28
101 Matt 24:36

Verse 25

Nevertheless that which ye have, hold fast till I come.

The second coming of Jesus from heaven to earth is emphatically taught in the Holy Bible.[102] It will happen. Depend on it. He will come shortly (suddenly), which means without warning. No flags will fly and no trumpets will sound to announce his near approach, but "as sure as the sun brings morning," he will come back to the proximity of earth "unto salvation for them that wait for him." He comes! He comes! Thank God!

Verse 26-27

And he that overcometh,
and he that keepeth my works unto the end, to him
will I give authority over the nations:

and he shall rule them with a rod of iron,
as the vessels of the potter are broken to shivers;
as I also have received of my Father:

He that is overcoming is he that is keeping the works unto the end. This is in present tense – keep on keeping on to the end. Being in sight of the finish-line is not victory; crossing the finish line is victory. When the goal looms large is the time for our best effort.

One promise of the Lord is to give to him that overcomes authority over the nations. When Jesus comes to the vicinity of earth again he will crush godless nations with a rod of iron.

The saints will participate in breaking the vessels of the potter to shivers in that they, being identified with the victorious Christ, concur in his righteous judgments. The saints shall join in the judgment of the world at the end of time. They will break the Potter's vessel.[103]

The victory of the clean and the devout is authority over the nations.[104]

102 Heb 9:27
103 1 Cor 6:2-3
104 Isa 60:14; Rev 3:9

Verse 28

and I will give him the morning star.

Jesus promises to the victorious saint the morning star. Few presume to know what this morning star may be.

The earth's sun is a star. It seems to rise every morning and set every night. It is often symbolizes royalty. It seems consistent to think that the rising and setting sun is the morning star. If so, it represents kingship.

The children of God are the stars of God. The sanctified are God's stars. Jesus holds you in his hand and affirms your kingship, if you are his child. Royalty is promised to the saints at Thyatira.

Verse 29

He that hath an ear,
let him hear what the Spirit saith to the churches.

Each person controls how he hears. It is possible for us to have ears but not hear and eyes but not see. It is also possible to harden the heart until it is like a flintstone and even the loving words of God make no impression. Take heed how you hear and what you see. Do not make the sad mistake of closing your eyes and ears to divine instruction. He is the potter and we are the clay.[105]

---

105 Isa 29:16; Jer 5:21

Letters to the Churches

PART 2
Chapter Three

In chapter two we read and learned from letters to four of the seven churches to whom Jesus addressed a letter. In this chapter we will study the letters to the three remaining churches.

Sardis
Verses 1-6

Verse 1

And to the angel of the church in Sardis write:
These things saith he that hath the seven Spirits of God,
and the seven stars:
I know thy works,
that thou hast a name that thou livest,
and thou art dead.

Jesus in this brief message to the saints at Sardis, refers to himself as "he that hath the seven spirits of God, and the seven stars."

Jesus writes to "the angel (messenger) of the church." He expects his letter to be read in an assembly of the saved at Sardis and preserved for the enlightenment of his people in coming generations. The epistle of Jesus to Sardis takes its place in the corridors of time in an eternal book.[106]

---

106 Matt 5:18; John 12:48

The seven spirits of God reference the Holy Spirit, later symbolized as seven lamps burning before the throne.[107] The Holy Spirit is God, that is, has the "form of God" or the "substance" or "essence" of God. This is true of all three members of the one Godhead. The figures describing the Comforter in these opening chapters of the book of Revelation witness his wisdom and awesome power.

Because of his pilgrimage, culminating in his redeeming sacrifice, Jesus received the totality of authority.[108] Included in this exaltation was the right to send the Holy Spirit.[109] Jehovah sent the Spirit but he did it at the behest of Jesus. The Holy Spirit came from the Father through the Son.

The mission of the Spirit was to guide the apostles into all saving truth.[110] Note the word "all" in this verse. Jehovah gave and Jesus sent the entirety of truth necessary for human redemption to the apostles of the Lord in the first century of our age. All of it came in the first century a.d., through the ministration of the Spirit, referred to in this passage as "the seven Spirits of God."

Seven, of course, symbolizes perfection or completeness. John calls the Holy Spirit the flawless exemplification of supreme excellence. Since the death of the apostles, no one has added one syllable to the powerful gospel of salvation. It is "the once for all delivered faith."[111]

All latter day claims of revelation are under the anathema of the Creator.[112] The book of Revelation takes its place as the final word from God in this age and concludes with the warning to neither take from it nor add to it.[113]

Jesus possesses that he may impart.[114] "He shall glorify me: for he shall take of mine, and shall declare it unto you." Notice the Holy Spirit does not glorify himself, but glorifies Jesus.

---

107 Rev 4:5
108 Matt 28:18; Col 1:18
109 John 14:26; 15:26
110 John 16:13
111 Jude 3
112 Gal 1:8-9
113 Rev 22:18-19
114 John 16:13-14; 14:16-17, 26; 15:26

It is incumbent on us to make and seize opportunities to study the word and meditate on it day and night.[115] Revelation is the only medium of salvation and salvation is the only legitimate purpose of life. The focus of the saved must be on the inspired word of God.

In preparing his soldiers to "fight the good fight of faith", Jesus begins by emphasizing the importance of "every word inspired of God." The Bible is the only instrument the saved need to rout the enemy and win the war.

The book of Revelation is a handbook on how to fight Satan and his powerful minions. It tells, in spiritual words, of an age-long spiritual battle. The fight is consistent … it never lets up and neither should we ever relax our vigilance. "Watch ye therefore …"

Jesus holds in his hand the "seven stars" representing the evangelists of his potent message of reconciliation to God. There is no more important work than proclaiming salvation in Christ.

The commander-in-chief of the Christian army is aware of the condition, attitude and action of his troops. To Sardis he said, "I know thy works." Were he to speak today he could say that same thing to us.

Jesus sees all sin and all goodness. His penetrating gaze pierces every disguise. He cannot be imposed upon because he has the power to know everything.[116]

Jesus knew the works of the saints in Sardis. I emphasize the word "works." Let no one deceive himself … Jesus is interested in works. He takes note of every act and every thought. The Lord tells us that we shall know false prophets "by their fruits."[117] You will know them by what they say and do. This same test identifies the good fruit of a good tree.[118]

The book of Revelation emphasizes the importance of works.[119] Those who question and deny the importance of works in the scheme of salvation are blind to the criteria for determining the lost and the saved. They are self-deceived and in their ignorance deceive others.

---

115 2 Tim 2:15; Psalms 1:1-3
116 Heb 4:12-13
117 Matt 7:15-16
118 Matt 7:17
119 Rev 2:2, 5, 19, 23, 26; 3:1, 2, 8, 15; 14:13; 20:12, 13; 22:12

Flamboyant congregations love to spread themselves and call attention to their works while denying that works have anything to do with salvation. "Grace and not works" is their battle cry. What the gullible fail to see is that show and circumstance is not necessarily pious and devout. Indeed, it is often worldly and therefore irreligious.

Jesus said to the Sardities, "... thou hast a name that thou livest, and thou art dead." The church at Sardis had a reputation for being vibrant and resonant, but in reality they were lifeless and wrongheaded ... dead!

Stuffed animals in a museum look like the real thing, but there is no life in them.

The church at Sardis in the days of John was dead. It was a congregation without healthful teaching and without heresies. It did not have enough life to produce even false teaching, evidenced by the fact that Jesus found no teaching error to expose and condemn.

There was no persecution in Sardis. Why should the devil persecute a dead church? Architects may design waving curves to have the appearance of flame but there is no heat; a "form of godliness" but no power. A dead church, even one that has a reputation for being on fire, is a mighty obstacle to truth.

The church of Christ must be countercultural. Much of the culture of our day is a rotten fabric that needs to be exposed and condemned. The world needs to hear again the kind of preaching that came from the mouth of John the bapitst, and from the lips of Jesus, and from the pens of the apostles.

Believers must go against the current in society. As long as the saved are content to go with the flow, they will be toothless and savorless ... and dead. Salt that is fit for nothing. Stand up. Speak out and boldly in Christ's name.

Not every large, active church is dead, but many of them are. The churches we may think of as outstandingly successful may be nothing more than a shell whose success is a sham. It may be dazzling to many but it cannot deceive the all-seeing eye of the Lord who looks not on the outward appearance but on the heart. If our works are not right before God, we cannot possibly be right in his sight.

We can almost hear the Sardis-like-disciples saying, "We? Dead? But Lord did we not prophecy in thy name, and in thy name cast out demons, and in thy name do many mighty works."

His answer … "Depart from me. I never knew you."[120]

Jesus marks as acceptable those who "heareth these words of mine and doeth them."[121] "Heareth" and "doeth" are present tense and call for continuing action, that is, "he that is continuing to hear and continuing to do these words of mine …" Not sporadic works but ongoing works are pleasing in the eyes of Jesus.

Verse 2

Be thou watchful,
and establish the things that remain,
which were ready to die:
for I have found no works of thine perfected before my God.

An ingredient in the balm that cures apathy (which is the besetting sin of the church in the modern age) is vigilance. Keep your eyes open. Strive to see things as they really are and not as they appear to be.

Saints are not alarmists. It is not theirs to engage unwarranted excitement of fears or loudmouth warnings of nonexistent dangers. It is counterproductive to fight against imaginary evils. There is enough of the real thing to keep us busy. We must not be blind to reality but oppose every morally reprehensible thing, but we must be sure that we are not fighting a phantom. Will-o'-the 'wisp strenuous activity wears out the warrior and wins no victory. It saps our energy and leaves us floundering in sheer impotency. We hear the sound of battle but no ground is gained.

We notice two mistakes: (1) not opposing actual sin and heresy; and (2) chasing non-existent bugbears. Nothing is as debilitating as *Ignis fatuus*. We run ourselves into total exhaustion and catch no rabbits, nor cross any finish lines.

Something remained of good sense and proper expenditure of energy in Sardis. The advice of the spiritual counselor is to "establish the things that

120 Matt 7:22-23
121 Matt 7:24

remain." These precious things are "ready to die." The death-rattle is in their throat. The wise in Sardis should revive valuable teaching and practice that was on the verge of teetering into eternity. Jesus tells them to brace up and summons all their strength to resist the devil. That will make him flee from you.

The people of God must turn a sharpened look at the remaining right things and say, "Except Jehovah of hosts had left unto us a very small remnant, we should have been as Sodom, we should have been like unto Gomorrah."[122] Thank God for the "small remnant."

VERSE 3

Remember therefore how thou hast received and didst hear;
and keep it,
and repent.
If therefore thou shalt not watch,
I will come as a thief,
and thou shalt not know what hour I will come upon thee.

Another ingredient in the balm that overcomes indifference is remembering. Paul urged Timothy to remember the good confession he made in the presence of witnesses.[123]

Peter told believers that he wanted to "stir" them up by putting them in "remembrance."[124]

It is easy to forget and it is hard to remember. The Lord's church has an extreme need to remember the power and appeal of restoring New Testament patterns. God grant that we never "drift away from" the things that were heard.[125] The call for a vigilant remembrance of "sound doctrine" is always in order.

Jesus built a church;[126] the church fell away from healthy teaching;[127] the crying need of every generation is to go back to the Bible and speak where

---

122 Isa 1:9
123 1 Tim 6:12
124 2 Pet 1:13
125 Heb 2:1-4
126 Matt 16:18
127 2 Tim 4:3-4

the Bible speaks and be silent where it is silent. We must turn away from the dictates of fallible men and plant our feet on eternal truth. Heralds of the gospel are ever and urgently persuading their fellow human creatures to "walk in the light" of God's word.

Remember what you heard about redemption, loyalty, patience and hope and give yourself wholly to the practice of pure and undefiled religion.

We are also to remember that Jesus is coming a second time unto a final salvation for them that wait for him and that are called according to his purpose. We are told that he comes. We are not told when. Therefore it is incumbent on us to always be ready to meet him.

Jesus warns that he comes as a thief in the night and we shall not know the hour in which he comes. His somber warnings are "watch" and "wait." John warns us that when Jesus comes again, "the kings of the earth, and the princes, and the chief captains, and the rich, and the strong, and every bondman and freeman" will hide themselves "in the caves and in the rocks of the mountains; and they say to the mountains and to the rocks, Fall on us, and hide us from the face of him that sitteth on the throne, and from the wrath of the Lamb: for the great day of their wrath is come; and who is able to stand?"[128]

The certainty of the uncertainty of his second coming should make us tremble; and resolve to remember what we have heard and keep it. "Be thou faithful unto death."

Repent, if you have wavered and wandered, and return to the fold. "For why will you die," O house of God?

VERSE 4

But thou hast a few names in Sardis that did not defile their garments:
and they shall walk with me in white;
for they are worthy.

A minority of a minority, "a few," did not defile their garments. How sad it is to see precious souls once washed and made clean in the blood of the lamb turning away from the fountain of life to drink stagnant water from "a broken cistern that can hold no water." That is the apex of imbecility.

---

128 Rev 6:15-17

For one washed and made clean to wallow in the mire with the hogs and to turn, like a dog, to his eat own vomit is disgusting.[129]

Imagine a person receiving a white, pure, clean, sparkling, translucent robe and putting that beautiful garment aside to dress in filthy rags. Do not scoff; it is done every day.

Thank God for the few that "press on toward the goal unto the prize of the high calling of God in Christ Jesus."[130] They did not choose to soil their righteous garments.

Jesus says of the few who did not defile their garments, "they shall walk with me in white, for they are worthy."

Worthy? How can one be worthy to walk with Jesus in white? Jesus pronounces them worthy. The idea of being worthy of strolling with Jesus down an avenue of gold in the presence of the holy angels and in the sight of Jehovah is taught in the Bible.[131] Those redeemed by the blood of the Lamb should not be too timid to claim their prize and honor.

VERSE 5

He that overcometh shall thus be arrayed in white garments;
and I will in no wise blot his name out of the book of life,
and I will confess his name before my Father,
and before his angels.

"He that overcometh," literally, "is overcoming" (a continuous action). Is overcoming what? This points to a battle ... a war ... a struggle ... a fight. Jesus wants his saints to be vigorously engaged in this fierce contest against wickedness. What are we to overcome? The answer is plain; we overcome self, the world, hostility, frowns, flatteries, indifference and death when we overcome Satan and his mighty army.

"For our wrestling is not against flesh and blood, but against the principalities, against the powers, against the world-rulers of this darkness, against the spiritual hosts of wickedness in the heavenly places."[132]

---

129 2 Peter 2:22
130 Phil 3:14
131 Eph 4:1; Phil 1:27; Col 1:10; 1 Thess 2:12; 2 Thess 2:5
132 Eph 6:12

Satan is not a pushover. He is a roaring lion and seeks to devour us.[133] We better be ready and summon all our power and might to overcome this foe.

That is what the book of Revelation is about – overcoming a spiritual adversary who is smart and strong.

"Wherefore take up the whole armor of God, that ye may be able to withstand in the evil day, and, having done all, to stand."[134]

Overcome and your name will be engraved in the book of life never to be removed, and Jesus himself will confess you by name before His Father and before the angels.[135]

VERSE 6

He that hath an ear,
let him hear what the Spirit saith to the churches

You have the ability to "hear what the Spirit" is saying … to hear in the sense of understanding and obeying. You can do it. That is not the issue. The question is, Will you do it?

"And he that heareth, let him say, Come. And he that is athirst, let him come: he that will, let him take the water of life freely."[136]

Philadelphia
Verses 7-13

A commander must keep his troops in fighting trim if he is to win the war. In the bloodless battle for the souls of men, it is necessary to train the soldiers in the art of righteousness and purity. Each spiritual warrior, as he does hand-to-hand combat with the principalities and powers of ungodliness, must instinctively do the right thing.

The great red dragon has terrible strength in his tail and leads battalions of giant scorpions and devouring hordes of locusts. They hurt men and leave the earth barren. To prevail against such lying prophets of evil and

133 Eph 6:12
134 Eph 6:13
135 Matt 10:32-33; Luke 12:8-9
136 Rev 21:6; 22:17

such demons from hell it is necessary for the Christian soldier to "press the battle ere the night shall veil the glowing skies."

It is for this reason Jesus, the Captain of our salvation, sent seven instructional letters to the seven churches of Asia. He must regiment his fighting men and women. The foe is formidable and the defender of faith must be highly disciplined.

Even the saints at Philadelphia, having no black mark against their name, needed additional training. Therefore, also, must we be careful to diligently study the divine oracles and meditate on them both day and night.[137]

The church will be militant or it will be defeated. The only way to overcome is to fight. A church that is comfortable in the world and knows nothing of tribulation is doomed to failure and destruction. Every believer is to be dressed in the panoply of God and must skillfully wield the "sword of the Spirit, which is the word of God."

VERSE 7

And to the angel of the church in Philadelphia write:
These things saith he that is holy,
he that is true,
he that hath the key of David,
he that openeth and none shall shut,
and that shutteth and none openeth:

In the beginning of this message, Jesus represents himself as holy and true. He is holy because he possesses perfect purity and in him, there is no darkness.

He is "guileless, undefiled, separated from sinners."[138] He is without sin.[139] None can convict him of sin.[140]

---

137 2 Tim 2:15; Psa 1:1-2
138 Heb 7:26
139 Heb 4:15
140 John 8:46

He is true because he is truth.[141] For this reason, his name is called "the Word of God."[142] God's word is absolute truth.[143] Truth sanctifies.[144] The wicked world hates lovers of truth.[145] An inflammatory condition exists, when believers face the worldly.

The soldier of Christ must never be mealy-mouthed nor pallid, but speak words of grace with straightforward boldness. He is never vicious and mean but neither is he tepid and apologetic. He must never be "ashamed of the gospel, for it is the power of God unto salvation."[146]

The children of the devil, on the other hand, are also aggressive and insistent. There is an unavoidable clash and listening ears can hear the sound of battle. It is not a pretend-tea-party. It is a vigorous conflict with eternal consequences.

We speak of a spiritual war, not a carnal one.[147]

That may sound strident but it is not, seeing that the "Word of God," who is also the Prince of Peace, stipulates the situation. The scenario is from the Bible and is therefore fair and just.

Jesus while on earth in human form spoke the truth and the world despised and crucified him for it.

> But now ye seek to kill me, a man that hath told you the truth, which I heard from God: this did not Abraham. Ye do the works of your father. They said unto him, We were not born of fornication; we have one Father, even God. Jesus said unto them, If God were your Father, ye would love me: for I came forth and am come from God; for neither have I come of myself, but he sent me. Why do ye not understand my speech? Even because ye cannot hear my word.[148]

---

141 John 1:14; 5:32-33; 8:32; 14:6
142 Rev 19:13
143 John 17:17
144 John 17:19
145 John 17:14
146 Rom 1:16
147 1 Tim 6:12
148 John 8:40-43

This may sound obtrusive to some, but his candor was not harsh. Jesus was a militant conversationalist but he was not loud and vociferous. We are to walk in his footsteps ... carrying a cross. We behave in all civility but our speech is salty, and free from evasiveness or obscurity, clear-cut and precise.

Look! O, look! Jesus wears upon his shoulder the "key of David."[149] He has "all authority, both in heaven and on earth." He shuts and none can open; he opens and none can shut.

When we speak in his name, we must be plain; we must be courteous but truthful; we must be kind, but unafraid to condemn the wrong; we must speak words of seasoned grace.[150]

Verse 8

I know thy works
(behold, I have set before thee a door opened, which none can shut),
that thou hast a little power,
and didst keep my word,
and didst not deny my name

Jesus is all-knowing. He can know anything he wants to know and, because he is God, he can refuse to know what he does not want to know. To deny this is to deny his omnipotence. He can do anything, provided it is neither self-contradictory nor contrary to his nature and his word.[151]

One commentator said: "The supernatural knowledge of the exalted Christ is emphasized."[152]

It is chilling to the ungodly to realize that Jesus knows their works. It is comforting to the saved to know that Jesus knows their works.

---

149 Isaiah 22:22
150 Col 4:6
151 He can destroy the world by a universal flood, but he will not because of his promise (Gen 9:11)
152 David E. Aune, *World Biblical Commentary on Revelatiion*, World Books, Vol 1, p 236

Notice the emphasis on "works." Each man is to be rewarded or punished "according to his works."[153]

The first century church at Philadelphia in Asia had "a little power." Compared to the awesome might of Jesus the power of man always seems small. Still, the strength of the pure in heart is equal the tasks of every day. God does not give us work to do without giving us the ability to do it. If we have a strong will to do the will of God our vitality will not fail and our understanding will not falter.[154]

Jesus commends these brothers in old Philadelphia because they kept his word and did not "deny" his name. All through the Bible the importance of fidelity to the revealed word of God is stressed.

The book of Revelation is God's answer to religious liberalism.

The greatest sin of the antediluvians was failure to keep God's word. This was the sin of the first pair and their posterity. It brought the great deluge, and cost the lives of multiplied millions.

The wickedness of not keeping the word of God brought severe punishment and loss.

Later, failure to keep the law of Jehovah resulted in chains and slavery for Israel.

Jesus warned that refusing to follow the word of God strictly would bring catastrophic rejection.[155]

Failure to keep the words of Jesus is tantamount to denying him. It is heart wrenching to witness modern religious liberals by the boatload committing the inexcusable sin of belittling the words of Jesus. They thoughtlessly deny him who has the key of David on his shoulder.

God grant that we have the good sense never to deny Jesus by failing to keep his words ... all of them.

---

153 Rom 2:6
154 John 7:16-18
155 Matt 7:21-27

Verse 9

Behold, I give of the synagogue of Satan,
of them that say they are Jews,
and they are not,
but do lie;
behold, I will make them to come and worship before thy feet,
and to know that I have loved thee.

In the Philadelphian church, there were those who said they were Jews but were liars.

Jesus called them a synagogue of Satan.

This brings to mind an incident in the earthly life of Jesus. In the Temple of the Jews in Jerusalem, Jesus was teaching on the importance of abiding in his word and being made free by its truth.[156]

This provoked an argument about who Jesus is and the authority by which he spoke. Jesus accused them to seeking to kill him "because my word hath not free course in you."[157] Once again, he stresses the importance of keeping his word and putting it first.

Jesus then spoke these biting words,

> Ye are of your father the devil, and the lusts of your father it is your will to do. He was a murderer from the beginning, and standeth not in the truth, because there is no truth in him. When he speaketh a lie, he speaketh of his own: for he is a liar, and the father thereof. But because I say the truth, ye believe me not. Which of you convicteth me of sin? If I say truth, why do ye not believe me? He that is of God heareth the words of God: for this caise ue hear them now, because ye are not of God.[158]

They claimed to be Jews, the sons of Abraham, worshippers of Jehovah, but Jesus called them liars who were not of God. Strong words of condemnation, but necessary under the circumstances.

---

156 John 8:31-32
157 John 8:37
158 John 8:44-47

Contrast this with the pitifully weak teaching of compromise so common in the pulpits of today. I grow weary of men who present the powerful gospel as if it were an apology.

Those liars in Philadelphia of Asia who claimed to be Jews but who were in fact a synagogue of Satan were in the church. Think of that! Satan may have a synagogue in the church, which, of course, displeases God and stirs his hot wrath.

The persecution of Christ and his church began with the Jews. Later the Romans picked it up and it became to them an obsession. The Jews started it. The Romans perfected it.

Jesus said that the day would come when those who persecute the righteous will worship at the feet of the saints. The word translated "worship" is from a word meaning, "to bow down" or "fall prostrate."

Those who try to shame the church of Christ in this life will one day fall on their faces before the very people they have demeaned. To wound the body of Christ – the church - is to insult God and suffer the consequence of his fierce wrath.

When Saul persecuted the church, Jesus said to him, "Saul, Saul, why persecutest thou me."[159] To persecute the church is to persecute Jesus, because the church is his body – the body of Jesus of which he is the head.[160]

Verse 10

Because thou didst keep the word of my patience,
I also will keep thee from the hour of trial,
that hour which is to come upon the whole world,
to try them that dwell upon the earth.

Jesus clearly foresaw the vicious, intensified persecution that was soon to come down on truth-loving saints in the body of Christ. He did not send a legion of angels to circumvent the tortuous deaths of many of his children. He knew it was coming and did nothing to stop it.

---

159 Acts 9:4
160 Col 1:18

Just to know that Jesus knows all about the throes of our hard struggle, and that he cares, is solace enough. It gives strength to endure what we must endure and to suffer what we suffer. Thank God for the empathy of Jesus.

To know that Jesus empathizes with his people in all their pain, sorrow and disappointment is sufficient. The hand of the loving mother on the fevered brow of her child is profoundly comforting to the little one. The mother's hand does not reduce the child's temperature one degree, but the child smiles.

The sympathy and condolence of the Mighty Son of God cheers us and enables us to walk unafraid through the fires of hatred and persecution. The sneers of scoffers and unbelievers do not daunt nor cow the sons and daughters of God because Jesus cares.

We can support the hurt of misunderstanding and ridicule, if we know that we have a friend in Jesus "all our sins and grief to bear."

VERSE 11

I come quickly:
hold fast that which thou hast,
that no one take thy crown.

Jesus promises to "come quickly" to the rescue of his children. He will come suddenly and unexpectedly, swiftly and forcefully, and all who do not love the truth but have pleasure in unrighteousness will be brought to a deserved justice.[161]

Knowing that on a "bright and cloudless morning" the trumpet of all ages shall sound and the Son of God shall appear in glory and the good and the bad shall arise to meet their destiny is adequate reason to "hold to God's unchanging hand."

Jesus counsels his beloved people to "hold fast" to what you have. The issues are large and eternity is forever, therefore tenaciously grasp truth and righteousness. Hold to your hope with vigor and determination. It is your task to maintain your sanctity. Let no man rob you of your prize.[162]

---

161 2 Thess 2:12
162 Col 2:18

You can lose your promised reward. Make it the main purpose of your life to "press on toward the goal unto the prize of the high calling of God in Christ Jesus'"[163]

The Book of Revelation is not merely a collection of high-sounding symbols and figures, but is eminently practical. It urges us to fix our eyes on the crystal sea, the gates of pearl, the street of gold, and the great, white throne of God. Gaze intently on coming glories hold tightly to the promised crown lest you lose it. It can be taken from you. Don't let it happen!

If you lose your reward, it is your fault and yours alone.

VERSES 12-13

He that overcometh,
I will make him a pillar in the temple of my God,
and he shall go out thence no more:
and I will write upon him the name of my God,
and the name of the city of my God,
the new Jerusalem,
which cometh down out of heaven from my God,
and mine own new name.

He that hath an ear,
let him hear what the Spirit saith to the churches.

Now the promises to the good church in Philadelphia, and to the faithful of all ages .The reward is real and uncommonly beautiful. Having just warned his disciples to "hold fast that which thou hast, that no one take away thy crown," he now promises a secure future.

If you hold firmly to your place in the ranks of the army of God then you will be in that number "when the saints go marching in."

You "shall go out thence no more."

Jesus will make you a "pillar in the temple" of God. The supporting pillar is "steadfast and unmovable." It is beautiful. It is powerful. It is firm. It is unyielding.

---

163 Phil 3:14

Just as the High Priest in Old Israel had words inscribed on his mitre, so will you have written upon you the name of God, the city of God, the new Jerusalem, and the new name of Jesus himself. What blessed assurance that is. To have these names written upon you is to declare to all who look that you are the child of the Most High and all the riches of God are yours. You are an heir of God and a joint heir with Jesus Christ.[164]

"He that hath an ear, let him hear what the Spirit saith to the churches."

The last of the seven letters was sent to the church at Laodicea ...

Laodicea
Verses 14-22

The commander of the forces of righteousness prepares his soldiers for the "good fight of faith." His primary concern, as we have seen in the six previous letters, is for his warriors to be well versed in eternal truth.

- The captain of our salvation is truth[165].

- God's word is truth[166]

- The victorious Jesus' "name is called the word of God"[167]

- Jesus' soldiers must "know the truth" that makes men free[168]

- We can know and understand saving truth[169]

- The great differential between Satan and Christ is that Satan is devoid of truth[170] whereas Christ is full of truth[171]

- The clash is between truth and untruth

- The good fight of faith is over truth.[172]

---

164 Rom 8:17
165 John 14:6
166 John 17:17
167 Rev 19:13
168 John 8:32
169 Eph 3:4
170 John 8:44
171 John 1:14
172 The only absolute truth the world will ever know is Bible truth. We may have truth in history, science, and education apart from biblical teaching, but all such truth is tentative and therefore liable to change ... in fact, it does change. Even Einstein's famous theory of relativity is undergoing revision. Absolute truth never changes.

The warriors of Christ are armed with the sword of the Spirit, which is the word of God, personified by Jesus.[173]

In the breathless battle of the ages, the conflict is between lies and absolute truth. The leader of one faction is the "father of lies;" the opposing leader is full of "grace and truth." Jesus is the way, the truth, and the life.[174]

Take your pick.

Verse 14

And to the angel of the church in Laodicea write:
These things saith the Amen,
the faithful and true witness,
the beginning of the creation of God:

The opening statement of this letter to Laodicea reaffirms the unapproachable dignity and basic fidelity of the majestic Jesus. He is "the Amen." Thayer says this "has the force of a superlative, most assuredly," which is to say that his word is unalterably true. What he threatens is certain … beware! Finally, look askance at anyone who denies the absolute truth of the Bible.

Jesus is also "the faithful and true witness," which continues to emphasize his fidelity and unwavering devotion to truth. He witnesses the solemn, eternal elements of salvation.

He attests the goodness and love of God, the unwillingness of God for any to perish but for all to come to salvation, the reality and beauty of heaven, the scheme of redemption, and the ultimate victory of truth over lies.

Jesus identifies himself as "the beginning of creation." In nothing do we see more clearly the limitless power of the Almighty than in the original creation of the universe. God spoke the cosmos into existence … an event that declares eloquently the glory of the Creator. Jesus, with intrepid boldness, steps forward to reveal that he is "the beginning of the creation

---

God's word is an expression of infinite wisdom and in its very nature is perfect, entire, and constant. To deny the absoluteness of his word is to deny God.

173 Eph 6:17; Rev 19:19
174 John 14:6

of God," which does not mean that he was the first created being, but that he is uncreated and eternal.

Jesus upholds all things by the word of his power.[175] His majesty is unparalleled.

Prophets said, "Thus saith the Lord."

Jesus said, "But I say unto you."

The exalted one speaks to you ... we dare not treat lightly his voice.

Jesus spoke the words of God;[176] His mission is salvation;[177] his birth, life, death all point to salvation.[178]

Our part in the salvation process is to believe and be baptized to be saved;[179]. repentance and baptism bring remission of sins;[180] when the believer repents arises and is baptized, his sins are washed away;[181] afterwards, the newborn child of God is to walk in the steps of Jesus – stepping in the light.[182]

Jesus did not come from heaven to earth for social reform but for forgiveness and eternal salvation. To put the emphasis of his mission anywhere else is unacceptable. It is not the economy but where will you spend eternity that is important. It is not redistribution of wealth, but refined gold, eye salve, and covered nakedness that really counts. Earthly things perish ... "labor not for the meat that is perishing, but for that which endures to eternal life."[183]

Verses 15-16

I know thy works,
that thou art neither cold nor hot:
I would thou wert cold or hot.

---

175 Heb 1:1-5; Eph 1:22-23; Col 1:18
176 John 5:30; 6:38-40
177 Luke 19:10
178 Luke 2:25-38; Matt 1:21; 1 John 4:9-14; Matt 26:28; John 3:17; Rev 1:5
179 Mark 16:16
180 Acts 2:38
181 Acts 22:16
182 1 John 1:7; Rev 2:10; 3:11
183 John 6:27

So because thou art lukewarm,
and neither hot nor cold,
I will spew thee out of my mouth.

Once again, Jesus announces his knowledge of behavior. He who saw at a distance Nathanael under the fig tree (a thing requiring supernatural vision) miraculously knew the heart of the Laodiceans.

He knew the works of his disciples, though they were on earth and he was in heaven. Jesus drives home repeatedly the importance of works, which play a vital role in the salvation process. Without works, faith is dead.[184]

Works reveal the man whether he is good or evil.

Jesus saw a lack of zeal in the self-satisfied saints of Laodicea. In their own eyes, they were okay, but in Jesus eyes, they were lacking passion, force, or zest. Jesus saw and noted an absence of enthusiasm or conviction.

This could well be his indictment of many of his professing followers today. Let each one of us labor and pray that we are not in that number.

Enthusiastic service requires deep conviction. "No man, having put his hand to the plow, and looking back, is fit for the kingdom of God."[185]

If you are "fit for the kingdom of God," you must believe what you believe with all the power of your being. You cannot be half-hearted and have true conviction. It is a proposition of, If I am right and you disagree, then you are wrong; if you are right and I disagree, then I am wrong.

The modern namby-pamby position that if I am right and you disagree, then we are both right is contradicted by the "Amen, who is the beginning of creation." Absolute truth is narrow in its very nature.

Conviction generated by absolute truth is necessarily uncompromising. Furthermore, believing what you believe is its driving force. The Historical-Critical method[186] of understanding religion is tepid and wrongheaded

---

184 James 2:14-26

185 Luke 9:62

186 The Historical-Critical method of theology is fundamentally a system of unbelief. It encourages the "cafeteria" approach to religion, which means, "go through the Bible and select the dishes that stimulate your taste buds and leave the rest." Select what you want; turn-up your nose at what you do not want. This is not

because it lacks being convinced of error and compelled to admit the truth. It is not a strong persuasion or belief.

Consider this: Jesus rose from the dead: therefore, there will be a general resurrection of all the dead. That is a compelling statement. To make the resurrection of Jesus optional is to make a universal resurrection optional. There is no conviction ... no strong belief ... no commitment ... no zeal ... no enthusiasm ... no zest in that. It is, at best, lukewarm and nauseating.

Jesus said, "It makes me want to vomit, or "spew thee out of my mouth." It may suit the half-hearted believer, but it makes Jesus sick.

The Lord wants us to believe what we believe, believe it with all of our heart, and not be reluctant to tell others about it.

Luke-warmness in faith and practice is not acceptable to "the Amen, the faithful witness." He was a man of deep conviction, as the pain of Gethsemane and Calvary attest. If you would follow Jesus, take up your cross and draw your sword.

If we are to war the good fight of faith, we must be possessed of the undying conviction that we are right and all who disagree are wrong. That fills us with a sense of commitment and impels being "faithful unto death." The true worshipper of God will say, I believe what I believe and am willing to die for it.

Jesus is saying, "Either get in or get out, but don't stand in the door and keep others from entering." Don't be a hypocrite. Be for me or against me, but do not make the tragic blunder of attempting to serve two masters "You cannot serve both God and mammon."[187]

A half-hearted disciple is repulsive to Jesus.

You can win no wars if the rank-and-file is not powerfully convinced of the rightness of their cause. If we go to battle unsure and wavering, defeat is inevitable. Jesus is saying, I want no slackers at my back.

---

conviction but convenience. Conviction is knowing why you believe what you believe, and not hesitating for a moment to tell others about it.

187 Matt 6:24

Verse 17

Because thou sayest,
I am rich, and have gotten riches,
and have need of nothing;
and knowest not that thou art the wretched one
and miserable and poor and blind and naked:

Ignorance is deceptive. God's people are destroyed for lack of knowledge.[188] When Christians begin to say, Hey, look me over; I am cocksure. I can get by just fine with sporadic and incomplete service. The consequence is alarming.

The emperor who thought his clothes were real was ignorant of his nakedness. There are many such ignorant people walking around in the world. They have good cars, fine homes, abundant clothes, lots of food and say to their souls, "Soul, thou hast much goods laid up for many years; take thine ease, eat, drink, be merry."[189]

"But God" says, "Thou foolish one, this night is thy soul required of thee; and the things which thou hast prepared, whose shall they be? So is he that layeth up treasure for himself, and is not rich toward God."[190]

So, you are rich. Maybe so, but are you rich toward God? If you are not rich toward God, do you know that you are naked?

God will one day dissolve earth, sun, moon, stars as suddenly as they appeared at creation. What then ... will you be clothed or naked? Will you be rich or poor?

Who is wretched, poor, blind, and naked? Is it not the fool who thinks his soul can be satisfied with the abundance of the stuff he possesses?

The disciples at Laodicea labored under the delusion that material things suffice. They had garments, chariots, palaces and gourmet food, but they did not have God, and, consequently, they were poor, blind, and naked.

188 Isa 15:13; Hosea 4:6
189 Luke 12:19
190 Luke 12:20-21

63

A fool says in his heart, there is no God.[191] "The heavens declare the glory of God, the firmament shows his handiwork."[192] The sun, moon and stars are shouting at you that God exists and the earth is his creation. Do you hear that thunderous chorus?

Verse 18

I counsel thee to buy of me gold refined by fire,
that thou mayest become rich;
and white garments,
that thou mayest clothe thyself,
and that the shame of thy nakedness be not made manifest;
and eyesalve to anoint thine eyes, that thou mayest see.

Jesus supplies the refined gold, sparkling robes, and healing eye salve, but we have to apply it. There is something for man to do. Jesus supplies grace[193] but we must apply it to our lives by the obedience of faith.[194]

For the grace of God hath appeared, bringing salvation to all men, instructing us, to the intent that, denying ungodliness and worldly lusts, we should live soberly and righteously and godly in this present world; looking for the blessed hope and appearing of the glory of the great God and our Saviour Jesus Christ; who gave himself for us, that he might redeem us from all iniquity, and purify unto himself a people for his own possession, zealous of good works."[195]

Please note: the grace of God brings salvation to all men; but not all will be saved. Grace is for all, but not all will receive it. Jesus died for all, but all will not benefit from his death. Grace is available to all, "instructing

---

191 Psa 14:1
192 Psa 19:1
193 Grace means favor or gift. "The apostles and N. T. writers at the beginning and end of their Epistles crave for their readers the favor ('grace') of God or of Christ, to which all blessings, especially spiritual, are due: Rom 1:7; 16:20,24; 1 Cor 1:3; 16:23; 2 Cor 1:2 2 Cor 13:13-14; Gal 1:3; 6:18; Eph 1:2; 6:24; Phil 1:2; 4:23; Col 1:2; 4:18; 1 Thess 1:1; 5:28; 2 Thess 1:2; 3:18; 1 Tim 1:2; 6:21-22; 2 Tim 1:2; 4:22: Titus 1:4; 3:15; Philem 3,25; Heb 13:25; 1 Peter 1:2; 2 Peter 1:2; 3:18; 2 John 3; Rev 1:4; 22:21" (Henry Thayer, *Thayers Greek-English Lexicon of the New Testament*).
194 Rom 1:5; 16:26
195 Titus 2:11-14

us, to the intent that, denying ungodliness and worldly lusts, we should live soberly and righteously and godly in this present world"

Again, those who obey the instructions of grace are to be "zealous of good works."[196] That was the problem with the church at Laodicea in the first century … they were not zealous of good works, and received the stinging rebuke of Jesus.

Verse 19-20

As many as I love, I reprove and chasten:
be zealous therefore, and repent.

Behold, I stand at the door and knock:
if any man hear my voice and open the door,
I will come in to him,
and will sup with him, and he with me.

Jesus is not willing that any should perish. He is longsuffering and filled with loving kindness. His plea is for his followers to buckle on the panoply of God, draw the sword of the Spirit, and throw the scabbard away; he wants his warriors to be brave and valiant and unrelenting. "Onward, Christian soldiers, marching as to war."

The Lord rebukes sloth especially in wartime. The "good fight of faith" is ceaseless and constant. We dare not be asleep or indolent because our enemy presses the battle without respite. Satan's minions are always at work and give no quarter. The army of the Lord cannot engage even temporary delay, rest or relief, or the enemy will take territory that may never be regained.

To be asleep while on duty in the military in time of war is a capital offence because it endangers others. The fight is on; we wage a spiritual war, and must man the battlements day and night. The face of valiant Christian soldiers must be visible in every breach or gap in the wall.

Standing up for Jesus is the duty of every saint. Plant your feet! Face the foe! "Watch ye, stand fast in the faith, quit you like men, be strong. Let all that ye do be done in love."[197]

---

196 Titus 2:14
197 1 Cor 16:13-14

We are to throw ourselves into the battle with fearless daring, but not with savagery. We are not to be like an army fired by greed and lust that comes down on a defenseless community to pillage and rape.

Notice the caveat. "Let all that ye do be done in love." Paul is not taking back his command for us to march "as to war," but he is telling us that we are to be civil and fair. Fighting for truth is not an excuse to be wild-eyed and ruthless, or to destroy for the sake of destroying. As we artfully wield the Spirit's sword, we must be always sensible of the rights and feelings of others.

"All things therefore whatsoever ye would that men should do unto you, even so do ye also unto them: for this is the law and the prophets."[198]

"Let your speech be always with grace, seasoned with salt, that ye may know how ye ought to answer each one."[199]

Paul does not say, "be weak;" but he does say, "be graceful."

Still, it is imperative that we "take up the whole armor of God," and "withstand in the evil day, and, having done all, to stand. Stand therefore …." and stand, and stand, and stand. Never give up!

The issue is eternity.

Verses 21-22

He that overcometh,
I will give to him to sit down with me in my throne,
as I also overcame, and sat down with my Father in his throne.

He that hath an ear, let him hear what the Spirit saith to the churches.

Jesus does not call on his valiant ones to engage the hard duty of war without offering rewards and a coming sabbath. He promises his obedient soldiers the highest honor.

Jesus does not ask us to do what he refuses to do. He "counted not the being on a equality with God a thing to be grasped" but put on over his

---

198 Matt 7:12
199 Col 4:6

divine form a robe of human flesh. "He was made in all things like unto his brethren."[200]

He faced every possible discouraging enticement but went straight on to the bloody sweat of Gethsemane, the inhuman scourging by Roman soldiers, and the pain of crucifixion. He was himself in the forefront of the fight of faith. He calls to us, "Take up your cross and follow me." He does not ask us to go where he has not trod.

Jehovah gave Jesus a name that is above every name. On his head are many diadems.

"I saw in the night-visions, and, behold, there came with the clouds of heaven one like unto a son of man, and he came even to the ancient of days, and they brought him near before him. And there was given him dominion, and glory, and a kingdom, that all the peoples, nations, and languages should serve him: his dominion is an everlasting dominion, which shall not pass away, and his kingdom that which shall not be destroyed."[201]

So our elder brother identifies with us in life and in death. He promises to share his glory with all who walk in his bloodstained footprints. He sat down with the Father on the great, white, shining throne and makes room for every battle-scarred veteran of the good fight of faith to join him there.

"For the Lamb that is in the midst of the throne shall be their shepherd, and shall guide them unto fountains of waters of life: and God shall wipe away every tear from their eyes."[202]

He promises an unfading crown ... the crown of life ... to all who bring their shields and swords to him and lay their trophies down at his feet.

---

200 Heb 2:17
201 Dan 7:13-14
202 Rev 7:17

THRONE OF GOD
CHAPTER 4

The fight is on! It is not a carnal battle, but a spiritual exercise. The opening chapter of the book of Revelation, after introductory statements, portrays the risen Christ as the commander-in-chief of the army of God. In this setting, Jesus continues to head a kingdom that is "not of this world."[203] He does not expect his recruits to bloody their swords, nor is he willing to call heavenly angels to engage a fleshly contest.[204]

The battle Jesus authorizes, and that his followers wage, is in the unseen world of mind and spirit. It is an appeal to testimony, facts and truth. Every Christian soldier has a sword in his hand, but it is not made of steel. It is sharp and pointed, but it does not cut flesh nor draw blood. It is the sword of the Spirit, which is the word of God.[205]

It is a real fight, but not a fistfight. It is a clash of ideas ... a struggle for the minds of men. It involves the human spirit, engaging thinking and communicating, as directed and enlightened by the Holy Spirit through the written, revealed word.

It is the word of God and the testimony of Jesus struggling against wickedness and vain human philosophy. It is a contest between right and wrong. It is the acceptance of the Bible as inspired of God and, in its original documents, inerrant.[206]

---

203 John 18:36
204 Matthew 26:21-23
205 Ephesians 6:11
206 It is juvenile to object to the inerrancy of the original manuscripts of the Bible because they contain misinformation. Satan's statement, for instance, that to eat

The good fight of faith is laying hold on life eternal.[207]

The Captain of Salvation calls the soldiers of the cross to arms and trains them in spiritual combat. His seven letters to the church[208] put an edge on the Spirit's sword; Jesus drills his troops in the art of incorporeal war. The letters also call upon the sainted warriors to be not only informed but also zealous. Jesus wants his army to be on fire for purity and truth.

Jesus commands his valiant ones to be steeped in sacred scripture, to be undefiled by the world and enthusiastic in service. He now gives them a glimpse of the awesome power of their guardian, protector and supporter. He carefully draws the curtain aside and allows us to look through its folds and garner an impression of the glory of God. He wants his infantry to be fully aware of the invisible authority that surrounds them and at whose command they labor.

Verse 1

*After these things I saw, and behold,
a door opened in heaven,
and the first voice that I heard,
a voice as of a trumpet speaking with me, one saying,
Come up hither,
and I will show thee the things which must come to pass hereafter.*

John hears a trumpet-like voice ... clear, loud, urgent, and demanding attention.

The idea of a penetrating voice that could not be ignored is mentioned several times in Holy Scripture.

---

of the forbidden tree of life would endow wisdom is false, but it is in the Bible. The statement is wrong, but it is true the Devil made the statement (he is the father of lies). Again, the long argument between Job and his friends contains many misstatements, corrected in the context. To cite such things as proof of errancy in the Bible is immature and unfair.

207 1 Timothy 6:12

208 Each letter ends with the admonition to "hear what the Spirit saith to the churches," not meaning a congregation in a local area, but churches in every generation and nation. The letter to "the church" in Ephesus, for instance, admonishes "the churches" (plural) to hear the message – not just the church (singular) in Ephesus.

- The voice at Sinai when the Law of Moses was given was "the voice of a trumpet exceeding loud."[209]

- The messengers of Jesus sent out on the urgent mission of sounding the good news of salvation to the ends of the earth is described as "the great sound of a trumpet."[210]

- The end of the universe and the final judgment begins with "the last trump" that is so loud that it wakes the dead.[211]

- In the beginning of the book of Revelation, John heard behind him "a great voice, as of a trumpet."[212]

This figure impresses upon us the importance of what is said and the need to follow its instructions exactly.

The voice of God comes with trumpet sound as a call to battle and warning of assault.

The trumpet voice is authoritative, reliable, convincing, and brings vital information.

It is a voice of convincing force and carries the idea expressed by the centurion who said to Jesus, "For I also am a man under authority, having under myself soldiers: and I say to this one, Go, and he goeth; and to another, Come, and he cometh; and to my servant, Do this, and he doeth it."[213]

The trumpet voice of God expects faith and obedience and threatens, if diluted and ignored, rejection and punishment.

The voice of God is also like the sound of "many waters."[214] It is soothing, eases pain and calms the troubled heart; it's promises "gild Jordan's wave."

Jesus said: "Come unto me, all ye that labor and are heavy laden, and I will give you rest.[215]

---

209 Ex 19:16
210 Matt 24:31
211 1 Cor 15:52
212 Rev 1:10
213 Matt 8:9
214 Rev 1:5
215 Matt 11:28

The voice of God and of those who God sends is demanding, and authoritative; it is also pleasing because it brings comfort and solace.

It is the voice of thunder and lightning, but it is also the voice of calm and peace. It threatens and warns, and it brings purpose and hope … living hope and enlightenment.

The voice invited John the apostle to enter the portals of the celestial city of God and peer into the throne room of the Almighty and Eternal One.

Verse 2

Straightway I was in the Spirit:
and behold, there was a throne set in heaven,
and one sitting upon the throne;

John tells us that he was immediately ushered into the throne chamber of God, which may be light years away from earth, but the apostle was there in the blink of an eye – suddenly! The transport of God does not take eons, but is virtually instantaneous.

John was in the spirit for there is no other way possible to enter into a spiritual estate. God's abode is not fleshly and material, but is incorporeal and untouchable. The King of the universe is immortal, invisible, eternal.[216] "The blessed and only Potentate" dwells in light unapproachable; whom no man hath seen, nor can see."[217] Jehovah told Moses, "no man shall see me and live,"[218] that is, no man in the flesh shall see me. To see Jehovah one must be out of the flesh, or in the spirit and free from the limitations of flesh.

Only spirits in the spirit can approach deity, nothing corruptible can survive the immediate presence of God. Flesh, blood, bones, skin, muscle, and sinew are decomposable and not fit to be in a state that is immortal.[219]

His conveyance into the headquarters of the Mighty Maker was without any perceptible duration of time. He stood before the divine presence in the spirit, stripped of skeleton and substance, but his personality and

---

216 1 Tim 1:17
217 1 Tim 6:15
218 Ex 33:20
219 1 Cor 15:51-54

identity were unaffected. It was a transfiguration, an exalting, glorifying, sacred change.

John was to see invisible, spiritual reality and had to look upon it with eyes made wise by an enormous change.

To sit upon the throne is to have regal dominion. Jehovah is "sitting upon the throne" in this vision. The occupant of the throne is clothed in unexcelled majesty, and incomparable grandeur.

John did not see an image, but he saw brightness, wisdom, power, goodness, purity, and wrath.[220] Human eyes cannot see these attributes, but a spirit can, which helps us to understand why so much of the book of Revelation is in figures, symbols, and metaphors.

"Our shield and Defender, the Ancient of Days, pavilioned in splender and girded with praise."

Verse 3

*And he that sat was to look upon like a jasper stone and a sardius:
and there was a rainbow round about the throne,
like an emerald to look upon.*

John looked upon "he that sat" upon the throne. What did he see? Was it an image? Was it male or female or genderless? Did the one sitting upon the throne have a long, flowing, white beard? There is not a word of any of that, but John describes the occupant of the throne in terms of rare jewels and meaningful colors.

Jasper is an opaque gemstone of striking beauty, especially when polished. It has the brilliance of the diamond. The Holy City of God that John was to later see coming down out of heaven is described as "having the glory of God; her light was like unto a stone most precious, as it were a jasper stone, clear as crystal."[221]

Jasper is famous for its splendor and strength. It could well symbolize the exalted purity of infinite holiness. Smooth cleanliness, unblemished beauty, force and firmness the polished perfection of infinite intelligence may well

---

220 1 Tim 1:17; 6:15-16
221 Rev 21:11

be the meaning of the jasper stone, which John saw as symbolizing "he that sat" upon the throne.

The occupant of the throne was also like sardius (sometimes translated "carnelian"), which is another gemstone of great value and beauty. Sardius is often deep red in color. To gaze upon the marvelous dark red sardius is to be drawn deeper and deeper into its esoteric color until there seems to be an endless descent into its excellent quality.

The sardius may be a metaphor for the wrath of God offset by the blood of a perfect sacrifice. The hot anger of God is unbearable and is stirred by disobedience to divine rules. When the holiness of God is offended by lawlessness his perfect justice comes into play and punishment is inevitable. The bowls of his wrath will not be restrained forever. When his purity is overburdened by irresponsible disregard for the testimony of his word his anger will overflow and retribution will descend. This is called "the recompense of reward."[222]

In addition to symbolizing the consequence of godly displeasure, the blood red sardius may be a figure of the blood of the Lamb of God who takes away the sins of the world. Anger and punishment are the strange work of God,[223] but his loving kindness never fails and he sends a remedy. "God so loved the world that he gave his only begotten son ..."

The blood red sardius stone may be a figure of the suffering servant of God nailed to a cross, exhibiting the mercy of a just God.

> *Much more then, being now justified by his blood, shall we be saved from the wrath of God through him. For if, while we were enemies, we were reconciled to God through the death of his Son, much more, being reconciled, shall we be saved by his life.[224]*

John, in the spirit, also saw an emerald rainbow overarching the throne. The soft and soothing glow of an emerald speaks of tranquility. Jehovah is a God of peace. When Jesus was born of a virgin in the ancient city of Bethlehem, Jehovah sent angels to sing, "Glory to God in the highest, And on earth peace among men in whom he is well pleased."[225]

---

222 Heb 2:2; 10:35; 11:26
223 Isa 28:21
224 Rom 5:9-10
225 Luke 2:17

Verse 4

And round about the throne were four and twenty thrones:
and upon the thrones I saw four and twenty elders sitting,
arrayed in white garments;
and on their heads crowns of gold.

Encircling the majestic throne of God were twenty-four thrones, each occupied by an elder wearing a crown of gold. Each throne is turned toward the great, white throne and all eyes are on him who sits thereon.

To think of the twenty-four thrones is to think of the twelve patriarchs of Israel and the twelve apostles of the Lamb. The Bible is an impressive mosaic and when all of its pieces are in place it presents a unified picture of sweet redemption. The sons of the Prince of God are joined by the apostles of the Prince of Peace.

The New Testament fulfills the Old Testament and the Old Testament prefigures the New Testament. Both Testaments are seeded by twenty-four men and they are supportive of the eternal purpose of God.

The theme of the Bible and therefore the soul of God's intention is salvation from sin. Any teaching that deviates from this is antagonistic to God's purpose. Teaching that promotes the salvation theme is complimentary to God's purpose.

The twelve patriarchs of Israel and the twelve ambassadors of Jesus have their names written on the foundations and the gates of the salvation city of God.[226]

The twenty-four elders are sitting, indicating authority. They wear crowns of gold, indicating regal power. They are arrayed in white garments, indicating pure hearts and kingly character.

It is a beautiful prophetic picture of the unity of the Bible and the solitary, specific and distinctive intention of the Almighty from time immemorial.[227]

---

226 Rev 21:12-14
227 1 Pet 1:18-25

Verse 5

*And out of the throne proceed lightings and voices and thunders.
And there was seven lamps of fire burning before the throne,
which are the seven Spirits of God;*

One throne dominated the scene and it is preeminently *"the* throne."
Out of the majestic throne came lightning ... thunders ... voices. John
saw a flash of fire; he heard the peal of thunder, and the sound of voices,
magnificent and marvelous.

When God put his divine power on display at Sinai the people were
terrified and Moses trembled.[228]

When Isaiah saw a vision of the throne of God, he cried out, "Woe is
me! for I am undone; because I am a man of unclean lips, and I dwell in
the midst of a people of unclean lips: for mine eyes have seen the King,
Jehovah of hosts"[229]

The rumbling roar of thunder and the brilliant flash of electric light and
the great voice of God should make each one aware of his sinfulness and
his need of reconciliation.

When we reject God and wander from him our crying need is to return
to the fountain of all blessings, which can only be accomplished through
hearing, believing and obeying his confirmed word.[230]

> *"[G]od was in Christ reconciling the world unto himself, not reckoning
> unto them their trespasses, and having committed unto us the word of
> reconciliation. We are ambassadors therefore on behalf of Christ, as
> though God were entreating by us: we beseech you on behalf of Christ,
> be ye reconciled to God.[231]*

Only through and by that "word of reconciliation" can we return to God.

The number seven in scripture means perfection or completeness. The
"seven lamps of fire, which are seven spirits," would mean a perfect Spirit,

---

228 Heb 12:18-21
229 Isa 1:5
230 Rom 1:16
231 2 Cor 5:19-20

which is the Holy Spirit, who guided the apostles in the first century to knowledge of saving truth. That truth is unaltered and it still saves.

The trinity is indicated. Jehovah, Jesus, and the Comforter flow into one God, indivisible and eternal. God speaks in a flash of enlightening fire and with thunderous tones and with the voice of reason and revelation.

The wise stand in awe and respond with reverent obedience. "This is the end of the matter; all hath been heard: fear God, and keep his commandments; for this is the whole duty of man."[232]

Verses 6

And before the throne,
as it were a sea of glass like a crystal;
and in the midst of the throne,
and round about the throne,
four living creatures full of eyes before and behind.

John also mentions a sea of glass mingled with fire.[233] A glassy sea is calm and unruffled; no storm clouds and no billows tossing high. It is smooth and serene. This contrasts with the thunder and lightning, and tells us that the electric power of God is set in a picture of profound calm. The awful force is restrained. The irresistible power of God is tempered and his judgment delayed.

Do not be deceived by the delay. "The Lord is not slack concerning his promise, as some count slackness; but is longsuffering to you-ward, not wishing that any should perish, but that all should come to repentance."[234]

John sees four living beings (creatures, not beasts) around the throne. They are full of eyes, indicating an ability to see in every direction. They are eternally aware and ready to serve … vigilant and vigorous. They are servants of God and perform their duties with amazing skill.

232 Eccl 12:13
233 Rev 15:2
234 2 Pet 3:9

Verses 7-8

And the first creature was like a lion,
and the second creature like a calf,
and the third creature had a face as of a man,
and the fourth creature was like a flying eagle.
And the four living creatures,
having each one of them six wings,
are full of eyes round about and within:
and they have no rest day and night, saying,
Holy, holy, holy, is the Lord God, the Almighty,
who was and who is and who is to come.

Ezekiel mentions living creatures that are something like the ones John saw round the throne of God.[235] Isaiah saw six-winged angelic beings, whom he called "seraphim" (fiery, burning ones), generally understood to mean high-ranking angels.[236]

These celestial servants of the Most High had animal characteristics. One was like a lion, another like a calf, a third had a face like a man, and the last was like a flying eagle.

Each one of these creatures has special ability and together they present an array of talent. The lion has agility and strength; the calf symbolizes endurance and perseverance; man has the ability to reason, draw conclusions, and make intelligent communication; the high-flying eagle is swift and strong and represents the rapidity of obedience to God.

John does not say the first creature was a lion, but was "like" a lion; the second was not a calf but had some of the features of a calf; the third creature was not a man but resembled a man; the last was not an eagle but had good eyes and strong pinions.

The apostle is helping us to understand something we cannot see. He uses metaphors to aid us in gaining a glimmer of knowledge about a world that is high above our experience and therefore beyond the reach of our full understanding. We may apprehend it, but we cannot comprehend it until death makes our eyes wise.

---

235 Ezek 1:10; 10:14, 21
236 Isa 6:2-3

As for the four living creatures, they are full of eyes, which suggest a towering knowledge and deep understanding.

These heavenly beings join in continual worship of God. Like Isaiah's seraphim, they constantly cry, "Holy, holy, holy, is Jehovah of hosts: the whole earth is full of his glory."[237]

"All things praise thee - Lord, may we!"

The living creatures praise God continually, having no rest day and night as they ceaselessly adore God and call him Holy. Their praise and worship of God is perpetual. Every informed man or woman in heaven and on earth should worship the God of salvation continuously by act and by word.

Verses 9-11

*And when the living creatures shall give glory and honor
and thanks to him that sitteth on the throne,
to him that liveth for ever and ever,
the four and twenty elders shall fall down before
him that sitteth on the throne,
and shall worship him that liveth for ever and ever,
and shall cast their crowns before the throne, saying,
Worthy art thou, our Lord and our God,
to receive the glory and the honor and the power:
for thou didst create all things,
and because of thy will they were, and were created.*

The inspired word-picture of God and his throne magnifies God. It speaks eloquently of the power, wisdom, and authority of the three beings that comprise the one Godhead. They are individually God and they are collectively God. He is the Supreme Intelligence that brought the universe into existence, who has the right and the power to sweep it all away. There is no thought more sobering and no consequence more appealing to the pious of the earth.

"Praise God, from whom all blessings flow;
Praise Him, all creatures here below'
Praise Him above, ye heav'nly hosts;
Praise Father, Son, and Holy Ghost.

237 Isa 6:3

Redemption
Revelation 5:1-13

The Bible is a book of salvation. Redemption throbs on its every page. From start to finish, the book of God's word reminds us of who we are and whether we go. Some embrace the destiny of glory and others cling to the fate of secular hedonism. Whether we walk in the broad-way of destruction or tread the narrow-way of deliverance is a choice each one must make and for which each one is responsible.

The book of Revelation is the climax of redemption's sweet song. It acclaims the awful sacrifice of Him whose blood was "poured out for many unto the remission of sins." If we read "the revelation of Jesus Christ, which God gave to him" and miss the emphasis on forgiveness of sin and regeneration, we miss the mark.

In the opening five chapters of the book of Revelation, we are given a vision of salvation's commander-in-chief, of his instructions to his people as they "fight the good fight of faith," and a glimpse of the throne-room of God in all its beauty and power.

In this chapter we continue to observe the command post of the righteous as the Lamb of God sounds a call to arms and is praised for his everlasting goodness in providing the plan of salvation. All celestial beings fall at his feet in appreciation for Gethsemane and Golgotha and the portent of unending, heavenly bliss.

Verse 1

And I saw in the right hand of him that sat on the throne
a book written within and on the back,
close sealed with seven seals.

The august and awesome power that occupies the great, blazing throne holds in his right hand[238] a book.

Take note of the book. John mentions this book again in the tenth chapter of this revelation. The book is the gospel of God and his power to save.[239] Its simplicity is amazing but it is also profound and daunting. Sometimes we need help in understanding the "mystery" of God. Jesus explained his teaching to the apostles, enabling them to know things concealed from the "wise and understanding," but revealed to babes.[240]

We often need help to have a sufficient understanding of what the Bible says or describes. The explanation is in the text, or context. Later, in the book of Revelation, God sent an angelic interpreter to explain what would otherwise be a riddle.

Every common sense person is able to read and understand what God says in his word. If we read and think, we will get the message. If we need additional comment, the Bible supplies it. The Bible explains itself.

Advanced degrees in difficult subjects are not necessary to grasp what God says to us in his written word. He speaks to plain, ordinary people in plain, ordinary language. "If any man willeth to do his will, he shall know of the teaching ...."[241]

Be not beguiled into thinking that to understand the Bible you must have the assistance of experts and that you are dependent upon those experts to know what God would have you to do.

---

238 The "hand" of deity is anthropomorphism. God does not have hands, feet, wings, feathers, eyes, ears, or any other mortal quality. He is Spirit (John 4:24). Yet, the handless God holds a book in his "right hand." This is an accommodation to our ignorance and helps us understand what would otherwise be eccentric.

239 Rom 1:16

240 Luke 10:21

241 John 7:17; read and ponder Deuteronomy 30:11-14 and Romans 10:6-7

The commands and laws of God are plain and understandable. The will of God lies upon the surface of the page and the average person of ordinary intelligence can understand it. For the most part, God chose men of the street to speak in the language of the street to common people in an understandable way.[242]

The book in the right hand of the throne occupant fascinates us. It is the wisdom of the ages explained to every soul seeking God. God is never far from us.[243] "[F]or every one that asketh receiveth; and he that seeketh findeth; and to him that knocketh it shall be opened."[244] Open your eyes; open your ears; open your hearts, read his word, and you shall know what God requires of you.

The book upon which John would have us rivet our attention is "close sealed with seven seals," which suggest a finished work. Take nothing from it; add nothing to it. It is "the once for all delivered faith."[245] To change it is to be anathema.[246]

Since the last apostle died, the Eternal One has not authorized any change or supplement to his revealed word. The Mighty Maker emphatically condemns all who undertake to add anything to sacred scripture or to take anything away from it. It is forever fixed and has been since the first century.

Ever since God sealed the book, all the inhabitants of earth are answerable to the same message, "for God is not a respecter of persons."

Verse 2

I saw a mighty angel proclaiming with a loud voice,
"Who is worthy to open the book,
and to break its seals?

---

242 Ephesians 3:4-5: "whereby, when ye read, ye can perceive my understanding in the mystery of Christ; which in other generation was not made known unto the sons of men, as it hath now been revealed unto his holy apostles and prophets in the Spirit."
243 Acts 17:27
244 Matt 7:8
245 Jude 3
246 Gal 1:8-9

The mighty angel speaks with a booming voice that commands attention and respect. His loud voice, like the flash of lightening and the peal of thunder, would make the earth shake and the people tremble.

The angel's penetrating question turned every head and captured every ear: "Who is worthy to open the book, and to break its seals?"

John sits with bated breath listening for the answer. He has a keen desire to know what is in the book. It holds the future … "things that are to come to pass."

Fortunetellers chirp, mutter, and pretend to forecast the future. They dive into deep water but come up dry and empty. Self-deceived people desperately try to contact the dead and discover the secrets of what the future has well hidden. Only God has the power to draw the curtain aside and know what the morrow holds. Fulfilled prophecy verifies God and confirms revelation. If God does not choose to foretell the future, it is unknown.

Still, we long to know what will happen on all of our tomorrows. Our hearts ache to know even what "must shortly come to pass." The desire of John to know the contents of the book clutched in the hand of God was intense and the question of who is worthy to open the book and to break its seals was of paramount importance. It is a transcendent consideration because it has to do with where humans will spend eternity.

This accounts for John's passionate desire to know the contents of the book God holds in his right hand. The loud voice of a mighty angel challenges us with the question: "Who is worthy to open the book, and to break its seals?"

Verses 3-4

And no one in the heaven,
or on the earth,
or under the earth,
was able to open the book,
or to look thereon.
And I wept much,
because no one was found worthy to open the book, or to look thereon.

The answer is … is … well … no one!

The book is too profound and its contents too precious for a presumptuous answer. So, there is silence. Only a being with moral qualities of an exalted nature, having intellectual depth and insight, could dare to answer this awesome query.

No one …. no one … in heaven … on earth … nor under the earth … not Plato … not Caesar … not Abraham … not Moses … is sufficiently courageous to stand up and offer his services in answering the question of who is able to break the seals and open the book.

The copious tears of the beloved John bear testimony to the importance of the answer and to the utter frustration triggered by the absence of a qualified interpreter. John was heartsick over the unavailability of a *bona fide* respondent. There is an impasse and the drama intensifies.

There is deafening silence as the universe searches for someone capable of giving answer to this important question, emphasizing the importance of the answer.

Where we will spend eternity transcends all other questions. It is paramount. It is superior to all other considerations.

Verse 5

and one of the elders saith unto me,
Weep not;
behold, the Lion that is of the tribe of Judah,
the Root of David,
hath overcome to open the book and the seven seals thereof.

The rejoicing of the book of Revelation is anchored in the sufficient sacrifice of the Lamb of God who takes away the sins of the world. Our filthy robes can be made white in the blood of the Lamb, and in no other way.[247]

The failure of religious liberalism is its blindness to saving, cleansing blood and its indifference to the utter importance of salvation. The Bible, with an intensity of expression, gives impressiveness to the crying need of human forgiveness. The liberal ignores eternal redemption in favor of social reform

---

247 Rev 7:14-17

and equal distribution of material wealth. One labors for perishing food. The other does not, but strives for spiritual robustness and healthy souls.

One of the elders, it matters not which one because they all are in agreement, comforts the apostle John and dries his tears, while pointing to "the Lion that is of the tribe of Judah," as being able to open the book and break its seals. The Lion of Judah is also the root of David.

His saving power is terrible and his loving-kindness endures forever.[248] An apparent dead root becomes green. A life hidden in the remote reaches of Galilee, in the humble city of Nazareth, flashes up like fire and water to open the door of salvation.

Because of the importance of forgiveness this lamb of God, this Lion of Judah, this dry root of Jesse springs up out of the shadows and declares himself to be Messiah of Jehovah. He is able to break the seals and open the book. In no other name is there salvation.[249] The heavenly choir is to repeat this glad refrain over and again in the remaining chapters of this powerful book.

Verses 6-7

And I saw in the midst of the throne and of the four living creatures,
and in the midst of the elders,
a Lamb standing,
as though it had been slain,
having seven horns,
and seven eyes,
which are the seven Spirits of God,
sent forth into all the earth.
And he came,
and he taketh it out of the right hand of him that sat on the throne.

John was told to "behold the Lion ... but when he looked he saw "a lamb." Two figures representing two aspects of the great savior-redeemer. The Lion is the king of the jungle, symbolizing strength and force, the Lamb is meek and mild, symbolizing gentleness and kindness. This brings into focus two grand features of the Supreme Being ... Almighty Benevolence.

---

248 Isa 11:10 and 53:2
249 Acts 4:12

The slain lamb is unexpectedly standing. One does not suppose that a dead animal could stand, but this one does. The Lamb of God, appointed to sacrificial destruction from the foundation of the earth, was also foreordained to overcome death.[250] It was also in the eternal purpose of God for the Anointed One to break the bonds of death and come out of the tomb in victory.

This explains the slain lamb standing ... killed but living ... dead but standing. His dead natural body was placed in a borrowed grave because he would have no long time need for it; a Sabbath and then the body lived again ... slain but standing.

The resurrected Lamb now appears "in the midst of the throne" to take the book out of the right hand of him who sat upon the throne, as the only being in all the universe and beyond who has the right and the power to brake the seals and open the book. He earned this privilege by making himself perfect through suffering.

In the brilliant throne room of God shines the name of Jesus Christ. He is preeminent among the preeminent. The preeminence of Jesus resides in the redeeming quality that flows from his wounded side.

Jesus is qualified to open the book because he died that we might live.

Jesus has seven horns ... seven eyes ... and seven Spirits of God. This stresses the authority of the Lamb. Throughout the Bible horns represent power and might. The idea embedded in "seven horns" would be authority carried to perfection. The seven eyes portray complete and unblemished knowledge.

The seven horns and the seven eyes are the seven Spirits of God representing all power and all wisdom. The perfect Spirit is the Holy Spirit who joins with Jesus and Jehovah in bringing salvation down.

---

250 Eph 3:9-12; 2 Tim 1:9 show that the eternal plan of God is salvation in Christ, which reconfirms the importance of redemption in the divine scheme. Any religious teaching that does not feature the priceless gift of salvation is not of God. When religious liberalism downplays redemption, it degrades itself and exposes its innate worthlessness.

Jesus said of the Perfect Spirit, "He shall glorify me: for he shall take of mine, and shall declare it unto you."[251]

The Perfect Spirit guided the apostles into all the truth in the first century.[252]

Jesus' message of salvation is to be carried into all the world.[253]

In the celestial city of God the slain but standing Lamb takes the seven-sealed book out of the right hand of him who sat upon the throne, provoking an eruption of praise..

Verses 8-14

And when he had taken the book,
the four living creatures
and the four and twenty elders fell down before the Lamb,
having each one a harp,
and golden bowls full of incense,
which are the prayers of the saints.

And they sing a new song, saying,
Worthy art thou to take the book,
and to open the seals thereof:
for thou was slain,
and didst purchase unto God with thy blood men of every tribe,
and tongue, and people, and nation,

and madest them to be unto our God a kingdom and priests;
and they reign upon earth.

And I saw,
and I heard
a voice of many angels round about the throne and the living creatures and
the elders; and the number of them was ten thousand times ten thousand,
and thousands of thousands;

saying with a great voice,
Worthy is the Lamb that hath been slain to receive the power,
and riches, and wisdom, and might and honor, and glory, and blessing.

---

251 John 16:14
252 John 16:13
253 Matt 28:18-20

And every created thing which is in the heaven,
and on the earth,
and under the earth,
and on the sea,
and all things are in them,
heard I saying, Unto him that sitteth on the throne,
and unto the Lamb,
be the blessing, and the honor, and the glory,
and the dominion, for ever and ever.

And the four living creatures said, Amen.
And the elders fell down and worshipped

The Celestial City of God erupts into loud Hosannas as the highest order of heavenly beings fall down before the Lamb, expressing again the Lamb's exaltation, an excessively intensified sense of well-being, and power.

The theme of the entire Bible and therefore the theme of every book of the Bible is salvation. Any view of the Bible that misses that point misses the distinctive and characteristic concern of the divine volume. The emphasis throughout the sacred scriptures is reconciliation. The gospel is a "ministry of reconciliation." Paul wrote:

> But all things are of God, who reconciled us to himself through Christ, and gave unto us the ministry of reconciliation; to wit, that God was in Christ reconciling the world unto himself, not reckoning unto them their trespasses, and having committed unto us the word of reconciliation.[254]

There is a close and undeniable connection between the "ministry of reconciliation" and "the word of reconciliation." The word of God is the powerful means by which sinners are reconciled to God.[255]

The Master taught his disciples to "labor not for the meat that perisheth, but for that which endures unto eternal life."[256]

The grand throne room scene closes with a loud chorus singing salvation's sweet song. The "new song" is the old story of God's redeeming love.

---

254 2 Cor 5:18-19
255 Rom 1:16
256 John 6:27

Liberals tragically misread God's great revelation when they misconstrue it to be a call for social reform instead of a return to God.

The death that overcame death is the clear subject of divine revelation and its closing book repeatedly sounds that unmistakable refrain. We repeat:

> *And they sing a new song, saying,*
> *Worthy art thou to take the book, and to open the seals thereof:*
> *for thou was slain,*
> *and didst purchase unto God with thy blood men of*
> *every tribe, and tongue, and people, and nation,*
> *and madest them to be unto our God a kingdom and priests;*
> *and they reign upon earth.*

The saints of God "reign upon the earth" by overcoming the "wages of sin" and identifying with the Christ who "burst asunder the bonds of death" and came out of the tomb a "victor over the grave." It is a rule over sin, and not over nations; it is a rule over self, and not over others; it is a rule over materialism, and not slavery to earthly things; it is righteousness, and not unrighteousness. When we think of the "rule upon the earth" as being like that of an earthy potentate, we are blind and deaf to spiritual reality.

The slain, standing lamb is worthy to receive all praise, glory, and honor because he is "the Lamb of God who takes away the sins of the world." He is appointed to break the seals and open the book because of his suffering at Gethsemane and death at Calvary.

Breaking the Seals
Revelation 6:1-17

The stage is set for the unfolding of the drama of earth and its creatures.

- The Potentate has been introduced — the splendid Anointed One

- The seven letters of instruction to the seven churches have been dispatched

- The awesome throne of God has been figuratively painted in striking hues

- The Book is in the hand of the Lamb[257], who is worthy to break its seven seals

- The thunderous praise of God for human salvation is reverberating through time and the universe

Verses 1-2

And I saw when the Lamb opened one of the seven seals,
and I heard one of the four living creatures saying as with a voice of thunder,

Come.

And I saw, and behold, a white horse,
and he that sat thereon had a bow;
and there was given unto him a crown:
and he came forth conquering, and to conquer.

---

257 The fact the book is in the hand of the Lamb reminds us that we are dealing with figures and symbols for no one ever saw a literal lamb with a hand capable of holding a book

The rider on the white horse is Jesus. It would be anti-climatic for this horseman to represent Caesar, Napoleon, or Hitler. The Godhead features loving-kindness and mercy, but when the rich gifts of God are thrown to the ground and trodden underfoot the wrath of God comes into play. The Creator is the source of "every good and perfect gift," but he is capable of hot anger and total destruction. Ponder the flood, the destruction of Jerusalem, and the final judgment. God prefers to bless, but he will punish, which is his strange work.[258] If punishment is his strange work, then rewarding is his natural and preferred work, which help to emphasize the benevolence of the All Powerful-Maker.

In the last age of the world, Jesus will come to wage war with Satan, otherwise called the good fight of faith.[259] We are about to read a Seer's description of that spiritual war, which he gives in prophetic imagery. We meet the white horse and its rider again in Rev 19:1-11 where the horseman is identified as Christ — the "word of God," "King of kings," "Lord of lords."[260]

Jesus fights a fierce age-long battle with Satan and at the last overcomes and throws the Devil and his imps into a lake of fire and brimstone (sulphur). The rider of the white horse engages Satan in a mighty spiritual war and it ends when this same rider comes back to earth in an ultimate conquest and irrepressible victory.

White, In Bible symbols, is the purity that springs from righteousness (careful obedience to the Heavenly Father's word). It is the emblem of purity and is associated with things holy and heavenly ... white garments, white cloud, white throne, and white stone.

The heavenly advocate of unwavering respect for the integrity of God's eternal word, who has shown us how to trust and obey, is the unique Son of God. There is none other.[261] He is the eldest son and therefore one of a kind, seeing there can be only one eldest son.

---

258 Isa 28:21
259 1 Tim 6:12; 2 Tim 4:7
260 We do not hesitate to affirm the great power of God unleashed to punish unrepentant wickedness (See Rev 1:13; 2:26-27; 3:21; 5:5; 6:16; 11:15; 12:11; 14:1, 14
261 Acts 4:12

This signifies the beginning of the "good fight of faith." The author of these words describes the war in graphic language because it is horrific. It is "not of this world,"[262] but is dreadful.

Verses 3-4

And when he opened the second seal,
I heard the second living creature saying,

Come.

And another horse came forth,
a red horse:
and to him that sat thereon it was given to take peace from the earth,
and that they should slay one another
and there was given unto him a great sword.".

The worthy Lamb breaks the second seal and a red horse and its rider appear. The drama deeply stirs the imagination. This horse is "red," that is "fiery" in color ... a horse that appears to be made of fire. Red is the color of blood. The rider is given a "great sword" and with it he took "peace from the earth."

This rider must be Satan who seeks a conflict with "the word of God" who is astride the beautiful white horse. This strikes a note that confirms the unseen battle for the hearts of people is now underway.

It is unthinkable that humans will torture and kill their fellow humans. The news of the day is full of accounts of people killed randomly and viciously. We wonder what could possess the mind of a man to enable him to be capable of such savagery. The raw brutality reported in the daily news staggers the imagination of right thinking people.

Some stupendous evil must enter the soul and grip the mind to enable this outlandish wickedness. The blood of the unsuspecting and the innocent requires the conclusion that an unseen morally reprehensible influence must drive the malicious murderer;[263] his is the Devil's part in the spiritual

---

262 John 18:36

263 The word translated "slay" is found only in the writings of John and refers only to the slaughter of Jesus and his disciples. Thayer says it means "put to death by violence." See 1 John 3:12; Rev 5:6, 9, 12; 6:4, 9; 133. 8;18.24; religious perse-

contest between the good and the bad. The rider of the white horse with his peaceful agenda stirs the rider of the fiery horse to action. Wherever good appears, evil soon follows. The great sword is the emblem of the carnage of this hateful war. People of the earth butcher one another because they have allowed themselves to be the slaves of wickedness.

The red horseman always follows the white horseman.[264]

The war is on ... it is the "good fight of faith" and deals primarily with the spirit, however its fruit may be seen in the physical realm. "A tree is known by its fruit."[265]

Verses 5-6

And when he opened the third seal,
I heard the third living creature saying,

Come.

And I saw, and behold, a black horse;
and he that sat thereon had a balance in his hand.
And I heard as it were a voice in the midst of the four living creatures saying,
A measure of wheat for a shilling,
and three measures of barley for a shilling;
and the oil and the wine hurt thou not.

Black is often typical of woe and mourning and fear. It does not portend a specific sorrow, but grief and misery generally. The rider of the black horse produces the fruit of heavy taxation, tyranny, famine, and pestilence.

The constant battle between the army of the Lord and the army of Satan produces heaped up grief for the citizens of earth. The rider of the black horse represents this deep and poignant distress. It is the "thousand ills to which flesh is heir."

- "In the world ye have tribulation"[266]

- "the world hateth you"[267]

---

cution is indicated, not war in general.
264 Matt 5:10-11; Luke 21:12; Acts 4:1; 5:17
265 Matt 12:33
266 John 16:33
267 John15:19-25

- "through many tribulations we must enter into the kingdom of God"[268]
- "we are killed all the day long; We were accounted as sheep for the slaughter."[269]
- "all that would live godly in Christ Jesus shall suffer persecution."[270]

Be sober, be watchful: your adversary the devil, as a roaring lion, walketh about, seeking whom he may devour, whom withstand stedfast in your faith, knowing that the same sufferings are accomplished in your brethren who are in the world.[271]

The rider of the black horse has a scale in his hand and a voice is heard proclaiming scarcity. Food is rare and expensive. Many people in many places in the world suffer starvation.

The rider of the black horse is not to "hurt the oil and the wine. In the scriptures "wine" symbolizes joy and "oil" represents healing. The goodness and loving-kindness of God preserves for us the saving gospel, which is the means of redemptive grace.

Verses 7-8

And when he opened the fourth seal,
I heard the voice of the fourth living creature saying,

Come.
And I saw, and behold, a pale horse:
and he that sat upon him,
his name was Death;
and Hades followed with him.
And there was given unto them authority over the fourth part of the earth,
to kill with sword,
and with famine,
and with death,
and by the wild beasts of the earth.

---

268 Acts 14:22
269 Rom 8:36
270 2 Tim 3:12
271 1 Pet 5:8-9

The word transated "pale" can mean "ghostly." It also means "livid," or "greenish," or "putrid." The rider on the pale horse is identified as "Death," who is followed by "hades." When death has done its work the human bodies are gathered into the unseen world where the good and the evil await the resurrection

About a fourth of the earth's population is at the door of death ready to be harvested at any given time. This is due to age, disease, violence, war, famine, beasts, and pestilence. It is also due to the work of Satan as he sits astride his fiery horse. Those who have lived for Christ have nothing to fear and are content as they await the inevitable appointment.[272]

God does not appoint the moment or manner of anyone's death. He is not a respecter of persons. Death may be caused by nature, folly, or the "fallout of life," but never by direct, divine decree. If God fixes the when and how of anyone's death, he would be preferential. God is not arbitrary or capricious, but is fair and just.[273]

Paul called death "the last enemy," and assures us that Jesus has overcome death.

The sting of death is sin; and the power of sin is the law: but thanks be to God, who giveth us the victory through our Lord Jesus Christ. Wherefore, my beloved brethren, be ye steadfast, unmovable, always abounding in the work of the Lord, forasmuch as ye know that your labor is not vain in the Lord.[274]

Death is the work of the Evil One and Jesus fights a spiritual battle against our "ancient foe who seeks to work us woe" and deprives him of this last enemy.

Jesus overcame death.

---

272 Heb 9:27: "it is appointed unto men once to die..."
273 The reasoning that brings us to this conclusion is simple and indisputable. 1) Either it is good to die young or it is not good to die young. 2) if it is good to die young and God by direct intervention causes some to die at an early age and another to die in advanced years, then he has respect to those who die soon after birth and he has not for those who die at a good old age. This applies to any circumstance of life and death.
274 1 Cor 15:56-58

Verses 9-11

*And when he opened the fifth seal,
I saw underneath the altar the souls of them that
had been slain for the word of God,
and for the testimony which they held:
and they cried with a great voice, saying,
How long, O Master, the holy and true,
dost thou not judge and avenge our blood on them that dwell on the earth?
And there was given them to each one a white robe;
and it was said unto them,
that they should rest yet for a little time,
until their fellow-servants also and their brethren,
who should be killed even as they were,
should have fulfilled their course.*

It is hard to think that people would kill because they do not like the "word of God." Men and women die because of "the testimony which they held."

The word of God seeks no harm to anyone, but seeks only to do good. Jesus, we are told, "went about doing good and healing all that were oppressed of the Devil."[275] Black-hearted men nailed him to a tree for his kindness, and brutally mistreated him. His suffering was so intense the word "excruciate" was coined to describe the pain.

Satan then led his demons to continue the slaughter by killing people whose only crime was believing Jesus is the Christ of Jehovah and the Savior of the world. These innocent souls now writhe beneath the altar and cry out for justice — not vengeance but justice.

John saw an altar of burnt offering and the souls of martyrs crying, "How long, O Lord, how long?" God knows the proper time to end this carnage. He sees with an equal eye and can measure the moment when the iniquity of the world is so prevailing that its evil is irreversible. When the world crosses the point of no return, is the "day that God has appointed to judge the world in righteousness, by the man whom he hath ordained; whereof he hath given assurance unto all men, in that he hath raised him from the dead."[276]

275 Acts 10:38
276 Acts 17:31

97

The sainted dead from beneath the altar wonder at the patience of him who is not willing that any should perish but that all should come to repentance."

Under the law of Moses the altar of burnt offering was where sacrifice was made and the blood was splashed on both sides of the altar. The saints who died for the word of God had their blood figuratively sloshed on the altar, which is a graphic portrayal of the death so many have suffered because they would not allow their love of God to grow weak.

Each received a white robe, indicating innocence, and they were told to "rest yet for a little time." Others will be added to their number. Old Testament heroes waited for New Testament saints.[277] When the vile and the foolish of earth have totally rejected God is the day when all accounts will be brought into balance. The imbalance will not continue indefinitely.

The day of final judgment looms and the last trumpet will one day sound. "Be ye ready, for in a day that the think not, the come of man cometh."[278]

This section ends with a description of the last judgment. It is forceful and convincing, and compliments what has just been said about the fight between truth and falsehood.

Briefly, some events of that great day are:

- mighty earthquake shook the earth
- sun is turned black
- moon became as blood
- stars removed
- mountains and islands removed out of their places

The reaction on earth is fear and helplessness. The people run, but have nowhere to go. All classes are caught up in the horror of that day. "Death lays his icy hands on kings."[279] The inspired message, coming from the throne of God, cannot be enhanced and we shrink from touching it lest

---

277 Heb 11:40
278 Matt 24:44
279 Poem: *Death the Leveller,* by James Shirley (1596-1666)

our fingermarks might stain its poignant warning.. So, we lay it out for you in its untouched form. Read it slowly and taste each word.

Verses 12-17

And I saw when he opened the sixth seal,
and there was a great earthquake;
and the sun became black as sackcloth of hair,
and the whole moon became as blood;
and the stars of the heaven fell unto the earth,
as a fig tree casteth her unripe figs when she is shaken of a great wind.
And the heaven was removed as a scroll when it is rolled up;
and every mountain and island were moved out of their places.
And the kings of the earth,
and the princes,
and the chief captains,
and the rich,
and the strong,
and every bondman and freeman,
hid themselves in the caves and in the rocks of the mountains;
and they say to the mountains and to the rocks,
Fall on us, and hide us from the face of him that sitteth on the throne,
and from the wrath of the Lamb:
for the great day of their wrath is come;
and who is able to stand?

SALVATION

REVELATION 7:1-17

God made the universe for the specific purpose of providing a testing-ground for sanctification. From the beginning, it was destined to destruction.

God made man and created for him a magnificent home. A cathedral of light and beauty rises about the creature as testimony of the existence of the Mighty Maker and his mindfulness of man.[280]

Yet the home of man and all that surrounds it is destined to a fiery end. The journey of man and the ashes of matter testify to the purpose of God in creating the world and its accruements.

God did not make man merely to make man happy. God made man to make him holy.

"For this is the will of God, even your sanctification."[281] " For God called us not for uncleanness, but in sanctification."[282] The infinite holiness of God cries out for the holiness of his creature. When that noble aim achieves or fails, the purpose of creation will be complete and the experiment will terminate.

In the first six chapters of "The Revelation of Jesus Christ, which God gave him to show unto his servants, even the things which must shortly come to pass" we learned:

---

280 Psa 19:1-4; Heb 2:6
281 1 Thess 4:3
282 1 Thess 4:7

- The glory of the preeminent Jesus

- Jesus tells his church how to fight the good fight of faith

- The throne of God and him who sits thereon is the authority for the revelation

- The breaking of the seven seals, revealing the four horsemen

- the souls under the heavenly altar and their ceaseless cry for justice

- the ultimate end of creation

Now there is an interlude to show who will be saved, and delivered out of the gigantic conflagration, and preserved beside still waters. The "good fight of faith," also called, "the great tribulation," is the Mighty Maker acting on his prerogative to cast into the fire what he brought into existence in the first place.

It is creation reversed.

Seventeen short verses describe and define this interval, introduced with an astounding declaration:

Verses 1-3

"After this I saw four angels standing at the four corners of the earth,
holding the four winds of the earth,
that no wind should blow on the earth,
or on the sea,
or upon any tree.
And I saw another angel ascend from the sunrising,
having the seal of the living God:
and he cried with a great voice to the four angels to
whom it was given to hurt the earth and the sea,
saying,
Hurt not the earth,
neither the sea,
nor the trees,
till we shall have sealed the servants of our God on their foreheads."

The angels stand at the four directions of the compass – encircling the earth. The Bible mentions four winds of destruction several times.[283] The winds of woe stand in the wings of time and point to its total destruction.

Early on Jehovah promised, "While the earth remaineth, seedtime and harvest, and cold and heat, and summer and winter, and day and night shall not cease."[284]

The great Benefactor of humankind solemnly promised that the earth would be productive and its nourishment available to creatures as long as the world stands.

The promise is also a statement that the earth would not always stand; there will come a time when the earth ceases and, obviously, everything in which there is the breath of life perishes.

Angels of destruction are standing by, waiting for the moment when the Maker shall say, "blow it away." That danger is eminent but not imminent.

We see its eminence in the fact that as long as the world stands there will be upheavals in nature, also wreck and ruin caused sometimes by wild beasts and other times by intelligent beings. The Bible tells us there will be hurricanes, tornadoes, earthquakes, tidal waves, pestilence, famine, wars and rumors of wars as long as the universe continues.[285]

When the inhabitants of earth have plunged themselves so deeply into wickedness that there is no turning back, then the four winds will bring the final devastation, reducing the creation to chaos, ruin, and desolation.

An angel from the "sunrising" cries, "Hurt not the earth," that is, "do not bring its final destruction."

The reason he gives for delaying the annihilation of the material universe is that the "servants of our God" have not yet been sealed "on their foreheads," which is to say that God "is longsuffering and not willing that any should perish, but that all should come to repentance." Only Jehovah knows when the time for annihilation comes, but when it does, there will be no further delay.

---

283 See Dan 7:2 and Jer 49:36-37
284 Gen 8:22
285 Matt 24:6-8

The angel from the East points out that total destruction of God's creation before the saved are sealed would be premature.

God awaits the time when it is impossible for anyone else to obey the gospel of salvation … when all of God's children are sealed.

In this book of symbols and figures, the Revelator uses the emblem of "sealed on the forehead" as identifying the saved. This is not a literal mark, but is a characteristic that everyone who sees will know and understand.[286] It is by trust and obedience that the children of God are "sealed with the Holy Spirit of promise."[287]

The question is: How many will be saved? The answer is: few and yet many. Many are called and few chosen in every generation, but as the number of generations increase the total number of the redeemed multiplies.

Sanctification is conditional. Many factors enter the redemption equation. God has a part in saving man and man has a part in his own salvation. There is something for God to do and there is something for man to do in bringing remission of sins to the human creature.

God's part includes grace, mercy, patience, love, gentleness, Jesus' sacrifice, and the gospel.[288] God saves us by all of these things, but by none of them alone.

There is also something for man to do. When Peter first preached the gospel on Pentecost (May 34) he told his Jewish audience, "Save yourselves from this crooked generation."[289] Jesus said, "He that believeth and is baptized shall be saved."[290] We are also told that repentance and confession are required of sinful man if he is to be washed and made clean in the blood of the lamb.[291] Man is saved by all of these things, but by none of them alone.

" The Lord is not slack concerning his promise, as some count slackness; but is longsuffering to you-ward, not wishing that any should perish, but that all should come to repentance."[292]

---

286 Matt 12:50
287 Eph 1:13-14; 2:19-22; 4:11-16; Rom 8:14-16
288 Eph 2:8-9; Heb 4:16; John 3:16; Rom 8:32; Rom 1:16
289 Acts 2:40
290 Mark 16:16
291 Acts 2:38; Rom 10:9-10
292 2 Pet 3:9

The question of, "How many will be transported to glory?" seems to trouble many people. The simple and obvious answer is that all who obey the gospel will be "richly supplied" "entrance into the eternal kingdom of our Lord and Savior Jesus Christ." The Holy Scriptures do not supply the exact number, nor is it important for us to know this information. (If the number were supplied, then humans could calculate the time of the end. The Bible says only God has this information.)

God does repeat that a remnant of both Jews and Gentiles will enter the heavenly Promised Land.

He deals first with Israel: twelve times twelve,[293] or 144,000

Verses 4-8

And I heard the number of them that were sealed, a hundred and forty and four thousand, sealed out of every tribe of the children of Israel:
Of the tribe of Judah were sealed twelve thousand:
Of the tribe of Reuben twelve thousand;
Of the tribe of Gad twelve thousand;
Of the tribe of Asher twelve thousand;
Of the tribe of Naphtali twelve thousand;
Of the tribe of Manasseh twelve thousand;
Of the tribe of Simeon twelve thousand;
Of the tribe of Levi twelve thousand;
Of the tribe of Issachar twelve thousand;
Of the tribe of Zebulun twelve thousand;
Of the tribe of Joseph twelve thousand;
Of the tribe of Benjamin were sealed twelve thousand.

The figures given are plainly round numbers as each one is the same as all the others … 12,000. This makes clear that the author of these words speaks in figurative terms. The point is that a minority will be welcomed through the pearly gates and into the shinning city of God.

---

293 The 144,000 of Revelation chapter seven has been hashed and rehashed and every conceivable and even some inconceivable theories have been spun from John's simple statement. It is not our purpose to take up the various fanciful and far-fetched opinions of starry-eyed speculators, but simply to point out the obvious meaning of the passage in its text, context, and the larger context of the entire Bible.

That comes as no surprise to the astute Bible student. Jesus said, "Many are called, but few are chosen;" to emphasize that fact causes those who are earnest in seeking "a rich" entrance into the eternal kingdom of God to be diligent. There will be no haphazard entrance into that everlasting kingdom, but it is only for those who have made their best effort to please God by keeping his word.

There were millions of Israelites on earth subject to the gospel's invitation of the grace of salvation. Each tribe mentioned in this Revelation passage had a sizeable population, but only "twelve thousand" would receive the Lord's smiling welcome into the timeless city that lies foursquare. Painstaking effort is therefore necessary to be among that number folded one day with the sheep of God.

Only a minority of a minority receives an abundant entrance into that city where Jesus now prepares mansions for his children.

In the book of Romans (9:1 to 11:36), Paul discusses Israel's future relationship with God:

- Paul's sympathy with the Jews (9:1-5)
- Israel's rejection was not inconsistent with God's promises (9:6-13), justice (9:14-24), or prophecy (9:25-29)
- Rejection is the fault of the Jews themselves (9:30-10:21)
- Salvation offered to all on feasible terms--same conditions apply to all (10:1-13)
- The disobedient, whether Jew or Gentile, was left without excuse (10:14-21)
- All Israelites were not all rejected ... some were saved (11:1-5)
- God rejected the nation because it rejected Him (11:6-10)
- Salvation is the gift of God and not from fawless keeping of the law (11:6)
- Israel's blindness caused rejection of the gospel (11:7-10)
- Gentiles saved through a better covenant (11:11-26)[294]

---

294 When, in verse 26, Paul says, "and so shall all Israel be saved" he uses an adverb of manner, which means "and so (in this manner, that is, by the gospel), shall all Israel be saved." He is distinctly not saying that "all" Israel shall be arbitrarily saved because his entire argument is that only a few (a remnant) of the Jews will

- If Gentiles are unfaithful, they will also be rejected (11:20-24)
- Salvation is by the power of the gospel (11:25; Rom 1:16)
- Israel, like all people, is to be saved by the gospel (11:26)
- Anyone, Jew or Gentile, can believe, obey and be saved (11:27-32)
- God's wisdom transcends all human understanding (11:33-36).

Twelve thousand from each of the twelve tribes (12,000 times 12, or 144,000) represent a minority of the Jews. To project this into a mass conversion of all Jews is wrongheaded, and misses the point.[295]

The 144,000 are not exclusive (except that they are all Jews), but represent the assurance of Jehovah that the Israelites are not excluded from the mercy of God.

In addition to the 144,000, there was a teeming crowd too numerous to count:

Verses 9-10

After these things I saw,
and behold, a great multitude, which no man could number,
out of every nation and of all tribes and peoples and tongues,
standing before the throne and before the Lamb,
arrayed in white robes, and palms in their hands;
and they cry with a great voice, saying,
Salvation unto our God who sitteth on the throne, and unto the Lamb.[296]

---

be saved. He is saying that every Israelite who is eventually saved will be saved just like everyone else who is saved, which is by the "power" of the saving gospel and man's response to it in obedience (Rom 1:16; 1:5; 16:26).

295 Judges 18 says the Danites did not secure the land awarded to them by lot when Joshua divided the land among the Jews. The people of the tribe of Dan migrated from their appointed homeland in the South to territory in the far North of Canaan where they became extinct. The genealogical record of Chronicles drops Dan, and Rev 7 does not mention the tribe of Dan. If the tribe no longer existed, it could not provide 12,000 converts to Christ.

296 Rev 7:9-10

God will gather to glory an uncountable multitude from all the earth, representing the saved of all ages. Old Testament worthies will be in that number and all who trust and obey since the cross will pass through gates of pearl to walk the street of gold and to see God even as he is and be like him. It will be an immense crowd because it includes the total number of the saved.

Their happy voices shout the glad truth that "salvation belongs to our God." God is the author and finisher of sanctification. The one theme of inspired writing is to assure the entire world that the Living God is the only hope for man's holiness and endless satisfaction. That is the whole purpose of creation and revelation.[297]

The saved will "stand" before the throne and before the Lamb. To stand before God is to have his approval and blessing. White robes of holiness cover their nakedness; they wave the emblems of victory, and shout with the voice of thunder, "Salvation belongs to our God."

Verses 11-12

And all the angels were standing round about the throne,
and about the elders and the four living creatures;
and they fell before the throne on their faces, and worshipped God,
saying,
Amen: Blessing, and glory, and wisdom, and thanksgiving, and honor,
and power, and might, be unto our God forever and ever. Amen.

The universe is no more. God gathers the saved to his great fold. All heaven is rejoicing. The victory of truth and righteousness is undeniable. The defeat of error and unrighteousness is clear. The happiness of all heavenly creatures is perfect.

The ultimate victory of the pure in heart is emphasized by a one-question catechism:

---

297 To make the purpose of religious energy anything other than forgiveness and redemption is a huge mistake. The exclusive intention of all that is in the Holy Bible is to make sinful man right with God. The work of the church is not primarily social reform, but purity; nor mere happiness, but cleanliness. "For this is the will of God, even your sanctification" (1 Thess 4:3).

Verses 13-14

"And one of the elders answered,
saying unto me,
These that are arrayed in white robes,
who are they,
and whence came they?
And I say unto him,
My lord, thou knowest.
And he said to me,
These are they that come of the great tribulation,
and they washed their robes,
and made them white in the blood of the Lamb."

An elder identifies the white robed multitude. They came out of the "great tribulation." They were in the tribulation and came out of it. They had been in the thick of the fight between right and wrong (the "good fight of faith"). They were the foot soldiers who served in the army of the Lord in the spiritual battle between good and evil. They acquitted themselves with honor. They held firmly to the word of God and would not be moved. The blood of the Lamb made their robes white and they now turned happy faces toward the Rock of Ages.

The grand climax is reached, the summit attained, and the loud voices sound the beautiful refrain:

Verses 15-17

"Therefore are they before the throne of God;
and they serve him day and night in his temple:
and he that sitteth on the throne shall spread his tabernacle over them.
They shall hunger no more,
neither thirst anymore;
neither shall the sun strike upon them,
nor any heat:
for the Lamb that is in the midst of the throne shall be their shepherd,
and shall guide them unto fountains of waters of life: and
God shall wipe away every tear from their eyes."

Because of their valor, they fought long and well and because of their trust, their commander gives them rest. Their happy feet are jubilant. The Lamb is now their shepherd. The Heavenly Father spreads his protecting tabernacle over them. The Lamb leads them to the "fountains of the waters of life," and God "wipes away every tear."

The book of Revelation is the story of overcoming and victory.

Revelation 8:1-13
Trumpets Sound

In the opening chapter of the book of Revelation the author paints an impressive word picture of the Lord Jesus Christ in his grandeur and preeminence. This is so magnificent that every reader should, figuratively, join the apostle John in falling "as one dead" at his feet.

He follows this with letters to seven of his churches telling his disciples what to do and what not to do. The letters are designed to discipline the church of Christ for its place in the world, and position each disciple as a soldier of the Lord, fighting the good fight of faith.

He next describes the breaking of the seven seals to reveal the content of a little book given to the Lamb of God from the hand of God. This book was sealed with seven seals and all of the seals had to be broken before we could know its contents. The first four seals reveal four horsemen and a spiritual battle that will rage until time is no more. That invisible war is a struggle for the hearts of men and a plea for each person to cast his soul into the great enterprise of heaven. It is for the betterment of humanity and the eternal salvation of all who follow Jesus. The fifth seal shows the carnage of war and tells of beheaded martyrs beneath the altar of burnt offering asking the penetrating question, "How long, O Lord, how long?" The sixth seal describes the final coming of the Lord to earth, judgment, and destruction of the universe.

He is now prepared to reveal the grand centerpiece of this closing book of the Bible. It describes in the symbolic language of prophets and poets the strenuous effort of the army of the Lord to put down the vile and the vulgar and to exalt the pure and the uncommon. It is the good fight of faith.

The seventh seal reveals seven trumpets of woe, which show the unhappiness caused by the fight between Jesus and the Devil - conflict produces a violent agitation of the heart.

Before revealing the hideous details of this war, Jehovah seeks to impress upon us the serious importance of what he is about to make known, and he does this with a dramatic pause.

Verse 1

And when he opened the seventh seal,
there followed a silence in heaven about the space of half an hour.[298]

Thirty minutes of unbroken silence is heavy and solemn. It gives us time to think, perhaps to rethink.

Tribulation, on a spiritual level, engulfs the earth and humans need to prepare for it. The wise will make themselves ready to meet God. Still, most people will not stop to think upon the "things that are more excellent," but will go heedlessly forward in their festival of vice and ungodliness.

The trumpets sound a warning of the treachery of sin and of the everlasting consequence of fighting on the wrong side in this battle of the ages. If you are on the wrong side in any contest with God, even if you seem to win, you lose.

Eyes open to the written will of God will cause ears to hear this half-hour of symbolic silence repeatedly. The informed and the sensitive will stop and think.

When the trumpets sound, telling of the damage done by the forces of evil under the leadership of Satan, we should acknowledge the violation and "take time to be holy," and prepare for the suffering resulting from persecution, knowing that "in the world you have tribulation."

God marshals the angelic missionaries, and they, with a mighty blast, warn the world of the treason of the Devil, and of the heaped up misery it causes.

---

298 *Rev 8:1*

Verses 2-4

And I saw the seven angels that stand before God;
and there were given unto them seven trumpets.
And another angel came and stood over the altar,
having a golden censer;
and there was given unto him much incense,
that he should add it unto the prayers of all the saints
upon the golden altar which was before the throne.
And the smoke of the incense,
with the prayers of the saints,
went up before God out of the angel's hand.

Mortals use the penetrating sound of the trumpet to announce glad tidings, or warn of eminent danger. Commanding officers use it to give instructions to armies on the field of battle. The trumpet is valuable in warning of danger, because we can hear its distinctive notes at a distance.

In the hand-to-hand combat between truth with error, the open ears of the obedient frequently hear the figurative warning sounds of the trumpet.

Satan uses lies to promote his agenda, seeing he is the father of lies, but Jesus uses truth to free the captives, seeing he is truth.

We hear the warning of these metaphorical trumpets throughout history. The warnings occur repeatedly because the danger is persistent.

Those who attune their ears to divine law benefit from the warnings of the trumpet. Those who do not are victims of their own disloyalty.

The seven angels with the seven trumpets "stand"[299] before God. They are his servants and have his approval. They can stand before him because he approves what they are doing. Each of the seven angels receives a trumpet, which symbolizes wisdom and authority. The purpose of these seven angels is to warn of the horror of everlasting loss by telling of the bitter grief that sin brings to the rebellious on earth. The message is that present pain and

---

299 Standing before an awesome power symbolizes being erect (firm and straight) and able to maintain a position. To stand before God is to have his approval, blessing, and sanction. The terrible wrath of Jehovah and the Lamb, described in Revelation 6:12-17, ends with the question, "And who is able to stand?" In this setting, none could stand before the fury of the Creator except those approved by Him.

113

sorrow, caused by sin, is a foretaste of the blank misgiving and utter loss imposed on those forever banished from the presence of God. It is their doing.

Another angel "came and stood over the altar" and was given a large amount of incense. This angel brings his golden censer to the altar of incense. The angel adds this pile of incense to the prayers of the saints and a huge cloud of a sweet smell bellows up to the throne of the Almighty.

We know how those "slain for the word of God" cried out from beneath the altar of burnt offering, "O Sovereign Lord, holy and true, how long before you will judge and avenge our blood on those who dwell on the earth?"[300] .

The perfume of this mighty offering of incense "went up before God" to please and praise his holy name, and is a memorial to the brave and the true who suffered atrocities in the fight of faith. The outcome of every human soul is either eternal life or eternal death.[301]

This elaborate preparation for the sounding of the seven trumpets testifies to the potency of prayer. "For the eyes of the Lord are over the righteous, and his ears are open unto their prayers." Jesus makes intercession for those who trust and obey him.[302] He is The High Priest for the church; through his name, a holy priesthood of believers stand in the presence of God.

Verse 5

And the angel taketh the censer;
and he filled it with the fire of the altar, and cast it upon the earth:
and there followed thunders, and voices, and lightnings, and an earthquake.

God answers the haunting cry of the beheaded saints who are under the altar of burnt offering and He casts fire upon the earth as the massive amount of incense, with the prayers of the saints, is poured upon the guilty heads of mundane mortals, reaping the consequence of loving the world and hating the word of God.

---

300 Rev 6:10 ESV
301 John 5:29; Matt 25:46. It is either the sweet odor of life or the foul stench of death (2 Cor 2:15-16)
302 Rom 8:34

There is an undeniable animosity between light and darkness, good and evil, right and wrong. People wedded to the world sincerely hate Jesus. They despise his teaching without a cause.[303]

Jesus said, "I came to cast fire upon the earth; and what do I desire if it is already kindled?"[304] The fire Jesus came to cast upon the earth consists of at least two things: (1) The fire of cleansing truth and the joy it brings; and (2) the fire of persecution and suffering that inevitably follows.

Think of Pentecost and the powerful preaching of Peter and the apostles; 3,000 "gladly" received that word and "continued steadfastly in the apostles doctrine and fellowship."[305]

Soon, however, persecution arose. Men and women were dragged in chains to prison where they faced death or scourging by madmen bent on banishing redemption's sweet song.

The martyrdom of the good man Stephen is an example of such harassment.[306]

The saints were driven from Jerusalem but the persecution continued. They were followed by Jewish antagonists and the brutal treatment persisted.

Paul beaten and cast into prison at Philippi is an illustration.

Later the Roman government used its authority in an attempt to stop the forward sweep of the soldiers of Christ, but to no avail – "his truth" was "marching on."

The persecution continues – sometimes physical and savage and other times mental and subtle but always painful. This, too, is the fire Jesus cast upon the earth, not that he is the source of it, but he allows it because his message of redemption is hatefully rejected by the world. God allows the free-agency of humans and they cast fire upon the earth, which the Lord is said to do because he allows men this freedom of fighting with fire.

An astute Bible teacher pointed out, people are "befogged in interpreting such symbols as beasts, and horses, and trumpets, and seals." By which he

303 John 7:14; 15:18-19; 23-25; 17:14; Matt 10:22
304 Luke 12:49
305 Acts 2:42
306 Acts 7

means that figures of speech are looked upon with such vivid and graphic imagination so as to cloud the obvious meaning.

The "peals of thunder, rumblings, flashes of lightning, and an earthquake" represent the disturbance in nature and society caused by people perverting the teaching of Jesus.

When self-appointed scholars re-write history and are not ashamed to also attempt to re-write revelation the consequences are serious and damning.

Violations of the moral precepts of God have repercussions in the physical world, witness the rebellion in the Garden of Eden.

Every catastrophic upheaval in nature testifies to the purity of God and his hatred of all that is false; the fallen world is not the world as God first made it, but it is as man has ruined through sin. We on the earth must suffer the consequences of sin, which is not the same as the guilt of sin. We may be innocent of any wrongdoing but still suffer the consequences of the wrongs of others.

Every tsunami and tornado tells of the holiness of the Lord and the exceeding evil of sin. It is the Lord casting fire upon the earth.

Verses 6-12

"And the first sounded,
and there followed hail and fire,
mingled with blood,
and they were cast upon the earth:
and the third part of the earth was burnt up,
and the third part of the trees was burnt up,
and all green grass was burnt up.

And the second angel sounded,

and as it were a great mountain burning with fire was cast into the sea:
and the third part of the sea became blood;
and there died the third part of the creatures which were in the sea,
even they that had life;
and the third part of the ships was destroyed.

And the third angel sounded,
and there fell from heaven a great star,
burning as a torch,
and it fell upon the third part of the rivers,
and upon the fountains of the waters;
and the name of the star is called Wormwood:
and the third part of the waters became wormwood;
and many men died of the waters,
because they were made bitter.

And the fourth angel sounded,
and the third part of the sun was smitten,
and the third part of the moon,
and the third part of the stars;
that the third part of them should be darkened,
and the day should not shine for the third part
of it, and the night in like manner."

This compelling emblematic language impresses upon the mind of the reader and listener the foul consequence of the army of Satan clashing with the army of the Jesus.

It emphasizes emotional and intellectual stress in the good fight of faith.

The first trumpet blast reminds us "in the world ye have tribulation."[307] The clash between the clean and the unclean produces reprehensible consequences. The disturbance may be in the realm of moral law, natural law, or both.

Hail and fire mixed with blood pictures something repulsive, painful, and fatal. Notice one third of the earth was involved in this disaster. We necessarily conclude from this fact that the verse is not talking about the ultimate end of the world, seeing that two thirds of the earth was unaffected. When the end of earth comes, nothing will survive. This first trumpet speaks eloquently of the misery the tribulation will cause, but not of the annihilation of the universe. Nothing material will remain when God erases the created universe.

---

307 John 16:33

The creation groans for its own destruction[308] which will one day come, but this passage references the tribulation of war, disease, persecution, famine and not total destruction of all material things.

The second trumpet points to great damage done to the seas and marine life. A majority of the earth's population depend upon the oceans to sustain them. The writer is not speaking of a specific mountain burning with fire but any and all such symbolic mountains. The great ball of fire coming into the bowels of the sea can come from volcanic explosion whether on land or in water.

The third trumpet speaks of the loss of potable water, which is a tribulation that defies description. Our dependence on fresh water is well known and the problems caused by the loss of such refreshment well documented.

The fourth trumpet speaks of the third part of the sun, and the third part of the moon, and the third part of the stars. It is vain to seek for a literal fulfillment of this figurative statement. Nothing in all of human history, or in mythological tales, literally fulfills this verse. If we were to lose one third of the sun, nothing on earth could survive. The fourth trumpet speaks of the emblematic poisoning of the air we breathe.

The four trumpets represent damage done to inhabitants of the world by harm to drinking water, marine life, and atmosphere. To remain in existence, the human creature must have all of these elements. He is simply reminding us in figurative language that "in the world ye have tribulation." Immorality and vice intensify and multiply the oppression. It can, and one day will, become insupportable.

The sounding of the first four trumpets emphasizes to us the hideousness of the consequence of Satan's rebellion and with what folly thoughtless men follow his lead. Most of the damage we suffer is harm we bring upon ourselves. To endure the battle between spirit and flesh we must offer our body a living sacrifice, which is our reasonable service.[309]

The Bible describes in picturesque words the terrible destruction that came upon the world when God punished man's rampant wickedness by sending a destructive flood of waters.

---

308 Rom 8:20-22
309 Rom 12:1 to the end of the chapter

Peter gives a vivid description of the Genesis flood,[310] :

- Unbelieving mockers will claim the world has always been as it now is …

- These mockers deny "Jesus will come a second time unto salvation"[311]

- They forget that the world from of old was destroyed (it perished)[312]

- The "old" world was compacted "out of water and amidst water"

- The heavens and earth "from of old" were created "by the word of God"

- By that same word, the "world that then was" perished

- The world compacted out of and amidst water was overflowed by water

Moses, describing this flood, says "the fountains of the great deep were broken up …the windows of heaven were opened.[313]

It is scarcely possible for mere mortals to understand this catastrophic destruction of the original world. We understand the terrible power in the forces of nature. We see this in "every stormy wind that blows." Earthquakes, typhoons, tsunamis, and volcanoes pack strength that humans cannot resist or contain. The forces of nature on earth can be savage.

We know something about the structure of the earth, with its inner core, outer core, mantle, and crust. We know that the heat of the inner core has power to melt rock (in fact, the inner core of the earth is molten rock and metal). When the plates on the crust of the earth move, the result is earthquakes and volcanoes either on land or under water. The boiling rock with its incredible heat pours through a fissure in earth's mantle caused by the moving plates and the result is terrifying. The destruction this causes overwhelms the human mind.

---

310 2 Peter 3:1-7
311 Heb 9:28
312 Thayer says of the word translated perished, "to destroy fully (to perish, or lose)"
313 Gen 7:11-12

Moses says of the flood "the fountains of the great deep were broken up," indicating the radical movement of earth plates and the ensuing devastation. The flood of Noah's day wrought chaos and indescribable ruin. Peter says, "The world that then was perished."

This was the greatest of all catastrophes in the annals of human history.

The world as we see it today and in which we live is not the world as God first made it, but is the world as sin has damaged it. We live in a fallen world. The original world – the one "compacted out of water and amidst water" – was perfect.[314] Our ruined world is far from being "very good."

Every upheaval in nature should remind us of the universal flood recorded in the book of Genesis and the horrible damage it did. It wrecked the world and brought havoc. It is a silent, solemn reminder that God hates sin and "every transgression and disobedience" receives a "just recompense of reward."

The first four trumpets remind us of the painful and intense fear, dread, and dismay caused by the unbridled power of wrecked nature. Each incident of disturbance in nature is the sounding of a trumpet of woe. It signifies the ultimate end of the universe.

The spiritual brutality in the good fight of faith, the despair and dismay of human creatures giving themselves to a carnival of vice and corruption, and the consequent destruction, is God warning us.

Let us heed the counsel of the Almighty.

Pay attention to the "hail and fire, mingled with blood ... the great mountain burning with fire and turning the sea to blood ... a great star, called wormwood burning as a torch, falling on rivers and fountains of waters ... the third part of stars, sun and moon smitten and darkened." .

It is a macabre dance of death, a forceful declaration of the woe brought down on human heads by the army of Satan and the need for the righteous to take their battle stations and stand in the breach.

> "We are not here to dream to play to drift;
> We have hard work to do and loads to lift.
> Shun not the struggle, face it; 'tis God's gift."[315]

---

314 Gen 1:31
315 Maltbie Babcock, *Be Strong*

"Wherefore, my beloved brethren, be ye stedfast, unmoveable, always abounding in the work of the Lord, forasmuch as ye know that your labor is not vain in the Lord."[316]

Verse 13

*"And I saw, and I heard an eagle,
flying in mid heaven,
saying with a great voice,
Woe, woe, woe, for them that dwell on the earth,
by reason of the other voices of the trumpet of the three angels, who
are yet to sound."*

This perks our ears and causes us to look out for the coming woes ... and learn from them.

---

316 1 Cor 15:58

Trumpets Five and Six
Revelation Chapter 9:1-21

Humanity's story as reported by a divine historian continues; the following information is recorded in the first eight chapters of the book of Revelation.

- The beauty, glory, and preeminence of the enthroned Jesus – Chap 1
- The Lord's letters of instruction to the seven churches of Asia – chaps 2-3
- The throne of God and the song of salvation – chap 4
- The throne of God and a seven-sealed book – chap 5
- The seals are broken and the contents of the little book revealed – chap 6
- Redemption available to all – chap 7
- Trumpets sound as a warning to the unbelieving and disobedient – chap 8

We have heard the powerful sound of four of the seven trumpets and are now to hear the sounding of the final three. The angelic trumpeters are about to tell of more terrible woes than have as yet been heard. "Woe, woe, woe, for them that dwell on the earth, by reason of the other voices of the trumpet of the three angels, who are yet to sound."

What power! What suffering! What glory!

The emphasis of the entire Bible, from its opening syllable to its final word, is on salvation. The many diadems on Jesus' head show the importance and value of redemption.

In the midst of the rejoicing of all those who by their faith and obedience have washed their filthy robes in the blood of the Lamb and made them white is the harsh warning to those who do not believe and obey and who cannot stand before God in their dirty rags.

The next three trumpets to blast their solemn warning are about to sound.[317]

Verses 1-2

And the fifth angel sounded,
and I saw a star from heaven fallen unto the earth:
and there was given to him the key of the pit of the abyss.

And he opened the pit of the abyss;
and there went up a smoke out of the pit,
as the smoke of a great furnace;
and the sun and the air were darkened by reason of the smoke of the pit.

The star sent from heaven to earth is not identified. Elsewhere in the book of Revelation stars equate with messengers of God who speak the word of God.[318] It is not necessary for us to be given information that does not impact the revelation of regeneration. It is enough for us to know that the star, referred to as "he" in verses 1&2, was sent for the specific purpose of releasing evil spirits from the abyss.[319] An angel from heaven receives the key to the abyss,[320] which explains as much as we need to know about this star.

---

317 The woes announced by the trumpets are not sequential but are simultaneous. There is no way to record them all at once.

318 Rev 1:20

319 Abyss means "the bottomless pit or the chaotic deep." Originally, this term represented a deep mass of waters, and was associated with the water which God created with the earth. Darkness is said to have been on the face of the deep or abyss (Gen 1:2).

The term is used in several other ways in the Bible. It describes the prison of disobedient spirits, or the world of the dead (Luke 8:31; Rom 10:7). Terms like "the pit" and "bottomless pit" represent the abode of all the wicked dead."

320 Rev 9:1

The star that fell from heaven was given the key to the bottomless pit and when he opened the abyss "smoke" billowed from the bowels of the prison.

The "smoke" that came from the Abyss and darkened sun and air is said to be "as the smoke of a great furnace." Evil spirits cannot be described in literal language, but when the star opened the Abyss something boiled out that had the appearance of smoke and caused two of earth's most vital elements to be darkened, which is consistent with demons working wickedness.[321]

Verses 3-6

And out of the smoke came forth locusts upon the earth;
and power was given them,
as the scorpions of the earth have power.

And it was said unto them that they should not hurt the grass of the earth,
neither any green thing,
neither any tree,
but only such men as have not the seal of God on their foreheads.

And it was given them that they should not kill them, but that
they should be tormented five months: and their torment was
as the torment of a scorpion, when it striketh a man.

And in those days men shall seek death,
and shall in no wise find it;
and they shall desire to die,
and death fleeth from them.

---

321 Alexander Campbell wrote a persuasive essay on Demonology in which he argues that departed spirits of the depraved are demons serving Satan – a part of his army. *A Campbell, Millenial Harbenger, Vol 5, pp 457-479, March 10, 1841; An Address on Demonology: Delivered before the Popular Lecture Club, Nashville, Tenn* in Bloomington, Indiana, also in *Popular Lectures and Addresses* by Alexander Campbell published by the Christian Publishing Company in St. Louis (1861).Such demons fogging forth from confinement might have the appearance of "the smoke of a great furnace." Bats leaving their cave at twilight appear to some as smoke. A swarm of locusts have the appearance of a cloud of smoke.

The figurative smoke of the abyss gave birth to fearful creatures, called locusts but perceived as scorpions. The terrible appearance of these unearthly animals is frightening beyond measure.

The mission of these unsightly locusts-scorpions was to punish the ungodly. They are forbidden to damage green and growing things, as locusts would, and are restricted to the punishment of pain on "only such men as have not the seal of God on their foreheads."

They are not of God and consequently are of the Devil, seeing there is no other alternative.[322] It seems strange for the Devil to punish his own people, but it cannot be otherwise, seeing that the fruit of unrighteousness is both bitter and disappointing.

These evil scorpion-spirits are not to hurt the environment of the earth, which would cause seasons, seedtime and harvest to fail.[323] The punishment was not to be general but specific, affecting sinners who did not have the seal of God on their foreheads. It would afflict the ungodly but would not injure God's people. It must be something in the mind that would discombobulate the wicked but not trouble the godly.

When Eve and Adam took the forbidden fruit they earned a reward of deep regret and searing pain, and brought down misery on the heads of all. The "wages of sin is death." Many men are willfully blind to the reality of the consequence of denying God and tampering with his word. Death makes sin sting the degenerate, but is a friend to the blood-bought saint.

The righteous suffer as well as the unrighteous; the pure in heart in the world have tribulation, persecution and sickness the same as the lawless. Tribulation is in the world and comes upon both the good and the bad. The ungodly are hopeless while the saints have a joyful expectation. Suffering is tolerable if we know it will end when a heavenly healing-balm is applied. "But even if ye should suffer for righteousness' sake, blessed are ye: and fear not their fear, neither be troubled."[324]

The stings of the scorpion-demons represent something more painful than the fallout of evil that comes randomly upon all men.

322 Matt 6:24
323 Gen 8:22
324 1 Peter 3:14

The horse-like scorpions are expressly forbidden to kill the God-denying and God-forsaken group of men, but to use five-months regrettable sting that would make the victim wish for elusive physical-death. Their agony would be perpetuated by subsequent stings that would have the net effect of continuous insupportable misery. There is perhaps no state more torturous than wishing to die, but not being able to do so.

The stings are like the grief of those addicted to lawless behavior and their inability to conquer the persistent desire for what they know will punish them. Still, they put their hands through the flames of hell to get a temporary thrill that will soon abate into pangs of remorse. They steal even from their closest friends and relatives, they lie, and they rob because the addiction is powerful upon them. They feel they must have what they know from past experience will bring to them regret and shame. The addiction may not kill them immediately but it will make them wish they were dead, for death is better than living a lie, yet, they cannot die. Many books tell the pitiful history of people addicted to illegal substances and conduct, of their fruitless struggle against their bonds and can find no relief.

As a dog that returneth to his vomit, So is a fool that repeateth his folly.[325]

It has happened unto them according to the true proverb, The dog turning to his own vomit again, and the sow that had washed to wallowing in the mire.[326]

There is hardly anything more revolting than to see a dog licking up his vomit. You can bathe a sow, spray her with perfume, manicure her hoofs, and put lipstick on her mouth, but, as soon as she can, she will return to wallowing in the mud and the manure.

These are unforgettable examples of people persisting in immoral behavior … the mighty sting of the huge scorpion-demon.

Verses 7-10

And the shapes of the locusts were like unto horses prepared for war;
and upon their heads as it were crowns like unto gold,
and their faces were as men's faces.

---

325 Prov 26:11
326 2 Peter 2:22

And they had hair as the hair of women,
and their teeth were as teeth of lions.

And they had breastplates,
as it were breastplates of iron;
and the sound of their wings was as the sound of chariots,
of many horses rushing to war.

And they have tails like unto scorpions,
and stings;
and in their tails is their power to hurt men five months.

This forceful section describes the consequence of rejecting heaven's offer of mercy.

Jesus was rich, "yet for your sakes he became poor, that ye through his poverty might become rich."[327] A cold-hearted rejection of the "unspeakable gift" of God's love is inhuman. It brings a woe almost too awful for words. Still, the inspired prophet-poet is equal to the task, giving a vision of perfected pathos.

The figurative smoke of the Abyss gave birth to fearful creatures, called locusts but perceived as scorpions. These animals could have the shape of a horse without being the size of a horse, yet, the overall impression of the passage justifies thinking of these beasts as "horses prepared for war."

Not many would be eager to face a cavalry of scorpions "with stings in their tails." The crowns they wear indicate their power. The human face is an indication of intelligence. They came in great number like a swarm of locusts.

The author resorts to the all-powerful technique of extravagant exaggeration and perfects his figures of speech. This is intended to hold our attention and bring fear into our hearts.[328]

He gives some of the features of these agents of evil: consider the appearance of the horses:

- Crowns on their heads
- Faces like men

---

327 2 Cor 8:9
328 2 Cor 5:11

- Hair like women
- Teeth like lions
- Breastplates of iron
- Stings in their tails

There is no known living being that has such appearance; these "scorpions" must not be literal but figurative animals. To attempt to find a visible parallel in the annals of human history is vain. To seek some event or instrument in mortal experience that would be like this animal of terrifying shape is useless. The author of these words seeks to impress us with the fearfulness and meanness of these evil beings. He wants us to understand the harm they do and the doubt and suspicion they cause. Their loathsomeness has no parallel.

The book of Revelation overflows with and abounds in symbols. These locust-horse-scorpion-man-woman-lion animals inflict upon a certain segment of human society terrible punishment.

The agents of the devil are unrighteous. To be lawless is to be unrighteous. To respect and keep divine law is good. Israel's sweet singer wrote,

> O Jehovah: give me understanding according to thy word.
>
> Let my supplication come before thee: deliver me according to thy word.
>
> Let my lips utter praise; for thou teachest me thy statutes.
>
> Let my tongue sing of thy word; for all thy commandments are righteousness[329]

If all of the commands of God are "righteousness," then, to obey the "commands of God" is to be righteous. Righteousness is doing what the law of God commands, which is always the right thing to do. Paul said, "So that the law is holy, and the commandment holy, and righteous, and good."[330] The Law, expressed in commandments of God, is holy and righteous. The law of God is good. On the other hand, "sin is lawlessness,"[331] and is not only not good but is damnable.

---

329 Psa 119:168-172
330 Rom 7:12
331 1 John 3:4

Religious liberals in the late eighteenth century A.D., following the example of the serpent in Eden, downgraded and belittled the revealed word of God and consequently became unrighteous. The technique of these unbelievers is to deny the truthfulness of divine revelation, just as the devil did when he beguiled Eve.

The modern method is to attempt to make "scripture inspired of God" originate with man. The religious liberal teaches the falsehood that much of the Bible is rooted in antique shepherd's tales. They insist that common folklore, in the passage of time, was elevated to divine revelation. They see their calling as convincing their contemporaries that the "documentary hypothesis" is a valid explanation for the origin of the Bible. If they are right the Bible is vulgar and can in no way make one holy through righteousness.

Most of the advocates of the documentary hypothesis profess to believe in God but deny the word of God, which claims to be God-breathed. If the Bible was handed down mouth-to-ear over many generations then it is not what it claims to be. If the Bible is not what it claims to be, it is false and unworthy of our attention. One can take it or leave it and that is exactly what the liberals do. They go picking and choosing between the words of the Bible and take the parts that suit them and leave the parts that do not please them. This is lawlessness. Lawlessness is unrighteousness. It brings its own penalty.

The symbolic sting of the symbolic scorpion released from the abyss is typified by the mental anguish of lawlessness, which includes hopelessness.

Verses 11-12

They have over them as king the angel of the abyss:
his name in Hebrew is Abaddon,
and in the Greek tongue he hath the name Apollyon.

The first Woe is past:
behold, there come yet two Woes hereafter.

"The angel of the abyss" is wicked. Rebellious angels were cast down out of heaven and are kept in "pits of darkness" and are "reserved unto judgment."[332] Fallen angels are still angels, but they are evil. The "angel of

---

332 Jude 6; 2 Pet 2:4; 1 Cor 6:3; Eph 6:12

the abyss" is king of the scorpions and his name "in Hebrew is Abaddon" (destruction) and "in Greek his name is Apollyn" (destroyer). These names affirm his sinful nature. He leads a band of bad angels and, as king, is the worst of the worst.

Two trumpets are yet to sound. Two woes remain. The first of the remaining three woes is past and the stage is set for the additional grief of trumpet six and the summit of all these woes in the sounding of the seventh trumpet.

Verses 13-14

And the sixth angel sounded,
and I heard a voice from the horns of the golden altar which is before God,

one saying to the sixth angel that had one trumpet,
Loose the four angels that are bound at the great river Euphrates.

Earth approaches her terminus. The saints of God are sealed with the mark of the Almighty on their foreheads.[333] Wickedness abounds as it did just before the great flood of Noah's day. The righteous dead are transported far beyond sun, moon and stars where they are forever safe. Soon the conquering Christ shall sit victorious on his magnificent white warhorse and the saved shall be insulated from the consequences of all evil and are themselves "more than conquerors." Soon sin shall be defeated and the last enemy abolished.

The divine historian speaks of things to come as if they had already happened.[334] He foresees a time when the inhabitants of earth will give themselves over to the lawlessness of sin and there will be none to "find favor in the sight of the Lord."

The golden altar is the altar of incense where the godly prayers of all ages ascend as an order of a sweet smell into the brilliance of God on his throne. Prayers glorify God.[335] We must never underestimate the important role prayer plays in God's eternal scheme.

Four angels are mentioned as standing at the four corners of earth for the purpose of preserving times and seasons until the day of the destruction

333 Rev 7:1-17
334 Isa 46:10; Rom 4:17
335 2Cor 4:15

131

of all material things.[336] As the time of the outrageous annihilation of the cosmos draws near the four angels are stirred to action with the shrill blast of the sixth trumpet.

Verses 15-19

And the four angels were loosed,
that had been prepared for the hour and day and month and year,
that they should kill the third part of men.

And the number of the armies of the horsemen was
twice ten thousand times ten thousand:
I heard the number of them.

And thus I saw the horses in the vision,
and them that sat on them,
having breastplates as of fire and of hyacinth and of brimstone:
and the heads of lions;
and out of their mouths proceedeth fire and smoke and brimstone.

By these three plagues was the third part of men killed,
by the fire and the smoke and the brimstone,
which proceeded out of their mouths.

For the power of the horses is in their mouth,
and in their tails: for their tails are like unto serpents,
and have heads;
and with them they hurt.

The four angels are not specified and we know little about them, except that they are agents of the "angel of the abyss" and do his bidding. The king of the bottomless pit commands a formidable army and applies clever stratagems to work his malignant mischief. Be afraid! Be watchful!

His army numbers two hundred million. The writer of this vision did not count the soldiers but "heard" their number – a voice of an unknown source told him how many were in the uncountable trained force of the evil one.

Never, in all the annals of humankind has such a force been gathered, but the ghastly angel-king calls hordes of hard-hearted and beastly soldiers of the abyss to stand in array. The Devil has plenty of workers to obey his malicious orders.

---

336 Rev 7:1-3

One third of the wicked world (godless humans) is killed by this repulsive organized body. Again, it is a matter of Satan killing his own people. The massacre is shocking. Remember the figurative nature of the book of Revelation and learn from this the formidable power of the great Destroyer and be warned. He is dangerous as a hungry lion on the loose. To enroll in his minions is worse than risky. It brings certain death,[337] which is not cessation, but separation from the fountain of all blessings and therefore everlasting meaninglessness.

The Evil One is sure to pay his agents and the ultimate recompense is the second death, which is not termination but permanent insupportable suffering.

Unbelievers profess shock at the thought of God consigning sinners to eternal punishment and seek to mollify what seems to them to be harsh and inconsistent with the divine nature. However, it is the Devil's payday. "The wages of sin is death." Those who are paid in the coin of hell have earned their shameful reward. It is their just recompense and therefore neither the wish nor the work of God.

The horses of the vision were mounted by warriors with breastplates of red, blue and yellow; "and the heads of the horses were like lions' heads, and fire (red) and smoke (blue) and sulfur (yellow) came out of their mouths." The fire, smoke and sulfur (three plagues) were fatal. The horses had serpents for tails whose bites inflicted injury and pain. The misery and death caused by 200,000,000 horses and their riders was inescapable, inflicted forward and rearward – coming and going.

This was a terrible massacre and speaks volumes about the maliciousness of fallen, sinful angels and their reprehensible leader.

Verses 20-21

And the rest of mankind,
who were not killed with these plagues,
repented not of the works of their hands,
that they should not worship demons,
and the idols of gold, and of silver, and of brass, and of stone, and of wood;
which can neither see, nor hear, nor walk:

---

337 Rom 6:23

and they repented not of their murders,
nor of their sorceries,
nor of their fornication,
nor of their thefts.

The inhabitants of the world are wicked. There are a few who "fear God and keep his commandments," but they are ever in the distinct minority. Jesus taught that the world, meaning the population of the world, is chronically sinful and complained that the whole world hates truth and right and loves immorality.[338]

Jesus saw the people of earth as two groups; one composed of his faithful followers and the other composed of those who reject God's word and adore the king of the abyss.

We know that whosoever is begotten of God sinneth not; but he that was begotten of God keepeth himself, and the evil one toucheth him not.

We know that we are of God, and the whole world lieth in the evil one.[339]

The picture drawn for us in the sounding of trumpets five and six is that of the whole world, which is evil, contrasted with those who are begotten of God and are not of Satan. The "whole" world is of the evil one, and those who are begotten of God by the word of God[340] are not of the world and therefore are not under the control of "the evil one."

The fifth trumpet introduces scorpion-like evil spirits who torment but do not kill one third of the whole wicked world.[341] The sixth trumpet reveals the massive army of Satan that kills one third of the population of the whole wicked world.[342] Neither the stinging-demons nor Satan's army is able to harm those begotten of God, but do kill one third of those who are under the control of Satan. This is not a contradiction; it makes a distinction between the woe of the fifth trumpet and the grief of the sixth trumpet, which is more severe than the misery of its forerunner. Under trumpet five, the victims are stung and suffer, but do not die as a direct result of the sting. They wish to die but cannot. Under the woe of the sixth

338 John 17:14
339 1 John 5:18-19
340 1 Peter 1:22-23
341 Rev 9:5
342 Rev 9:15, 18

trumpet, one third of the world's population of scoundrels dies. Killed by their king! Again, death is separation and not termination.

The Devil doesn't mind killing a third of his earthly worshippers because he takes a hellish delight in seeing the survivors writhe in their abject fear. Satan is a terrorist and takes pleasure in seeing even his own soldier's quake and shudder. Ben Jonson in the early seventeenth century wrote a famous play, titled, "*The Devil is an Ass.*" Jonson had that right. In addition, it is ironclad stupidity to bow in service to an evil being that enjoys killing his own kind even though this puts them beyond his power to further torment them.[343] He is a fiend indeed.

The writer closes this vision by describing the inglorious satanic host as idolaters guilty of murders, sorceries, fornication and thefts (the fruit of Satanism).

WHO ARE THESE PEOPLE?

They are the hard of heart; the slow learners. They witnessed the slaughter of a third of their number but did not repent of their evil. The day of no return was drawing on but at this moment in time they could still have been reconciled to God. They foolishly refused.[344]

All those wicked inhabitants of the earth contemplated in chapter nine are the morally reprehensible followers of Satan. The righteous are exempted from the hurt brought by the locust-scorpion sting because they are sealed with the mark of Jehovah on their foreheads, and have a protecting wall of fire about them.

We are not told specifically what the sting is, but only that it is painful, which can be mental or physical. We are told in the New Testament: "*The sting of death is sin; and the power of sin is the law: but thanks be to God, who giveth us the victory through our Lord Jesus Christ*",[345] which shows that a sting can be mental and make its victim wretched.

The duration of the pain caused by the scorpion's sting is five months (about half a year) which is short, but seems interminable to the victim.

343 Luke 12:4
344 Matt 23:37-39
345 1 Cor 15:56-57

John saw *"underneath the altar the souls of them that had been slain for the word of God, and for the testimony which they held: and they cried with a great voice, saying, How long, O Master, the holy and true, dost thou not judge and avenge our blood on them that dwell on the earth?"*[346]

The sting of the demon-scorpions is part of the answer and the complete response is when the faithless and fearful are stung by the second death, which is eternal separation from God. "

The seventh trumpet is yet to sound and we tremble at its prospective woe.

---

[346] Rev 6:9-10

THE LITTLE BOOK

REVELATION 10:1-11

Children of God are commanded to "war the good warfare."[347] Life is a battle in which the meek of the earth are to fight with full strength and skill.

It may sound like a contradiction to speak of the meek rolling up their sleeves and vigorously fighting, but it is not. The war we wage is not carnal but spiritual, yet it has fatal consequences.

The book of Revelation describes in majestic language an invisible contest between the good and the bad and gives assurance that the victory goes to those who follow Jesus because he is "the way, the truth, and the life."

The fight is figurative but it is real and its outcome more serious than any literal war. Even atomic war pales into insignificance when the desperate struggle for priceless souls is considered.

Every human life is worth more than the whole world with all its contents,[348] consequently, the battle for the hearts of intelligent-creatures outstrips in importance any and all carnal wars.. We are called to buckle on our war-armor and plant our feet on solid ground and stand, and stand, and stand.[349]

In the opening nine chapters of the book of Revelation, the beginning and continuation of this ceaseless hostility are recited.

---

347 1 Tim 1:18
348 Mark 8:36
349 Eph 6:10-17

- Jesus in his splendor is the main character in this battle of the ages (chap 1)
- The Lord instructs his churches in spiritual warfare (chaps 2-3)
- God's throne and a Lamb that was slain introduces a sealed book (chaps 4-5)
- The seals of the book are broken and the war narrative unfolds (chap 6)
- Humans will have an equal opportunity to "lay hold on eternal life" (chap 7)
- Four trumpets sound warning of earthly woe and affliction (chap 8)
- Trumpets five and six announce more grievous woes (chap 9)

The inhabitants of earth have a choice; they can put on the panoply of God as missionaries following "Christ the royal Master" as he "leads against the foe," or they become the mercenaries of the Devil. That is the choice – either missionaries of Jesus or mercenaries of Satan. There is no alternative. You are either for Christ or you are against him.[350]

Six of seven trumpets have sounded and now there is an intermission before the seventh trumpet is heard. In the breaking of the seals, the seventh seal introduced the seven trumpeters, and the seventh trumpet will introduce the seven bowls of wrath.

Before the seventh trumpet sounds there is an interlude and two other visions are reported by the inspired prophetic historian. We look first in chapter ten where we have the vision of the "little book;" in chapter eleven we will see the vision of the "two witnesses."

Verse 1

And I saw another strong angel coming down out of heaven, arrayed with a cloud; and the rainbow was upon his head, and his face was as the sun, and his feet as pillars of fire;

---

350 Matt 12:30

It is no surprise to learn that a "strong" angel comes down out of heaven to deliver this revelation. All angels of God are strong angels; he has no weak angels in his kingdom. Weak angels are all in the service of Satan and are dominated by the word of God, which binds them and renders them impotent. Jesus overcame the temptations of the evil one by repeating the formula, "It is written.[351]"

The gospel is the "power" of God for salvation to every believer.[352] The wise will recognize:

- There is nothing more important than salvation[353]
- Believers exhibit in their lives the obedience of faith[354]
- Faith, perfected by works of obedience, justifies the sinner[355]
- The gospel is unspeakably powerful[356]
- The word of God puts a hook in the nose of the Devil[357]

The Christian warrior armed with the sword of the Spirit can overcome the wiles of the great deceiver and destroyer and bring him to his knees.

Failure comes when we fail to recognize the potency of God's word and turn it into a manmade fabrication. When we fall for the delusion that the Bible is nothing more than the folktales of antique shepherds and much of it was not put into its present form until about 600 years before the birth of Jesus, we rob ourselves of heavenly power. This is the thunderous warning of the closing book of the Bible.

The angel who gives the details of this vision was "arrayed in a cloud." This was a symbol of majesty and glory, and is often represented as accompanying the divine presence.[358] The Savior ascended in a cloud, Acts 1:9; and he will again descend in clouds to judge the world.[359]

---

351 Matt 4:4, 7, 10
352 Rom 1:16
353 Mark 8:36; Matt 13:44-46
354 Rom 1:5; 19, 26; James 2:14-26
355 James 2:21-24
356 Rom 1:16
357 Rev 20:1-2
358 Ex 16:9-10; 24:16; 34:5; Num 11:25; 1 Kings 8:10; Ps 97:2.
359 Matt 26:64; Rev 1:7.

The feet and legs of the angel – the mighty one – appear as pillars of fire. Fire often represents the presence of God.[360]

His face was as the sun in its brilliant brilliance, which makes us think of Moses in the presence of God.[361]

A rainbow was over the angel's head just as a rainbow overarches the mighty throne of God.[362] Since the days of Noah, the rainbow is a token of the promise of God, and symbolizes peace and hope.

Verse 2

and he had in his hand a little book open:
and he set his right foot upon the sea,
and his left upon the earth;

This glorious angel had in his hand "a little book open." The book only Jesus could open and reveal its mysteries was "sealed with seven seals."[363] This "little book" was open not sealed, perhaps because Jesus had broken the seals of the book and is in the process of revealing through the apostle John the destiny of all those made in the image and likeness of God. Some of them will live in glory, but others will "judge themselves unworthy of eternal life," and be self condemned. There is no other option.

The angel had one foot upon the sea and other upon the earth representing the universal application of the little book.[364] The gospel is for all. If anyone is lost it is because of sin not being washed away in the blood of the Lamb and the sinner's own choice to refuse to listen to the words of the New Covenant, written in a "little book."[365]

It is heartbreaking to see some professing Bible scholars abuse the "little book;" their claim to respect the Bible gives way to shamelessly disparaging Hoy Writ. Thank God for sincere and competent Bible scholars who hold high the flaming torch of God's unfailing and imperishable word.

---

360 Exodus 3:2; 13-14; Num 14; Neh 9; Acts 2:3
361 2 Cor 3:7-11; Exodus 34:29-30; Acts 17:1-5
362 Rev 4:3
363 Rev 5:1-2, 9
364 Matt 28:18-20; Mark 16:15-16; Luke 24:46-47
365 Matt 22:3; 23:37; John 1:11; 5:39-40; 3:19; 8:45-46; 12:34-41

The New Testament teaches the unique origin, nourishment, and vitality of the church, which is built on the teaching of Jesus and the apostles;[366] their word shall not pass away.[367] Its salvation message is odious to Satan.

Verses 3-4

[A]nd he cried with a great voice, as a lion roareth:
and when he cried, the seven thunders uttered their voices.
And when the seven thunders uttered their voices,
I was about to write:
and I heard a voice from heaven saying,
Seal up the things which the seven thunders uttered,
and write them not.

The strong angel had a strong voice. Supernatural beings in the book of Revelation speak loudly.[368] The voice of Jehovah is powerful and full of majesty.[369] What is said is important and the commanding, resonate tone helps to rivet attention and implies the need for acceptance. Still, it is a voice and not a direct irresistible force and it can be ignored, or even ridiculed.

We are not told who the seven thunders are nor the part they play in heavenly realms; speculation is worthless. There is much we do not know about celestial creatures and we will have to wait on that knowledge until our eyes are made wise by death.

The sound of the powerful angel voice was enough to stir the seven thunders to give an utterance. What was said, we do not know. John, the recorder, heard, understood, and knew what the seven thunders said and was about to write and preserve the message, when he was forbidden to do so.

The words were no doubt full of wisdom, but it is not essential that we know them or John would not have been told to "seal up the things which the seven thunders uttered, and write them not."

---

366 Eph 2:20
367 Luke 21:33
368 Rev 1:10; 6:1; 7:10; 11:15; 12:10; 14:2, 7, 9, 15, 18; 16:1, 17; 21:3;
369 Hosea 11:10; Joel 3:16; Amos 1:2; 3:8; Jer 25:25:30; 1 Sam 7:10; Job 40:9; Jer 10:13

Saul of Tarsus was caught up into the third heaven; he was forbidden to tell what he heard or describe what he saw.[370]

Daniel was told "shut up the words, and seal the book, even to the time of the end: many shall run to and fro, and knowledge shall be increased."[371]

It was not time for this link in the redemption process to be revealed, so the prophet was told to seal his lips and lay down his pen.

Verses 5-6

And the angel that I saw standing upon the sea and upon
the earth lifted up his right hand to heaven,
and sware by him that liveth for ever and ever,
who created the heaven and the things that are therein,
and the earth and the things that are therein,
and the sea and the things that are therein,
that there shall be delay no longer:

The strong angel, clothed with majestic clouds and a rainbow crown, lifts his right hand to heaven and swore by the mighty Maker of heaven, earth, and sea, and all that is in them, that there shall be delay no longer. The uplifted hand and the solemn appeal underscore the importance of of the angelic oath.

When the seventh angel blows his trumpet, the bowls of the wrath of God are poured out simultaneously upon a benighted earth; delay and time end. The earth is baptized in the undiluted anger of God as the totality of his wrath brings an end to the original creation – sun, moon, stars, planets, air, and the first and second heavens are erased by a furious Godhead.

The time for the destruction of a system that has sold out to the Devil arrives and in a benevolent rage God Almighty brings it to an irreversible close. The fire of the undiluted anger of God eliminates every jot and tittle of wickedness and purifies its space. John sees the world standing on the threshold of oblivion as the seventh trumpet is prepared for sounding.

When the sovereign and supreme authority of the Eternal One is emphasized inspired men often make reference to his creative might. He who made the

370 2 Cor 12:4
371 Dan 12:4

heavens, earth, air, and sea, and all that is in them, is Omnipotent and his power cannot be successfully challenged.

The angel stands with one foot on land and the other on the sea, indicating the universal nature of the Kingdom of God and the global application of the "little book" that Jesus said is to be preached to "every creature" in all the world.

Verse 7

but in the days of the voice of the seventh angel,
when he is about to sound,
then is finished the mystery of God,
according to the good tidings which he declared to his servants the prophets.

Prophets in the Bible told things they themselves did not fully understand. They studied their own writings in an attempt to "understand what time or manner of time the Spirit of Christ which was in them did point unto, when it testified beforehand the sufferings of Christ, and the glories that should follow them."[372] Our questions are sometime answered with the gentle rebuke, "it is not for you to know the times and the seasons God hath set within his own authority."[373]

In government there will be necessary secrets of state that must not be blabbed. To reveal things that ought to be kept confidential is treason. This may be part of the reason for the silence of the seven thunders. Many seem to have a thirst to know the time of the end and use every devise to dislodge this information. God keeps his own counsel and none will have this knowledge until the seventh trumpet blows.

If we knew the exact time of the ultimate end of all things, some might be tempted to wait until the evening of the last night to repent. It is the will of Jesus for the people of earth to be ignorant of the end time to avoid partiality and to assure fairness. "*Watch therefore: for ye know not on what day your Lord cometh ... Therefore be ye also ready; for in an hour that ye think not the Son of man cometh.*" [374] "He that is ignorant, let him be ignorant still."

---

372 1 Pet 1:10-11
373 Acts 1:7
374 Matt 24:42, 44

The Old Testament concealed things that are revealed in the New Testament.[375] There are things now concealed that will not be known until the shrill notes of the seventh trumpet are heard.

Verse 8

And the voice which I heard from heaven,
I heard it again speaking with me, and saying,
Go, take the book which is open in the hand of the angel
that standeth upon the sea and upon the earth.

The apostle of Jesus is told to take the book out of the hand of the angel. Its message is not to be concealed, but is for all the people of earth. The revealed wisdom of God is always for the entire population of the world in every generation, but most people will not accept it.

People of the earth have the unearthly strangeness or oddness of being able to see and hear confirmed truth and, amazingly, to shut it out. Isaiah was forewarned that though his message was from God it would be rejected by most of his listeners and only a few would receive it.

"If ye be willing and obedient, ye shall eat the good of the land: but if ye refuse and rebel, ye shall be devoured with the sword; for the mouth of Jehovah hath spoken it."[376] They had the fantastic ability to shut their eyes, close their ears, and harden their hearts against the very word of God.

And he said, Go, and tell this people, Hear ye indeed, but understand not; and see ye indeed, but perceive not. Make the heart of this people fat, and make their ears heavy, and shut their eyes; lest they see with their eyes, and hear with their ears, and understand with their heart, and turn again, and be healed.[377]

We, too, have the bizarre ability to refuse the word of God, but not to his face. We can do it, but it is not wise. Jesus rebuked the perversity of some in his day, saying, *"Ye search the scriptures, because ye think that in them ye have eternal life; and these are they which bear witness of me; and ye will not come to me, that ye may have life."*[378]

---

375 1 Cor 2:6
376 Isa 1:19-20
377 Isa 6:9-10
378 John 5:39-40

The day will come when his commands will be implicitly obeyed, and just as Lazarus had no choice but to respond when Jesus called his dead body out of the tomb, so shall all the good and all the bad assemble before him at his call when he comes again.[379]

You have the ability to refuse his voice now, but will not be able to do so when the last trumpet sounds. When he says to the lost, "Depart from me, all ye that work iniquity," they will have no choice but to go.

Verses 9-11

And I went unto the angel,
saying unto him that he should give me the little book.
And he saith unto me,
Take it, and eat it up;
and it shall make thy belly bitter,
but in thy mouth it shall be sweet as honey.
And I took the little book out of the angel's hand, and ate it up;
and it was in my mouth sweet as honey:
and when I had eaten it, my belly was made bitter.

The little book is the new covenant. God prepared the world for its reception over many centuries. Prophets, from Eden to Bethlehem, stood pointing to the coming of Messiah and his message of salvation. When the time was right, God sent his Son to enable those who receive him to become the children of God.[380] The message was freely given and should be freely taught.[381]

The highest office of the church is the proclamation of her king with bold clearness. "Thou that tellest good tidings …, lift up thy voice with strength; lift it up, be not afraid."[382] No whisper will do. Bated breath is no fit vehicle for God's gospel. The saving word of God must never be presented as if the teacher were ashamed of it.[383]

"[W]e preach Christ crucified, unto Jews a stumblingblock, and unto Gentiles foolishness; but unto them that are called, both Jews and

---

379 John 5:28-29
380 Gal 4:4-5; John 1:11-12
381 Luke 12:3
382 Isa *40:9*
383 Rom 1:16

Greeks, Christ the power of God, and the wisdom of God." We should be *"determined not to know anything among you, save Jesus Christ, and him crucified."*[384]

True-hearted, whole-hearted soldiers of Jesus hold high a bloodstained cross and shout , "Behold the Great Power of God." This must not be preached as if it were an apology. The church is to preach the majestic, saving truth of God in plain, clear, bold words shaped by the tenderness of the universal love of God exhibited in the Lamb that was slain for the sins of the world.

The good news of salvation is pleasant and sweet, but not deceptive. The gospel is to be taught with force, vigor and civility. It must be proclaimed in clarion tones framed in words of kindness and love.

The strong angel willingly handed over the saving gospel and John gladly received it. It is precious.[385] To the taste it is sweet. "The fear of Jehovah is clean, enduring for ever: the ordinances of Jehovah are true and righteous altogether. More to be desired are they than gold, yea, than much fine gold; sweeter also than honey and the droppings of the honeycomb."[386]

Again, though the words of the little book taste sweet, they are not to be taught in a weak and effusively sentimental style. God's word is not only of great value and therefore pleasing to the taste, but it is also like "[F]ire, saith Jehovah; and like a hammer that breaketh the rock in pieces." It is bittersweet.

The emphasis in this verse is the sweetness of the book as it is consumed. Jesus spoke of "eating" his flesh and "drinking" his blood. Many of the people who first heard these words were offended because they failed to recognize the figurative nature of the expression, and they "went back and walked with him no more." We do not literally put a literal book in our literal mouths and crush and grind the pages into pulp with our literal teeth, and swallow the melted words.

We consume Jesus by absorbing his teaching and making it a central part of our thinking. It becomes a part of us - "the engrafted word." We must "give diligence to present thyself approved unto God, a workman

---

384 1 Cor 1:23-24; 2:2)
385 1 Pet 2:6; 2 Pet 1:4;
386 Psa 19:9-10; 119:103

that needeth not to be ashamed, handling aright the word of truth." We find it "sweeter than honey" and we become addicted to studying its priceless pages.

Lo, the sweet words of the little book become bitter in our bellies. How can this be? What can this mean? We see the thought exemplified in the life of Jesus:

- Jesus came bringing truth, light, and life to the world – John 1:9-14
- He went about "healing all that were oppressed of the devil" – Acts 10:38
- His popularity turned into bitter hatred – Luke 20:13-15; John 3:20; 15:25; 17:14
- He was mercilessly killed – Matt 27:26; John 19:16

The tragedy of the senseless crucifixion of Jesus illustrates perfect goodness generating bitterness. We see the same lesson demonstrated in the lives of Moses, Isaiah, Jeremiah, John the baptist, Paul, and the apostle John.

When God commissioned Ananias to go to Saul, the man from Tarsus, heal his blindness and instruct the believing, penitent Paul to "arise and be baptized and wash away thy sins."[387] He was also to tell him the Lord said, "[H]e is a chosen vessel unto me, to bear my name before the Gentiles and kings, and the children of Israel: for I will show him how many things he must suffer for my name's sake." The honey-sweet gospel was to bring suffering, disappointment, imprisonment, and physical death.

We see it also in the experience of the church, which is one of the lessons in the book of Revelation. The church holds high the banner of truth and lovingly calls for all to bow before the throne of the Prince of Peace and make his will their passion. The noble band of believers is often rewarded for their sincere effort to extend the borders of the kingdom of righteousness with prejudiced hostility. Sadly, some see that as a reason to apologize and cease the militant struggle against the forces of evil.

We dare not!

---

387 Acts 22:16

"Fight the good fight of the faith, lay hold on the life eternal, whereunto thou wast called, and didst confess the good confession in the sight of many witnesses."[388]

We are in the midst of a raging spiritual battle, and the sounds of war are heard on the right hand and on the left, before and behind.. To retreat is treason. The Captain of our salvation bids us to "war the good warfare." He taught our fingers to fight;[389] for us to seek the comfort of freedom from labor and difficulty is to deny him.

Pure and undefiled religion has few ceremonies: its form of worship is simple: it depends for success on the presentation and defense of the truth.

The study of the Bible is the foundation of all the efforts to spread the knowledge of the truth to "peoples, and nations, and tongues, and kings," in every generation.

This will be true until "the kingdoms of this world become the kingdoms of our Lord, and of his Christ; and he shall reign forever and ever," or when the Lord's sovereignty brings the present, final earthly dispensation to an end.

The Bible is exalted because it is the power of God to save; symbolized by the appearance of the "angel descending from heaven clothed with a cloud …his face radiant as the sun, and his feet as pillars of fire … "standing on the sea and the earth."

---

388 1 Tim 6:12
389 Psa 144:1

Measuring the Temple
Revelation 11:1-14

The spiritual battle recorded in the book of Revelation rages and the combatants are about to be identified more fully. It is not a flesh and blood war but it necessarily involves flesh and blood, seeing the body is the vehicle of the spirit. It is not fought with guns and bullets and bombs but is a battle of minds and the weapons are intangible, yet they are real, though unseen. John is describing a fierce struggle between righteousness and unrighteousness. The fight is in the realm of "unseen principalities and powers" using lies, deception and carnality on one side, and truth, honesty and the obedience of faith on the other side.

The clash is inevitable since truth cannot be compromised without losing its savor and because evil hates truth.[390]

Satan and his soldiers are "foolish, disobedient, led astray, slaves to various passions and pleasures, passing their days in malice and envy, hated by others and hating one another"[391] while Jesus and his valiant warriors exhibit "faith, virtue, knowledge, self-control, steadfastness, godliness, brotherly-kindness, and love."[392]

One army consists of the slaves of the Devil and the other army is composed of those who have "escaped the corruption that is in the world because of sinful desire;" the slaves of righteousness.[393]

---

390 John 15:18; 17:14
391 Titus 3:3
392 2 Pet 1:5-6
393 Rom 6:16

Jesus came from heaven to Bethlehem to free sinners.[394] His fighters in this good fight are those who have been released from captivity and blindness, and in the joy of emancipation they throw themselves into the battle with vigor and commitment.

In the first ten chapters of this amazing book we have been apprised of the following:

- Glory and power of Jesus – Chapter 1
- Authoritative words of Jesus – Chapters 2 & 3
- Grand Throne of God – Chapters 4 & 5
- Breaking of the seven seals – Chapters 6 & 7
- Sounding of six trumpets – Chapters 8-10

As we await the sounding of the seventh trumpet, we are told in chapter eleven of the measuring of God's glorious temple, it's furniture and its people:

Verse 1

And there was given me a reed like unto a rod: and one said,
Rise, and measure the temple of God,
and the altar, and them that worship therein.

The measuring reed was given to John along with the command to measure the temple of God, the altar, and the worshippers.

The worshippers are individual, living, thinking, animate beings. A ruler may be used to determine a person's height and weight but it cannot measure the essential being, which is spirit born of God the Father.[395] There is one Father of all human spirits just as there is one giver of all human spirits. The God-given spirit of man is invisible and eternal; it therefore cannot be measured with a reed like unto a rod. This also tells us that the temple and the altar are spiritual and not corporeal.

Temple

God has a temple today that is real but not visible to mortal eyes. The all-seeing eye of deity can behold the temple but flesh and blood cannot see

394 John 8:32-36; Luke 4:18
395 Heb 12:9

it. It is a temple more glorious than the material building made of cedar boards, gold, marble, linen, exquisite embroidery, and costly gems made by Solomon or by Herod the Great. We read of this wonderful temple in the pages of the New Testament. Here are some of its features:

- The soldiers of Christ, in the aggregate, are a temple of God and the Holy Spirit directs that temple through the revealed word.[396]

- It is made of "living" stones redeemed by the blood of the Lamb; these living stones are a "spiritual house," which humans cannot see, smell nor touch, but they can appreciate its grandeur; the living stones that make the spiritual house have the ability to offer to God "spiritual sacrifices acceptable to God through Jesus."[397]

- The body of every blood-bought child of God is a temple in which the Holy Spirit abides through the word of truth; this amazing temple glorifies God.[398]

- The saved of earth are "a temple of the living God;" and the abiding place of the divine.[399]

- The foundation of this beautiful temple is the apostles and prophets, "Christ Jesus himself" is "the chief corner stone;" it is a "holy temple in the Lord" and "a habitation of God in the Spirit."[400]

- This marvelous temple is the "house" of Jesus Christ.[401]

The temple, its fixtures and its people must be figurative. God has the power and the ability to contemplate this spiritual temple and he sees it as an ornate and indescribably beautiful edifice. Jehovah, Jesus, and the Holy Spirit dwell in this palatial home of God and in their view it is magnificent. Human hands made of bone and flesh cannot touch it, but the human heart, which is related to the eternal spirit in man, can understand what the Bible says about it.

---

396 1 Cor 3:16
397 1 Pet 2:5
398 1 Cor 6:19-20
399 2 Cor 6:16
400 Eph 2:20-22
401 Heb 3:6

God speaks to us about this stupendous, universal body of which Jesus is the head. Mortals, so accustomed and addicted to material things, cannot see it and often do not appreciate it, but it is invaluable in God's sight.

Paul describes it in these words, *"Christ also loved the church, and gave himself up for it; that he might sanctify it, having cleansed it by the washing of water with the word, that he might present the church to himself a glorious church, not having spot or wrinkle or any such thing; but that it should be holy and without blemish."*[402]

John was told to measure "the temple of God, and the altar, and them that worship therein." You measure the church by the standard of God's revealed and confirmed word – and by nothing else. The little book that was sweet in the mouth but bitter in the belly is the reed like a rod by which the church, which is the temple of God, is defined. It is made up of every earthly, saved soul from the beginning of time to the end of time, all celestial beings that are in favor with God, and the Godhead. It is spiritually gorgeous beyond comparison and altogether lovely in God's view of the "things more excellent," which are, "the things that remain."

Here is the measurement of the temple of God:

- Jesus is its only founder, head, and mediator[403]
- It began in Jerusalem of Judea [404]
- The only organization in the church is a specific, local congregation[405]
- The organization of a local church consists of an evangelist, a plurality of elders, deacons, and members, all this and nothing more[406]
- The local church is involved in evangelism and benevolence[407]

---

402 Eph 5:25-27
403 Matt 16:18; Eph 1:22-23; 1 Tim 2:5
404 Luke 24:47
405 The silence of the New Testament concerning a hierarchy for the earthly phase of the church is sufficient to establish the autonomy and sufficiency of the local congregation. God's word does authorize a polity for a local congregation, but not for the universal, earthly church.
406 1 Tim 3:1-16; Titus 1:5; Phil 1:1; 1 Tim 5:17-20; Ehp 4:11-12
407 Mark 16:15-16; Matt 28:18-22; James 1:27; Gal 6:10

- The local church assembles upon the first day of the week[408]
- Whatever else the New Testament requires the church to do and be is included in measuring the church[409]

This summary of the measurements of the temple of God is not intended to be exhaustive.

Altar

John was also to measure the altar of the temple of God, which equates to the worship of the temple, which is made up of living stones offering up spiritual, living sacrifices, "acceptable to God through Jesus Christ." Here is a cogent statement of her altar upon which spiritual sacrifices are continually made:

- "We [Christians] have an altar"[410]

- Jesus, acting as our High Priest, "loved you and gave himself for us an offering to God for an odor of a sweet smell."[411]

- In the obedience of faith, which is the sanctification of holiness, believers are priests and priestesses under Jesus[412]

- "Through him then let us offer up a sacrifice of praise to God continually, that is, the fruit of lips which make confession of his name"[413]

- The local church or temple of God worships in perfect harmony with what God's word requires in worship and service; worship is not limited to the assembly of the saints but is manifest in the life of the disciple at all times; in the first day of the week assembly of the local church the saints sing, pray, give money, teach one another, and observe the Lord's Supper (which is the centerpiece of their weekly worship); the attitude, behavior,

408 Heb 10:25; Acts 20:7
409 Rom 13:9
410 Heb 13:10
411 Eph 5:2; Heb 9:14; Heb 2:17; 4:15
412 1 Pet 2:5, 9; Rev 1:6; 5:10
413 Heb 13:15-16

prayers, meditations, and service of the saint on a daily basis is also worship.[414]

- Whatever the saints do, in word or deed, is to be done in the name of the Lord.[415]

- "Through him then let us offer up a sacrifice of praise to God continually, that is, the fruit of lips which make confession to his name. But to do good and to communicate (share what you have) forget not: for with such sacrifices God is well pleased."[416]

People

John was also told to measure the people. In the context of a spiritual temple and holy worship, the people must be those who "washed their robes and made them white in the blood of the Lamb."[417] The plan of salvation is outlined in the following Bible statements:

- To enter the kingdom of God one must be born of "water and spirit," that is, his spirit must be born of water[418]

- Spiritual regeneration requires the "obedience of faith"[419]

- Repentance is necessary to salvation or remission of sins[420]

- Confession of Jesus as the Son of God is a prerequisite of salvation[421]

- The penitent believer must be immersed in water to be saved[422]

- To be eternally saved the born-from-above child of God must be faithful unto death[423]

---

414 **John 4:**24; Col 3:17; 1 Cor 11:23-28; 14:14-15; 14:19; 16:1-2; Heb 13:15-16
415 1 Thess 5:17
416 Heb 13:15-16
417 Rev 7:14
418 John 3:5
419 Rom 1:5; 16:26; James 2:14-26
420 Acts 2:38
421 Matt 10:32-33; Rom 10:9-10
422 Rom 6:4; Col 2:12; Mark 16:16; Acts 2:38; 22:16; John 3:5; 1 Pet 3:21
423 Rev 2:10; 12:11

We have measured the temple of God, the altar, and the people who worship therein and are ready to consider the outer court.

Verse 2

And the court which is without the temple leave without,
and measure it not;
for it hath been given unto the nations:
and the holy city shall they tread under foot forty and two months.

The temple of God equals the church of God the "court which is without" represents those who are outside the pale of the church. The church is the body of Christ and "all spiritual blessings" are in that body.[424] Since "all" spiritual blessings are in the church, there are no spiritual blessings outside the church. Still, there are religious minded people in the "outer court." These are people who think about God and care about salvation but do not display in their life the "obedience of faith." Theirs is a dead faith, or faith without works.[425] "[H]olding a form of godliness, but having denied the power thereof."[426]

"But he that looketh into the perfect law, the law of liberty, and so continueth, being not a hearer that forgetteth but a doer that worketh, this man shall be blessed in his doing."[427] Those who exhibit in their lives a dead faith – a faith without works – are in the outer court. They have a form of godliness but have denied its power.

The outer court is beyond the pale of the church and is not to be measured. It is given to the nations; they are without. (All the saved are "within.")

The "holy city" is the church and is to be "trodden under foot forty and two months." The church will be persecuted and the truth denied for this entire period." The forty-two months denote the entire period of the Gentiles, which is the final dispensation, or system. It is the last age; when it is over, all things earthly are over.[428] The exact length of the Christian

---

424 Eph 1:3
425 James 1:23-25; 2:14-26
426 2 Tim 3:5
427 James 1:25
428 Dan 7:24; 12:7, 11-12 mentions a "time, times and ½ time," which is 1,260 days or 42 months, and indicates the finishing point. Though there is no necessary connection between Daniels' statement of an end time for Judiasm and

155

system depends upon the decisions and actions of free agents and therefore cannot be calculated until the condition indicated develops. It is a long time but no one knows how long, so the prophet uses a term that stands for length of days but is not intended to spell out a specific time ... a long, unknown period.

Verses 3-4

And I will give unto my two witnesses,
and they shall prophesy a thousand two hundred and threescore days,
clothed in sackcloth.

These are the two olive trees and the two candlesticks,
standing before the Lord of the earth.

Some say the two witnesses are Moses and Elijah, others say Enoch and Elijah, and still others say Peter and Paul, but there is no conclusive evidence to support any of these opinions.

Given the figurative nature of the book of Revelation the Olive Trees and Candlesticks may represent a thing.[429] The two witnesses "shall prophesy a thousand two hundred and threescore days, clothed in sackcloth." The witnesses would bear witness throughout the entire Christian dispensation, and no human could do that. The messages of the Bible are filled with condemnation and demand repentance, therefore the two witnesses are "clothed with sackcloth."

Furthermore, the two witnesses "stand before the Lord of the earth," which would require supernatural power.

The Olive Tree, in scripture, generally represents health or life and the Candlesticks symbolize light, or wisdom.

The two witnesses are the Old and New Testaments personified[430] ... the Law of Moses and the Law of Christ. The revealed word of God

---

John's declaration of the close of the Christian system, both writers use it to indicate the terminus of a dispensation.

429 See Zech 4:3-14

430 Just as Ezekiel personified Samaria and Judah by two sisters, Oholah and Oholibah (Ezek 23:2-49), or as Solomon personified wisdom as a woman pleading for acceptance (Prov 1:20-28)

brings spiritual health and life and also brings wisdom and understanding. The two Testaments or Laws stand perpetually before the Lord and bear witness to the everlasting purpose of God. The passage identifies the witnesses as being the Holy God-breathed Scriptures. Still, the witnesses take no delight in their words of judgment and condemnation … they are "clothed with sackcloth," but persist in teaching truth.

Verses 5-6

And if any man desireth to hurt them,
fire proceedeth out of their mouth and devoureth their enemies;
and if any man shall desire to hurt them,
in this manner must he be killed.

These have the power to shut the heaven,
that it rain not during the days of their prophecy:
and they have power over the waters to turn them into blood,
and to smite the earth with every plague,
as often as they shall desire.

The tremendous power of the imperishable word of God is sketched in a few words. The fire of revelation was symbolized on the day of Pentecost when the Holy Spirit came upon the apostles and they were baptized in the Spirit and fire. The Comforter guided them into all truth[431] and the fire confirmed by miraculous demonstration God's sanction and approval.[432]

The word of God is living, active, and sharper than any two-edged sword.[433] It is the seed of the earthly phase of the eternal kingdom.[434] You may hold a small seed in the palm of your hand but its power belies its appearance. The seed is strong, durable and has life in it; the word of God is like seed.

Mount Horeb seemed to catch on fire when God confirmed his covenant with Israel; smoke from the mountain went up like the smoke of a furnace, the rocks were rent, and the earth convulsed with a mighty earthquake.

We read of the apostles being immersed in flames of fire when he new law was given at Jerusalem.[435]

---

431 John 16:13
432 Heb 2:3-4
433 Heb 4:12
434 Luke 8:11
435 Acts 2:1-4

We understand the confirmation of the law of Christ and its power when it was certified by divine might in "signs, wonders, manifold powers, and gifts of the Holy Spirit."[436]

The word of God is "the sword of the Spirit"[437] and those who do not bow before its power continue in a spiritual death.

When we are told that the "sword of the Spirit" is "the word of God" the language is obviously figurative, which means that the consequences of refusing that word are also symbolic.

Paul wrote, "For I am not ashamed of the gospel: for it is the power of God unto salvation to everyone that believeth; to the Jew first, and also to the Greek."[438] Like Paul, we, too, must be unashamed of the powerful gospel of God.

"For as touching those who were once enlightened and tasted of the heavenly gift, and were made partakers of the Holy Spirit, and tasted the good word of God, and the powers of the age to come, and then fell away, it is impossible to renew them again unto repentance; seeing they crucify to themselves the Son of God afresh, and put him to an open shame. For the land which hath drunk the rain that cometh oft upon it, and bringeth forth herbs meet for them for whose sake it is also tilled, receiveth blessing from God: but if it beareth thorns and thistles, it is rejected and nigh unto a curse; whose end is to be burned."[439]

Verse 7

*And when they shall have finished their testimony,
the beast that cometh up out of the abyss shall make war with them,
and overcome them,
and kill them.*

The beast of the abyss kills the two witnesses, which are the Law of Moses and the Law of Christ.

In the good fight of faith the revealed word of God is despised, desecrated and dishonored. It is misrepresented and its divine origin denied. It is

---

436 Heb 2:4
437 Eph 6:17
438 Rom 1:16
439 Heb 6:4-8

blasphemed and ridiculed. The father of lies directs his full attention to the "wonderful words of life" and undertakes to destroy them, to kill them, by causing people to reject them.

The intimation of the Bible, especially the book of Revelation, is that the day will come "when they will not endure the sound doctrine; but, having itching ears, will heap to themselves teachers after their own lusts; and will turn away their ears from the truth, and turn aside unto fables."[440]

When unbelief is so rampant there is no possibility of reform that will be the day God has appointed in which he will judge the world in righteousness – that is, the final, and irreversible end of all things material ... the things that are perishing.

Just as the Noachian flood came when the "thoughts of men's heart were only evil continually," or when Israel was empowered and directed to drive the Canaanites from their land when "the iniquity of the Amorittes" was full, or it was when the evil of Judea was insurmountable that she fell to the might of the Babylonians and the judgment of condemnation came on Israel, so also shall it be with the end of the world; it is when people are as bad as they can be and cannot get any worse that the hammer of doom falls.

The unfailing eye of God will see and know when the Bible is thought to be dead because 99.99% of the earth's population considers it to be dead and, like any dead body, worthless. The seventh trumpet will sound and the catastrophic judgment will come down upon the universe to blast it into the oblivion of annihilation and cast a black pall over the very memory of it.

- God's written word can be, and often is, rejected by mortals[441]
- God's spoken word is irresistible[442]
- The testimony of the two witnesses is finished when none cares what the Bible says and looks upon the sacred volume with utter disdain and foolish mortals declare it to be killed.

---

440 2 Tim 4:3-4
441 Acts 13:45-46
442 Jer 23:29; Isa 55:11; 1 Pet 1:24-25

- The decisive victory belongs to the rider of the white horse, whose name is called "The Word of God."[443] He is "faithful and true."

- Modern religious liberalism plays into the hands of this blistering prophecy and is the handmaid to bring in an attitude of disrespect for the eternal word of God and foolishly think it can perish.

Verse 8

And their dead bodies lie in the street of the great city,
which spiritually is called Sodom and Egypt,
where also their Lord was crucified.

The "great city" is not named because it is not a specific place, but it is every city. To make this mean a particular city of infamy in past history is to rob the passage of the ability to indict evil in other melting pots of iniquity and make them appear less dangerous. The symbol includes Rome and Las Vegas; it embraces ancient Jerusalem and every reincarnation of Jerusalem; it is universal because it is the epitome of every sordid population center from the cross to the second coming and gathers into its view all centuries and generations. The author does not name a certain city because his aim is to include them all through the whole channel of time.

Cities attract corruption. People tend to deceive themselves into thinking they are not visible if they are in a crowd; that to live in a city of millions is to be anonymous. This subterfuge causes the foolish to immerse themselves in rotten and foul behavior and suppose that not even God sees their perfidy.

The stinking cities of all time are symbolized by Sodom, and Egypt; Sodom is the embodiment of moral degradation and Egypt is the symbol of abuse and inhuman slavery. These two vile and vicious cities have the dishonor of representing totally objectionable misbehavior and are the emblem of all the sinkholes of putridity in all ages.

The reference to the crucifixion of Jesus is not determinant because Jesus has been and is being "crucified afresh" all over the world and in every generation. Apostates of all ages "crucify unto themselves the Son of God afresh and put him to an open shame."[444] The "once for all" sacrifice of Jesus

---

443 Rev 19:11-13
444 Heb 6:6

is not repeated, but its excruciating pain is remembered every time someone hears the gospel and spurns its invitation to grace, or "having been once enlightened, turns away from the holy command delivered to them."

"For many walk, of whom I told you often, and now tell you even weeping, that they are the enemies of the cross of Christ: whose end is perdition, whose god is the belly, and whose glory is in their shame, who mind earthly things."[445]

Verses 9

And from among the peoples and tribes and tongues and nations do men look upon their dead bodies three days and a half, and suffer not their dead bodies to be laid in a tomb.

Notice the plurals ... "peoples, tribes, tongues, nations," look upon the dead bodies of the two witnesses, which fosters and confirms that not a single city is meant but many cities and many centuries.

The unwillingness to bury the dead bodies may have been intended by the onlookers to be an insult to the witnesses, or it may be that the closeness of the Bible – the two witnesses – to God somehow prevented disposing of the bodies that appeared to be dead, but that still had potential to live, as we shall see.

The fact that there were two witnesses conforms to what the Bible says about having multiple witnesses to establish veracity.[446] Though dead, the two witnesses (Law of Moses and Law of Christ) continue to bear a silent, irrefutable testimony; being unburied may have arisen from divine providence as a reflection of the superstitious fear and involuntary tribute of the peoples, tribes, tongues and nations who looked upon the now voiceless but still potent witnesses.

Verse 10

And they that dwell on the earth rejoice over them, and make merry; and they shall send gifts one to another; because these two prophets tormented them that dwell on the earth.

---

445 Phil 3:18-19
446 Deut 19:5; Matt 18:16; John 8:17; 2 Cor 13:1

The peoples of earth create an orgy of feigned celebration and a carnival of vice as they party over the death of the two witnesses (here called "prophets"). This information demonstrates the depth of immorality and carelessness that prevailed over cities of earth, and shows clearly the hardened hearts and rambunctiousness of the depraved citizens of the entire world … it had come to a sordid state and its cruelty and callousness affirm the time for judgment and condemnation was at hand.

The witnesses lie there under the hateful eye of the inhabitants of earth. The witnesses (revealed wisdom of two systems) - had provoked the world's hatred because they "tormented them that dwell on the earth, which fulfills divine prophecy.[447] The Laws of Moses and Christ call for a high morality and consequently frown upon lawlessness and iniquity.

The world feels the rebuke and resents it. If the testimony of the witnesses does not provoke persistent ill will by the peoples of earth, it is dead and failing in its function. It is not possible to be faithful to God and loyal to his word if the world is not offended by the exalted standard of conduct demanded by deity.

What makes the followers of Jesus weep and lament causes the peoples of earth to rejoice.[448]

Verse 11

And after the three days and a half the breath
of life from God entered into them,
and they stood upon their feet;
and great fear fell upon them that beheld them.

The rejoicing of the wicked world came to a screeching halt and its people were astonished to see the two witnesses standing upon their feet. Either a resurrection occurred or the witnesses were apparently but not really dead.

Three and a half days is not very long and the futility of trying to kill the word of God was plain to see when a revival happened after just a few

---

447 Matt 10:22; John 15:18; 17:14
448 John 16:20

hours. God has given his word into the hands of men and appointed them to keep it, teach it, and protect it. The command of the Lord is for his devotees to "contend earnestly for the faith which was once for all delivered unto the saints.[449]

As strange as it may sound, God sometimes makes himself a partner with fallible man and depends upon his creature to carry on to victory. Jesus placed the burden of preaching the gospel on the shoulders of his disciples.[450] They either perform admirably or fail miserably. As the wickedness of man becomes intolerable, his failure to hold high the banner of truth brings doom upon an ungodly universe. The fault is neither with God nor his word but with God's free agent.

The durability of the wisdom of the Creator as expressed in his revealed will is the hard-hitting fact in this verse. The personified Law of Moses and the Law of Christ, like the Lamb that was slain, are standing on their feet. They live, God be thanked, they live.

"For, All flesh is as grass, And all the glory thereof as the flower of grass. The grass withereth, and the flower falleth: But the word of the Lord abideth for ever. And this is the word of good tidings which was preached unto you."[451]

Weak and ignorant man may imagine he is strong and wise, but God makes the wisdom of this world foolishness. The wrath of God, like the fury of a sleeping giant roused from his slumber, will demonstrate the utter folly of the human creature. Pomposity is crass stupidity in full flower.

Humanoids may in loud-mouthed ignorance proclaim God to be dead, while the evidence that he lives is seen in every twinkling star. Mortals may encourage each other in their sin by saying "the Lord seeth us not; Jehovah hath forsaken the land," while the Lord God is standing with his prophet, as silent observers, in the open of door of their underground chambers of imagery,[452] silently observing the ignorance of these self-proclaimed intellectuals. The smarter man thinks he is, the dumber he gets, and his fate includes the disaster of "great fear."

---

449 Jude 3
450 Matt 28:28-20
451 1 Peter 1:24-25; John 12:48-50
452 Ezek 8:12

163

Verse 12

And they heard a great voice from heaven saying unto them,
Come up hither. And they went up into heaven in
the cloud; and their enemies beheld them.

The two witnesses, prophets and apostles, the old system which gave birth to the new, and the new system that fulfills the old one,[453] are called by a loud voice into the heaven of heavens.

The jeers and laughter of the godless multitude of earth sticks in the throat and they choke upon their own perfidy. "The fool has said in his heart, There is no God."

When hard-headed men reject God's word, the penalty is that very word is taken from them. The consequence of not using anything is that you forfeit that thing and lose the power to use it.[454] To trample God's word underfoot is to condemn oneself to the loss of that precious word.

Verse 13

And in that hour there was a great earthquake,
and the tenth part of the city fell;
and there were killed in the earthquake seven thousand persons:
and the rest were affrighted,
and gave glory to the God of heaven.

Earthquakes are associated with the end of time and final judgment.[455] The earthquake in this passage was "great," causing the tenth part of "the city" to fall. We are not told what city because, as we earlier observed, it may mean every city or no city (as was discussed in our comments on Revelation 11:8-9, see above)."Peoples" in association with one or more "tongues," "tribes," "nations," and "kings" are repeated in this book. [456]

"City" as used in verse 9 above is used anonymously and includes all the important cities from the cross to the judgment. This is fortified by the fact that the "city" in this verse had a total population of only

453 Eph 2:19-20
454 Amos 8:11-12; Mic 3:6; Prov 29:18; Lam 2:9; Hos 4:6
455 Rev 6:12; 16:18-20
456 Rev 7:9; 10:11; 11:8-9; 17:15

70,000. No important city in the lifetime of John the apostle would have been that small ... not Rome and not Jerusalem and not any other city of consequence. Verse 13 implies that the people who rejoiced over the supposed death of the two witnesses now gave "glory to the God of heaven," and we have established they are all peoples of all major cities of the entire world.

The book of Revelation abounds in figures and symbols so it should come as no surprise to the Bible student if the city that fell is emblematic and not literal. It represents the totality of degraded cities during the entire Christian dispensation. For the tenth part of the inhabitants of a major city to suddenly die would cause shock and awe throughout the world.

For example, if a New York City earthquake were to kill ten percent of its peoples, about one million people would die in the disaster.

When the twin towers fell on September 11, 2001, the death toll was much lower (3,000) but the impact was global and the jar was violent; if that number were multiplied to a total of a million, all the inhabitants of earth would be dumbfounded because of its immensity, which is clearly the impression made by the pen of John. He speaks of something horrific.

Fear would be inevitable and deep and giving God the glory would be natural and expected. The fact that earthlings gave glory to God does not necessarily mean that they "brought forth fruits worthy of repentance." Praise of God was wrung from their unwilling lips, but they did not therefore become worshippers of God.

John is further preparing us for the sounding of the seventh trumpet and wants us to steel our nerves in anticipation of its magnitude and power.

Verse 14

The second Woe is past:
behold, the third Woe cometh quickly.

Catch your breath! Plant your feet! Brace yourself! The terrible third Woe is about to be unveiled as the trumpet of all ages is soon to be heard, but first the writer delays by describing another interlude before the angel messenger puts the trumpet to his lips. The drama builds.

The build up to this moment is dramatic. Once again we look back at world history especially in its religious context.[457]

- Jesus is Lord of lords and King of kings – chap 1
- Jesus walks among congregations of the church and invites fidelity – chaps 2-3
- The throne room of the Almighty displays his sovereign power – chaps 4-5
- Breaking of the seven seals; ignites the war of wars – chap 6
- Sounding of the trumpets; the fight rages and the suffering is great – chap 7-10

The imaginations and emotions are deeply stirred as we stand on the tiptoe of expectancy and beg relief. The delay in the sounding of the last trumpet makes our hearts beat fast and piques our interest.

Now, at long last, the final trumpet sounds and the good fight of faith is won by the valiant servants of Christ.

The church is gathered home to profound peace and unbounded joy, but the unsanctified and unwashed are subjected to the horrors of a demolishing material universe.

Verse 15

And the seventh angel sounded;
and there followed great voices in heaven,
and they said,
The kingdom of the world is become the kingdom of our Lord,
and of his Christ:
and he shall reign forever and ever.

The last trumpet sounds and Satan surrenders his kingdom to "our Lord and to his Christ." It's over! The experiment is complete. Truth wins and error is defeated when the everlasting kingdom of the Godhead

---

457 Without apology to secular historians who seem to think that human events without deference to God is necessary whereas, in fact, history that is not considered within the framework of God is meaningless and empty. It is not history but is propaganda in the worst possible sense.

absorbs and converts the kingdom of this world. Notice the singular; there are many kingdoms of this world but taken as a whole they are one because of their unanimous consent to walk in the footsteps of the devil.

The triumphant army of Christ made up of a teeming throng of good angels, the redeemed of all time, the twenty-four elders and the indescribable creatures that surround the eternal throne of the great Governor of all things, have crushed Satan and his servants. The full extent of the world's loss is yet to be reported, but it will be when the consequence of the outpouring of the bowls of wrath is represented by a figure of the loud lamentation of the astonished evil ones. They stand baffled and tearful as all material things are shown to perish; but that is yet to come. We must first be reminded of God's reason for making man, the world and the universe.

This is a summary statement explaining that when the last trumpet sounds the purpose of God is accomplished, which is good for the good and bad for the bad. It explains the statement of Jesus that his followers must not be working exclusively for things that are perishing as if such dying things are an end all.[458] People of faith do not worship silver and gold but expend their energy for the undying things of eternity.

Incidentally, physical bodies must have the support of material things but nevertheless count all earthly things as refuse to gain Christ.[459]

When the "kingdom of the world" and the kingdom of God (Heaven) are folded into "the kingdom of our Lord and his Christ" the resulting merger is indestructibly durable … eternal … forever and ever. There will be no alterations, concessions, or changes. The kingdom of God in its perfection can never diminish.

Please take note that all this is accomplished to the tune of "great voices in heaven." The thunder-like voice of the Creator speaks of authority that cannot be denied. The loud voices emanating from the eternal throne of God affirm his irresistible power.

---

458 John 6:27
459 Phil 3:8 – incidentally, one translation uses the word "dung" instead of "refuse" (garbage).

Verses 16-17

And the four and twenty elders,
who sit before God on their thrones,
fell upon their faces and worshipped God, saying,
We give thee thanks,
O Lord God, the Almighty,
who art and who wast;
because thou hast taken thy great power,
and didst reign.

The four and twenty elders ordinarily sit upon their thrones, but there are occasions so transcendently important that these distinguished agents of righteousness are forced to their faces on the floor.

A fair reading of the Bible leaves no doubt that the twenty-four elders are the 12 patriarchs of Israel and the 12 apostles of the Lamb ... the old covenant and the new covenant.

The term "Judeo-Christian" is the source of so much false teaching it ought to be rejected and in its place a clear statement of the relationship between the two covenants should emerge.

The Old Testament is the background for the New Testament; the two testaments are interdependent. The first covenant prophesies the second covenant and the second testament explains and reveals the Old Testament. They complement each other.

The covenant God made with the nation of Israel at Sinai is superseded by the far more glorious covenant Jesus offers.[460] One is a covenant of anticipation and the other is a covenant of fulfilled realization. The second covenant replaces the first covenant.[461] The two covenants are not capable of simultaneous observation because what one requires would transgress what the other demands.[462] Still, though the first covenant is no longer viable, the second covenant in full force and effect.

---

460 2 Cor 3:7-11

461 Heb 10:9

462 The Lord's Supper versus Passover, for instance; also, the offering of live animal sacrifices versus the once for all sacrifice of Jesus; and many other differences in the two covenants.

The founders of the twelve tribes of Israel and the twelve men chosen and appointed to be the apostles of Jesus join hands in constituting the foundation of the earthly phase of the kingdom of heaven that Jesus announced and created.[463]

At any rate, the heads of the tribes of Israel and the ambassadors of the church, which is the kingdom of heaven, make a total of twenty-four and are represented in this closing book of the Bible as "the four and twenty elders." The expression, "four and twenty elders" simply means the foundation and power of salvation.

When Jesus is revealed as the master of redemption and when at the end of time, at the sounding of the seventh trumpet, Jesus is honored as the exclusive cure for sin and the solitary cause of perfect forgiveness,[464] the twenty-four elders fall from their thrones upon their faces at the proclamation and worship.

All things praise Father, Son, and Comforter because they made heaven and earth and all that is in them and because they provided for the redemption to all who exhibit the "obedience of faith."

Verse 18

And the nations were wroth,
and thy wrath came,
and the time of the dead to be judged,
and the time to give their reward to thy servants the prophets,
and to the saints,
and to them that fear thy name,
the small and the great;
and to destroy them that destroy the earth.

The psalmist David by the grace of the Holy Spirit foretold the coming of the Anointed One and the blessings that would abound to mankind. Still, because he spoke truth and would make no compromise, the world hated him, just as it hates his loyal followers today, and in their anger demanded that the gracious Christ be hung in shame on a tree.

---

463 Eph 2:20; Matt 16:18-19

464 Acts 4:12: "And in none other is there salvation: for neither is there any other name under heaven, that is given among men, wherein we must be saved." See also Acts 10:42-43; 1 Cor 3:11; 1 Tim 2:5-6; 1 John 5:11-12; Rev 7:9-17

David foresaw the event and described it in these words:

Why do the nations rage, and the peoples meditate a vain thing?

The kings of the earth set themselves, and the rulers take counsel together, against Jehovah, and against his anointed, saying,

Let us break their bonds asunder, and cast away their cords from us.

He that sitteth in the heavens will laugh: the Lord will have them in derision.

Then will he speak unto them in his wrath, and vex them in his sore displeasure:

Yet I have set my king upon my holy hill of Zion.

I will tell of the decree: Jehovah said unto me, Thou art my son; this day have I begotten thee.

Ask of me, and I will give thee the nations for thine inheritance, and the uttermost parts of the earth for thy possession.

Thou shalt break them with a rod of iron; Thou shalt dash them in pieces like a potter's vessel.

Now therefore be wise, O ye kings: be instructed, ye judges of the earth.

Serve Jehovah with fear, and rejoice with trembling.

Kiss the son, lest he be angry, and ye perish in the way, for his wrath will soon be kindled. Blessed are all they that take refuge in him.[465]

The story is told in terse words and has two parts; first, the rage of Israel and Rome as they joined hands to kill Jesus and frustrate the purposes of God and, second, his awful recompense when he comes in glory to judge, condemn and reward. This verse speaks with force about the second division of this wonderful psalm. He will "break them with a rod of iron" and "dash them in pieces like a potter's vessel." With all their engines of war and evil cunning, they will not prevail against the majestic Captain of Salvation and he vanquishes them as easily as the potter's clay vessel is

---

465 Psa 2:1-12

smashed. David foretold it, the saints of the first century saw the first part of it[466], and the book of revelation describes the second and last part of this stupendous Old Testament prophecy. The loud blast of the seventh trumpet declares that smashing time has come.

Jesus "destroys them that destroy the earth." Vile civil governments destroy the earth by arraying themselves against God and his word and plunging earthlings into the putrid and stinking filth of immorality. Their reward is to be destroyed by the great destroyer.

We must never be deceived by the longsuffering of God into supposing that he will not keep his promise to destroy the wicked … that promise is sure.[467]

The commitment of the Almighty to comfort those who love Him and his word and his church is equally sure. He will eternally bless those who fear his name.

And now the curtain of revelation is drawn back once more to enable us to see a something wondrous.

Verse 19

And there was opened the temple of God that is in heaven;
and there was seen in his temple the ark of his covenant;
and there followed lightnings,
and voices,
and thunders,
and an earthquake,
and great hail.

Men in their weakness and ignorance have searched for the lost Ark of the Covenant for many years, but did not find it, nor will they ever find it.[468] It is beyond their reach.

---

466 Acts 4:25-29

467 2 Pet 3:9

468 In all probability the physical gold plated ark was destroyed by Nebuchadnez-zar's army when he destroyed Jerusalem, but the figurative reality of that ark was transported to glory.

The ark as constructed by Moses contained the Ten Commandments, a container of manna and Aaron's rod that budded. Its golden lid was the mercy seat of the Mighty Maker of all things.

- The ten words affirm that God is a God of law and his people must be law abiding, or righteous

- The manna confirms the care and keeping of the people of God's law … Jehovah provides

- The budding rod reiterates that divine revelation is attested by miracle

- The mercy seat is a faithful reminder of the goodness and unspeakable grace of our Creator

The Ark of the Covenant, like the Tree of Life, has been removed from earth and now resides in the lofty and celestial courts of YHWH. It is untouchable by mortals but abides to remind us of the sweet sound of amazing grace; under Moses' law it was atonement; under the law of Christ it is forgiveness.[469] The blood of the cross reaches back to remove atoned sins and flows forward to offer the possibility of eternal salvation to all who would live godly in Christ Jesus, being slaves of righteousness. The emblems are, of course, figurative but real.

Are you looking for the Ark of the Covenant? There it is, gracing the courts of glory as a perpetual reminder of God's forgiving love and mercy, shining forth in splendor in the shining city of God that lies foursquare and eternal in the heavens. It is fascinating that as the seventh trumpet sounds announcing the destruction of the universe that the Ark of the Covenant is featured. "God is not willing that any should perish but that all should come to repentance."

Before the bowls of wrath are poured out upon the universe the Holy Spirit moves the pen of John to remind us of Israel's vital place in God's eternal scheme, the fearsomeness of a desperate Satan joined by godless government and godless religion, beating the drums of war as the opponents of Prince Immanuel continues to press the battle between right and wrong … it is "the good fight of faith" and truth will out.

---

469 Rom 3:24-26

So, in prophetic imagery, the Comforter through the fisherman, John, confirms the futility of materialism and shouts to us "labor not for the meat that is perishing, but for that which endures unto eternal life."

As gigantic flying angels of God cry with booming voice, Woe, Woe, Woe, the beautiful mercy seat of God is serene and secure in the third heaven.

The threats and promises of the Mighty Maker of all things repeat over again; and are sealed by *"lightnings"* ... *"voices"* ... *"thunders"* ... *"earthquake"* ... *"and great hail."*

It is awful!

A Glorious Woman, a Dragon, a Child

Revelation 12:1-17

The seventh trumpet – the trumpet of all ages – has been heard and the time has come for the outpouring of the wrath of God, but before that terrible destruction is chronicled the inspired writer is directed by the Holy Spirit to record again the inauguration of the church (the earthly phase of the kingdom of God) and the bitter, hateful opposition of the Devil and his constituents to God and his children.

The words of this book have been recorded in an eternal volume to preserve an accurate knowledge of God's dealing with man from the birth of the Savior at Bethlehem to the time of his second coming from heaven to earth in ultimate judgment. The story briefly put is:

- The commander-in-chief of the Christian army – chapter 1
- Letters to the seven churches – chapters 2-3
- The awesome throne of the living God – chapters 5-6
- Salvation is available to all, but only a few will accept it – chapter 7
- Trumpets sound and tribulation is multiplied – chapters 8-10
- After long delay, the seventh trumpet is heard – chapter 11

Before the events of the rolling up of the heavens and the rout of material and earthly things, the wisdom of God dictates that the history of the good fight of faith should again be etched in the everlasting annals of a Supreme Being.

John begins with the sign of a woman in birth pangs delivering a child.

Verses 1-2

And a great sign was seen in heaven:
a woman arrayed with the sun,
and the moon under her feet,
and upon her head a crown of twelve stars;
and she was with child;
and she crieth out, travailing in birth,
and in pain to be delivered.

The vision of this gloriously arrayed woman was great or colossal, much too large for the earth to contain it and it therefore stretched out toward the stars.

This woman was spectacular. The sun and stars convey the glory of this massive, heavenly sign; she was dressed in sunbeams and crowned with stars. This was the same kind of inner brilliance emanating from Jesus on the mount of transfiguration and the same as the after-glory of God Moses saw on mount Horeb in the Sinai Peninsula where Moses heard God speaking through the burning bush and where the Law of Moses was given to Israel, all foreshadowing the prospect of eternal salvation in Christ Jesus, the Lord.

Abraham, Moses and Jesus emphasize the promise and the fulfillment of salvation. "For the grace of God hath appeared, bringing salvation to all men, instructing us, to the intent that, denying ungodliness and worldly lusts, we should live soberly and righteously and godly in this present world."[470]

The gloriously arrayed woman transcends mundane things (the moon is under her feet).

Her crown composed of twelve stars represents the patriarchs of Israel … the heads of the twelve tribes.

Some say Mary of Nazareth the betrothed of Joseph is represented in this vision, but she was not driven into the wilderness nor persecuted with vengeance.

The beautiful, pregnant woman in this vision is Israel personified. She is giving birth to the church; which fulfills the ancient promise to Abraham

470 Titus 2:11-12

that "I will bless them that bless thee, and him that curseth thee will I curse. And in thee shall all the families of the earth be blessed."

This stately woman was in the throes of birth-pains and was on the verge of delivering a man child. That is the picture ... a woman giving birth in "greatly multiplied pain and labor."

It is a picture of Judaism giving birth to Jesus and his new covenant and bringing to fruition the great promise of God to bless the entire world through the seed of Abraham.[471] It is a warning that where truth and salvation go persecution is sure to follow.

Now, a second sign

Verses 3-4

*And there was seen another sign in heaven:
and behold, a great red dragon,
having seven heads and ten horns,
and upon his heads seven diadems.
And his tail draweth the third part of the stars of heaven,
and did cast them to the earth:
and the dragon standeth before the woman that is about to be delivered,
that when she is delivered he may devour her child.*

The horns of an animal represent his power. If the horns are shorn, the power to defend and attack is gone. It is to emphasize his power that the Bible mentions the horns of God and his altar.

This great, red dragon has seven heads and ten horns upon every head for a total of 70 horns, which underscores the dragon's dreadful power.

The great (another colossus) red dragon is positively identified as Satan[472] – the archenemy of both man and God. He sweeps away a third of the stars of heaven with one swipe of his tail.

Never mind about trying to find a parallel in history; there is none! It is vain to search for one. This statement is designed to reiterate the force of

471 Gen 12:3; 18:18; 22:18; 26:4-5 (notice the emphasis on obedience); Joel 2:28; Acts 2:39; 3:25-26
472 Rev 12:9

the devil and to warn us of his might. A symbolic figure that can knock out a third of the stars of heaven with one swish of his tail has tremendous strength.[473] Obviously, that is figurative language but expresses a grim reality in an unseen world.

It is inexcusable for us not to know the devices (tricks) of Satan, nor to fail to understand the source of his energy.[474]

The diadems of the Devil symbolize the battles with the pure in heart he has fought and won, which herald again his cunning power and crafty schemes. In dealing with such a foe we must be vigilant and valiant. He never lets up, nor must we.

The attempts of Satan to circumvent and destroy the purposes of God are many and consistent:

- Eden and the serpent
- Noah and the flood
- Abraham and Isaac
- Israel and Egypt
- David and Athaliah
- Herod and Jesus

The battle flags yet fly; Satan still seeks to devour the woman's child.

John saw in the heavens the great red dragon standing before a woman in pain watching for the moment of birth that he may to eat up the baby greedily and ravenously, like a lion devouring his prey.

Verse 5

And she was delivered of a son,
a man child,
who is to rule all the nations with a rod of iron:
and her child was caught up unto God, and unto his throne.

---

473 The power of the Devil, incidentally, is given to him by humans. When people volunteer to sin and follow the Dragon's lead, they empower him and weaken themselves.

474 2 Cor 2:11; 1 Pet 5:8

"For unto us a child is born, unto us a son is given; and the government shall be upon his shoulder: and his name shall be called Wonderful, Counsellor, Mighty God, Everlasting Father, Prince of Peace. Of the increase of his government and of peace there shall be no end, upon the throne of David, and upon his kingdom, to establish it, and to uphold it with justice and with righteousness from henceforth even for ever. The zeal of Jehovah of hosts will perform this."[475]

"A man child," that is, a man's man. He is strong and manly. He rules with a rod of iron and a sharp sword; his wrath is fierce. He is able to war with Satan and defeat him because in righteousness he is stronger than the great red dragon.[476] Right, born of truth, is a mighty force that cannot be crushed to earth never to rise again. The good and the clean will prevail, though often cast down. The Captain of our salvation is courageous and powerful.

Some see Jesus as weak and sniveling but if he had been effete he could not have gathered and led the strong, hardworking men that were his willing followers. He was a leader of fishermen and other outdoorsmen and seemed to have little to no patience with those who wore soft clothing and lived in king's palaces and were like reeds shaken by the wind.[477] Paul was given to study, reflection, speculation, but even he was robust and endured the rigors of rugged travel and shipwreck without whining. Jesus was a man and a leader of men.

This manly man was "caught up unto God, and unto his throne" where the insane hatred of the Devil cannot reach.

> And when he had said these things, as they were looking, he was taken up; and a cloud received him out of their sight. And while they were looking stedfastly into heaven as he went, behold, two men stood by them in white apparel; who also said, Ye men of Galilee, why stand ye looking into heaven? this Jesus, who was received up from you into heaven shall so come in like manner as ye beheld him going into heaven.[478]

---

475 Isa 9:6-7
476 Psa 2:7-9; Rev 2:26-27; Rev 19:15; Rev 1:16; Dan 7:13-15; Rev 5:1-8; Acts 1:4-9
477 Matt 11:7
478 Acts 1:9-11; Dan 7:13-15

The Lone Galilean was removed from this planet to the throne of God to assure that nothing would befall him that had the possibility of frustrating the good gifts of God to the human race. He abides with God and his throne to this day, executing his function as the only mediator and High Priest, making intercession for his loyal servants. What a comfort and joy that is to his saints.

Now, more about the fate of the gloriously arrayed woman …

VERSE 6

And the woman fled into the wilderness,
where she hath a place prepared of God,
that there they may nourish her a thousand two hundred and threescore days.

The woman gloriously arrayed in sunbeams with the moon under her feet and twelve stars in her hair represents Israel giving birth to Immanuel.

There is a double symbol here … the woman not only represents Israel but also the church, reflecting the fact that the church in the beginning of the gospel was made up entirely of Jews and that continued for about ten years, ending when Peter, at the command of the Holy Spirit and by his apostolic power, authorized the baptism of Gentiles.[479]

The woman represents both the nation of the Jews and the infant church of Christ.

The infamous Jerusalem persecution of the church scattered the church to the ends of the earth and since it was no longer concentrated could not be completely destroyed by a single blow. It could exist even if in some remote corner of the earth. God arranged that.

Initially, the church was all together in one place and could have been eradicated with comparative ease, but once scattered into the wilderness prepared of God this was no longer possible.[480]

The 1,260 days is a figure for the completion of the cycle or historical period. It is found in the book of Daniel with this meaning and passed to prophetic use to denote a series of events or an age.[481]

479 Acts 10:34-48
480 Acts 8:4
481 Daniel the prophet uses synonyms for the 1,260 days, such as 42 months

The writer harks back to earlier events and speaks of how Satan was thrown out of the heaven of heavens and down to the earth. He does this to explain the reason for the utter intensity of the dragon's malicious hatred of truth and the church and his unrelenting determination to destroy both, if he can. The church is made up of individuals and to persecute, belittle or denigrate the people is to shame the church with spitting.[482] It is immeasurably wicked to bring reproach upon the church … the people of God.

VERSES 7-12

And there was war in heaven:
Michael and his angels going forth to war with the dragon;
and the dragon warred and his angels;

And they prevailed not,
neither was their place found any more in heaven.

And the great dragon was cast down,
the old serpent,
he that is called the Devil and Satan,
the deceiver of the whole world;
he was cast down to the earth,

And the great dragon was cast down,
the old serpent,
and his angels were cast down with him.

And I heard a great voice in heaven, saying,
Now is come the salvation,
and the power,
and the kingdom of our God,
and the authority of his Christ:
for the accuser of our brethren is cast down,
who accuseth them before our God day and night.

(42X12=1260) or "a time, times, and a half time, that is, a year, two years and a half year (3.5 years times 360 days per year equals 1260). These time frames in prophetic usage merely mean "the entire time," however long that may be, and that is how the Spirit told John to use the expression here.

482 When Saul persecuted the church, he was persecuting Jesus (Acts 9:4-5); See also Isa 50:6.

And they overcame him because of the blood of the Lamb,
and because of the word of their testimony;
and they loved not their life even unto death.

Therefore rejoice, O heavens, and ye that dwell in them.
Woe for the earth and for the sea:
because the devil is gone down unto you,
having great wrath,
knowing that he hath but a short time.

We know little about it, but the Bible says a civil war in heaven resulted in the creation of the universe and the casting down of Satan to the earth. This powerful demon continued to have some contact with other-world-beings, but lost the fullness of his former stature.[483]

Reference is made in the scriptures to the various ranks of angels.[484] Old and New Testament writers speak occasionally of unearthly creatures. John in this book, in describing some things in the throne room of God, notes some of these angelic creatures.

He mentions:

four living creatures full of eyes before and behind. And the first creature was like a lion, and the second creature like a calf, and the third creature had a face as of a man, and the fourth creature was like a flying eagle. And the four living creatures, having each one of them six wings, are full of eyes round about and within: and they have no rest day and night, saying, Holy, holy, holy, is the Lord God, the Almighty, who was and who is and who is to come.[485]

Questions flood our minds, but little is said about such beings in Holy Writ. God does not cater to our curiosity. There are intimations and implications, but no hard and extensive information. To fully understand the deep things of God our eyes will have to be made wise by death.

Some celebrated worldwide Bible scholars imagine that John received his information from sources and borrowed heavily from Pseudepigraphic writings (1 & 2 Enoch), Assyrian, Egyptian, Babylonian and Greek myths; they ascribe to him an intimate knowledge of remote and

---

483 Jude 6-16; 2 Pet 2:1-4
484 1 Cor 15:24; Eph 3:10; Eph 6:12; Col 2:15
485 Rev 4:6-11

obscure philosophers and historians; they claim that John knew all this information and crafted it into his fabrication, which we know as the book of Revelation. If that were true, John was a profound liar because he says the information came from Jehovah, Jesus, the Holy Spirit, angels and visions.[486]

John's information came from divine beings that conformed the message to the vocabulary and literary style of John, however limited that may have been. It is a book that a man like John could not have written without supernatural assistance.

Still, the curtain of revelation is drawn back a little and we are permitted a quick glance behind it in a few verses of scripture; most of it is too wondrous for us and is far beyond our depth.

We do know there was a war in heaven and in consequence Satan was cast down to the earth. That he now roams the world seeking to devour the children of God, and this is the reference of John in this place.

It is a solemn warning, but it is also a bracing and stimulating thought to those who would live godly in Christ Jesus. The "kingdom of God and the authority of his Christ" bind and overcome "the Devil and Satan." Their amazing victory is possible only "because of the blood of the Lamb ... and the word of their testimony." This is a tribute to the revealed word of God and its power to save.[487]

The heavens are commanded to rejoice over the prospect of salvation but the earth is warned that the devil is yet in the world, filled with enormous anger, and "knowing he hath but a short time."

Verses 13-17

And when the dragon saw that he was cast down to the earth, he persecuted the woman that brought forth the man child.

And there were given to the woman the two wings of the great eagle, that she might fly into the wilderness unto her place,

486 It is ludicrous to impute to John, a rugged outdoorsman who spent much of his life as a commercial fisherman, such delicate, high-flown, fabulous and difficult knowledge that could only come from a lifetime of searching through heavy tomes and world libraries. John did not even have a computer!
487 Rom 1:16; Heb 4:12

where she is nourished for a time, and times, and half a time,
from the face of the serpent.

And the serpent cast out of his mouth after the woman water as a river,
that he might cause her to be carried away by the stream.

And the earth helped the woman,
and the earth opened her mouth and swallowed up the
river which the dragon cast out of his mouth.

And the dragon waxed wroth with the woman,
and went away to make war with the rest of her seed,
that keep the commandments of God,
and hold the testimony of Jesus:

"When the dragon saw," that is, when he understood, restrictions were placed on him and his sphere of influence was limited … that he was cast down to earth … he was filled with fury and was consumed with a passionate desire to destroy the woman (Israel) and her child (the early church).

The "two wings of the great eagle" are obviously figurative and indicate the woman and her child were empowered to escape the dragon's rage because she (the church) was scattered over the entire world – the wilderness.

As explained in verse six of this chapter (see footnote 10) the timeline given ("time, times, and half a time") denotes the entirety of the period, which, in this case, is a reference to the last dispensation, or the Christian age. The archenemy of mankind will not relax his zealous hunger to devour the faithful slaves of Jesus while the world stands.

The serpent, or the dragon, sends after the woman a river of lies and deceit "to lead astray, if possible, even the elect."[488] The world (people of earth) unwittingly helped the woman by swallowing the bundle of lies that spewed from the serpent's mouth and leaving the few who are both called and chosen to direct their attention to more wholesome teaching. Let the wicked world drown in the vicious lies of Satan while the church goes happily on its upward way to scenes of glory and profound peace.

The dragon's unabated fierceness and violence is turned on those "that keep the commandments of God, and hold the testimony of Jesus." To

---

488 2 Thess 2:9-11; Rev 13:14; Matt 24:24

hold tenaciously to the word of God is to incur the Devil's wrath. People who profess to follow Jesus but who are not willing to die for their faith are sucked into the powerful whirlpool of the dragon's lies.

Let the church be warned.

BEASTS FROM THE SEA AND LAND

REVELATION 13:1-18

We have come a long way in our discussion of this incredibly astonishing prophecy. Someone said that prophecy is history told in advance. Just as only God can make a tree, so also is it true that only God can prophesy with one-hundred-percent accuracy. Unfailing prophecy is a miracle and miracles are proof positive that there is a God and he has power to foretell events.[489]

The book of Revelation is not a timeline but it does record historical events, though not necessarily in the order of occurrence. Some historical events will repeat over and over again albeit with minor alterations and other historical events may occur sparingly. We all know that history often repeats itself, which is a history lesson.

Anyway, let us look once again at the correct worldview presented to us in the Bible:

- As a result of his earthly pilgrimage and sacrifice, Jesus is glorified – chap 1

- The Lord instructs soldiers of the cross – chaps 2-3

- The power of the untarnished courts of God cannot be corrupted – chaps 4-5

- The breaking of the seven seals and beginning of the good fight of faith – chap 6

---

489 Religious liberals are in line with the Dragon and the beasts who serve him because they discount Bible prophecy … this is why they denigrate Deuteronomy and butcher the book of Isaiah.

- Many are called but few are chosen, but over time the number will be uncountable – chap 7

- Seven trumpets sound a warning of the tumult resulting from the clash between the army of Satan and the army of Jesus – chaps 8-11

- The sounding of the seventh trumpet announces the imminent outpouring of seven bowls of wrath, but first we are reminded of a glorious woman and her child – chap 12

The Bible worldview is that God is at the center of everything and his word will bring an unspeakable blessing to the redeemed of earth. "Fear God and keep his commandments; for this is the whole duty of man."

John delays discussing the ultimate end of the universe as he gives some additional information about the spiritual war between God and the Dragon.

The *evil one* has helpers and they are introduced. They have been there and at work all along but are now brought on stage so we may see and smell their repulsive filth and corruption.

There are two visions in this chapter; first, the vision of the beast that arose from the restless sea and, second, the vision of the earthy beast that arose from the land.

FIRST VISION – SEA-BORN BEAST

Verses 1-3

and he [the dragon] stood upon the sand of the sea.
And I saw a beast coming up out of the sea,
having ten horns,
and seven heads,
and on his horns ten diadems,
and upon his heads names of blasphemy.

And the beast which I saw was like unto a leopard,
and his feet were as the feet of a bear,
and his mouth as the mouth of a lion:

and the dragon gave him his power,
and his throne,
and great authority.

And I saw one of his heads as though it had been smitten unto death;
and his death-stroke was healed:
and the whole earth wondered after the beast;

The great red dragon, the serpent, who is Satan, the Devil, stands on the shore of the sea to summon the leaders of his unlawful and antisocial gangs. These gang leaders are called "beasts."[490]

One of these ugly dogs comes from the sea and the other from the land but both arise from the abyss.[491]

The sea is symbolic of wild unrest forever dredging up slime and sludge. John saw the sea as an enemy and rejoiced when the sea was no more.[492] It can be helpful, even protective, but it is treacherous.

The sea born beast represents godless governments of all ages ... he is a composite of all corrupt governments.[493]

The heads, horns and diadems proclaim the tremendous power of this devil dog, which is given to him by the great red dragon. They are enabled and empowered by the irredeemably Wicked One and by all who bow at his feet and worship his vileness. The point John makes is the excessively vicious meanness of this fierce, disgustingly unpleasant and roguish dog that gives off a skunk-like odor.[494] All evil is malodorous.

---

490 Thayer says they are "wild beasts (Mark 1:13; Acts 10:12 Rec.; 11:6; 28:4; Heb 12:20; James 3:7; Rev 6:8; in Rev 11:7 and Rev 13-20, depicted as Antichrist, metaphorically, a brutal, bestial man, savage, ferocious, Titus 1:12 (colloquial, 'ugly dogs')."

491 Rev 11:6 - all of Satan's demons are held captive in the abyss and released only as humans give them power by not binding them with the word of God.

492 Rev 21:1

493 Not all government is corrupt ... it can serve the purposes of God (Rom 13:1-5), but it more often serves the Devil

494 To attempt to tie this description to a particular character in history is to miss the point, although it is a good description of many world leaders both past and present. Its purpose is to put them all in the same poke and does not single out a certain one ... all of them from Caligula to Hitler, before, after and in between, living and dead .. all of them ... are included.

189

This beast is cruel and has speed and tenacity, like a leopard; his feet are like the feet of a bear, slow and crushing with strong rapier-like claws; his roar is as frightening as that of a lion, who is dominating and fierce.[495]

The Holy Spirit through Jesus and John is defining a powerful monster whose meat is to blaspheme God, which is to speak evil of him and ban him from the public square. Down through the years many nations have done this and it seems to be popular as leaders of nations gain more and more power, which, we are told, corrupts.[496]

This is obviously figurative because there is no actual animal that fits this description. To look for one is to waste time.

The potency of godless governments of all ages comes from the dragon, who is Satan. Nations who have no trust in God are enabled by the Prince of Darkness.

Many evil world rulers have been cast down only to rise again with renewed power; it is also true that when a treacherous ruler loses his power he is frequently succeeded by another devil dog more evil than himself. The head was given a death-stroke but it is the beast that survives with increasing power.[497] Wicked world leaders come and go but their sinful master is continuous in every generation to the end of time.

More about the beast from the abyss that arose from the sea ...

Verses 4-8

A]nd they worshipped the dragon,
because he gave his authority unto the beast;

---

495 Never be surprised at the wickedness of which world leaders are capable, which includes but is not limited to the merciless killing of 6,000,000 Jews in the concentration camps of WWII Germany, suicide bombers in Arab countries and expanding immorality in nations thought to be civilized, which brings godless, and therefore corrupt, government and slaughters beyond count. "The price of liberty is eternal vigilance."

496 English theologian and philosopher John Dalberg-Acton is popularly associated with the famous dictum, "And remember, where you have a concentration of power in a few hands, all too frequently men with the mentality of gangsters get control. History has proven that. All power corrupts; absolute power corrupts absolutely" (Lord Acton, in a letter to Bishop Mandell Creighton, 1887): He is also said, "Great men are almost always bad men."

497 Rev 13:14

and they worshipped the beast, saying,
Who is like unto the beast?
And who is able to war with him?

and there was given to him a mouth speaking great things and blasphemies;
and there was given to him authority to continue forty and two months.

And he opened his mouth for blasphemies against God,
to blaspheme his name,
and his tabernacle,
even them that dwell in the heaven.

And it was given unto him to make war with the saints,
and to overcome them:
and there was given to him authority over every
tribe and people and tongue and nation.

And all that dwell on the earth shall worship him,
every one whose name hath not been written from the foundation of
the world in the book of life of the Lamb that hath been slain.

The dragon is worshipped by the people of earth – Satan is worshipped because multitudes admired the beast (godless government) and gave him the power of public support and adoration.

The masses believed the beast was invincible, saying, "Who is like unto the beast? And who is able to war with him," which is an expression of both impotence and despair.

Notice the beast has a big mouth and is thought to speak "great" things, but in fact irreverently insults God, blaspheming the holy name. The beast spoke against God, his name, his tabernacle, and the heavenly host.

If you think this is overstated, just listen to what is coming from the seats of learning and the pillars of government in nations all over the world.

He makes war with the saints (the good fight of faith) and, amazingly, he overcomes them. The saints lose and the Devil wins. Consider the piled-up corpses of the sainted dead in the early centuries of the church and the literal and figurative slaughter of the beloved of God in every generation from the cross to the second coming.

How could this happen? The answer is that God gave man free agency and man used this power to enrich the dragon and his big, ugly dogs. Every disrespect shown to the "inspired of God" scriptures gives power to the Devil and his demons.

The Bible has power to restrain the dragon but if unused, it gives official authority and legal power to him; (shades of Eden and the serpent's gaining of power … a trickle in the beginning and a torrent today.)

Satan wins when the professing followers of Jesus are too "nice" to contend "earnestly for the faith once for all delivered to the saints."[498]

We are told to be "ready always to give answer to every man that asketh you a reason concerning the hope that is in you, yet with meekness and fear."[499] Notice, especially the words "always" and "every" man; Instead of standing up and speaking out from the rooftops, Christians are mute and cowed into silence.

The fight has gone out of the church and that is why Satan wins. A silent saint is a contradiction in terms. To be a secret disciple is to be a traitor. When Joseph of Arimathea and Nicodemus[500] were too cowardly to openly confess their belief that Jesus is the Christ, the Son of God, it was to their shame. They stood silently by while the Lord was beaten and killed and then, apparently being stung by his bloody death, they asked for and buried his dead body.

That same disgrace descends on every person saved by the blood of the lamb but who is too timid or afraid to let it be known openly.

The time will come when all humans on the entire earth will worship the dragon and none will worship God. This may happen because the pitiful few who persist in believing that Jesus is the Son of God will be caught up to the shores of the crystal sea, leaving only unbelievers, or because everyone on earth surrenders to the might of Satan. It happened once before,[501] (only eight souls were on Noah's ark). According to verse eight it will happen again.

When sinful people believe, repent, confess Jesus as Lord and are baptized to obtain the forgiveness of sins, their names are written in the lamb's book

---

498 Jude 1:3
499 1 Peter 3:15
500 John 19:38-39
501 Gen 6:1-13

of life.[502] God has written in the book of life that all who obey the gospel conditions of salvation will have their name written in that august record. Is your name written there?

Verses 9-10

If any man hath an ear, let him hear.

If any man is for captivity, into captivity he goeth:
if any man shall kill with the sword,
with the sword must he be killed.
Here is the patience and the faith of the saints.

The call to open your ear and hear the message is proof that the believers of the word of God have the power to and should be "casting down imaginations, and every high thing that is exalted against the knowledge of God, and bringing every thought into captivity to the obedience of Christ; and being in readiness to avenge all disobedience, when your obedience shall be made full."[503]

You can do it, therefore see to it that you do.

Those evil worshippers of the devil and his ugly-dogs who throw the righteous into cold, stone cells of a prison shall themselves be confined in a somber jail; and those who draw the sword against the saints shall be killed with the sword. "[F]or whatsoever a man soweth, that shall he also reap." Godless people who kill saints shall suffer the same fate as the saints they killed.

This is what John calls "the patience and the faith of the saints."

SECOND VISION – THE EARTH-BORN BEAST

Verse 11

And I saw another beast coming up out of the earth;
and he had two horns like unto a lamb,
and he spake as a dragon.

---

502 Heb 11:6; Acts 2:38; Rom 10:9-10; Acts 22:16; Phil 4:3; Rev 3:5; 20:12, 15
503 2 Cor 10:5-6

The second beast came from the earth and represents religious-minded people who hanker for material things; they are false prophets. The beast that is of the earth attempts to turn spiritual verities into worldly delusions. All earthly things perish with the using but spiritual truth is uncompromising and eternal; it is therefore correct to think of the material things of earth as illusion and the unseen things of the spiritual world as reality and live a life that is consistent with this conviction.

The beast represents all godless philosophy, which inevitably results in worthless speculation. He, like a wolf in sheep's clothing, tried to look harmless, but he spoke with the roar of a dragon. He is ever deceitful and beguiling.

Things are not always what they appear to be; be watchful.

Verse 12

And he exerciseth all the authority of the first beast in his sight.
And he maketh the earth and them that dwell
therein to worship the first beast,
whose death-stroke was healed.

The first beast (godless government) is empowered by the dragon (Satan) and gives authority to the second beast (godless religion). This second beast is called a false prophet several times in the book of Revelation.[504]

The dragon and the two beasts constitute a trio and walk hand-in-hand as they deceive the nations.

John references the "first beast, whose death-stroke was healed." It is misguided and too limited to make this a particular world leader or a certain kingdom of men. The visions of the book of Revelation cover the entire present dispensation, which is the last system. All evil world leaders and world empires are included in these figures.

Virtually all presidents of countries and kings of nations rise and fall and rise again. Nations flourish, decline, and revive. It is an ongoing process. To single out one wicked world leader or one godless government as the fulfillment of the prophecy of this vision is wrong and misses the point that bad magistrates and governments are plentiful and spread out over

504 Rev 16:13; 19:20; 20:10

the years. Paul says specifically Satan's henchmen existed in his day and would continue until Jesus comes again unto judgment.[505]

Now, a caveat: not all government is malignant and some rulers are "ministers of God."[506] Government is necessary and God appoints that there shall be government, but it can be treacherous. Governments derive "their powers from the consent of the governed." Even dictatorships can be overthrown by united rebellion of the masses. Godless government exists in every age and is a dangerous enemy of truth. Be on guard.

Verses 13-15

And he doeth great signs,
that he should even make fire to come down out of heaven upon the earth
in the sight of men.

And he deceiveth them that dwell on the earth by reason of the
signs which it was given him to do in the sight of the beast;
saying to them that dwell on the earth,
that they should make an image to the beast who
hath the stroke of the sword and lived.

And it was given unto him to give breath to it,
even to the image of the beast, that the image of the beast should both speak,
and cause that as many as should not worship the
image of the beast should be killed.

Simon, the sorcerer of Samaria, like all tricksters and charlatans, gave out that he "was some great one."[507] He deceived all the people of the city of Samaria; fooling them into thinking his "signs" were real.

Paul warns us that false religious teachers, showing fictitious wonders, shall persist until the end of time.

These self-proclaimed wonder-workers claim to display miracles, but their works are far from the genuine signs of Jesus and the apostles. They do not raise the dead nor still the raging sea – the winds and waves are not subject to them as they were to the Lord. Their so-called miracles are invented by

505 2 Thess 2:7-8
506 Rom 13:1-7
507 Acts 8:9-10; 2 Thess 2:1-12

the imagination and are not derived from the power of God. What they do is "the working of Satan" and are false signs and "lying wonders."

The second beast gave "breath" to an image made by the subservient people; it was an image of the second beast himself. They were to idolize and deify the beast. People were to bow down to this godless, lying, deceitful animal (people enable godless government and false religion). Such idolizing will continue until earth, moon, sun and stars are recalled and we all enter timelessness. Idolizing false religion will continue until the earth "melts in fervent heat."

The adoration of the majority of earthlings of the image caused them to kill those who refused to worship the beast. The blood of the pure in heart has often dripped from the sword of the wicked and pooled at the feet of false prophets who worship the idol of materialism. Never mind, the pure in heart shall "see God." The kingdom of heaven belongs to those who are persecuted for righteousness sake.

Verses 16-17

And he causeth all,
the small and the great,
and the rich and the poor,
and the free and the bond,
that there be given them a mark on their right hand, or upon their forehead;

and that no man should be able to buy or to sell,
save he that hath the mark,
even the name of the beast or the number of his name.

The influence of the second beast includes the "small and great; rich and poor; free and bond;" in other words, it is ecumenical; this evil beast is so popular and powerful that he requires all who would do business in the world to display a mark upon their foreheads and right hands. In a book that abounds in figures and symbols it is unlikely this is a literal mark. We are told to mark and avoid "them that cause divisions and occasions of stumbling."[508]

We are told to "mark" and imitate "them that walk after example of Paul."[509]

---

508 Rom 16:17
509 Phil 3:17

The wicked worshippers of Satan are identified (marked) by what they do and say. The speech and behavior of the unrighteous marks (identifies) them as ungodly and lost.

Even so every good tree bringeth forth good fruit; but the corrupt tree bringeth forth evil fruit.

A good tree cannot bring forth evil fruit, neither can a corrupt tree bring forth good fruit.

Every tree that bringeth not forth good fruit is hewn down, and cast into the fire.

Therefore by their fruits ye shall know them.[510]

A thorough knowledge of God's revealed word implants wisdom in the human heart enabling the saved to know the difference between right and wrong; it also allows them to know who is saved and who is without the promise of salvation. ("He that believeth not shall be damned."[511]) The mark of the unbeliever is his unbelief which manifests itself in disobedience, or lawlessness.

The Dragon and his beasts tell their disciples to ostracize the sanctified by refusing to buy from them or sell to them, and to deal exclusively with those who show the signs of corruption and dishonesty. The purpose of this dictum of the devil is to punish the lovers of God and, if possible, to cause them to apostatize. It is his strategy for winning the war.

"We are not ignorant of his (Satan's) devises."[512]

Verse 18

Here is wisdom.
He that hath understanding,
let him count the number of the beast;
for it is the number of a man:
and his number is Six hundred and sixty and six.

---

510 Matt 7:17-20
511 Mark 16:16; Thayer says, "katakrino; to judge against, ... condemn, damn ... sentence adversely"
512 2 Cor 2:11

John tells us the "number of the beast" is "Six hundred and sixty and six (666)."[513]

Hendriksen[514] points out "the number of the beast is the number of a man;" he reminds us that man was created on the sixth day. He also says that the number seven is a symbol for completeness or perfection and that the number six is not seven "and never reaches seven." "Six means missing the mark, or failure." He concludes "The number of the beast is 666, that is, failure upon failure upon failure! It is the number of a man, for the beast glories in man and must fail."[515] I repeat, fallible, weak, imperfect people empower godless government and false religion and bring misery down upon their own heads. Their number is 666, which is imperfect! imperfect! imperfect!

The saints ultimately win and unbelievers who have fought against the warriors of Jesus are cast into "the lake that burneth with fire and brimstone."

Under the influence of the Dragon and the two beasts unbelievers do no business with the saved but rather oppose, ridicule and harm them ... "breathing threatening and slaughter against the disciples of the Lord ... whether men or women" ... to bind, punish and imprison them.[516]

"All who would live godly in Christ Jesus shall suffer persecution."[517]

"These things have I spoken unto you, that in me ye may have peace. In the world ye have tribulation: but be of good cheer; I have overcome the world."[518]

"But be ye glad and rejoice forever in that which I create; for, behold, I create Jerusalem a rejoicing, and her people a joy."[519]

The New Jerusalem descending from the courts of God is "the mark of the high calling of God in Christ Jesus" and a place of perfect contentment and total satisfaction. "Rejoice in the Lord always, and again I will say, Rejoice."

---

513 Rev 13:18
514 William Hendriksen, *More than Conquerors*, Baker Book House
515 *More than Conquerors*, p. 151
516 Acts 9:1-2
517 2 Tiim 3:12
518 John 16:33
519 Isa 65:18

HE THAT OVERCOMES
TRANSPORT
REVELATION 14:1-18

John, empowered by Jehovah, Jesus and the Holy Spirit, foretells a day when the universe is brought to violent ruin. The seventh trumpet has pealed out the last warning. A day of "judgment" and the destruction of ungodly men"[520] is swiftly coming. The godless have ruled God out of the created world, proclaimed him dead, and laughed him out of his own universe. They have brought down upon their guilty heads earned punishment and are on the brink of receiving the recompense of their error which was due.

The worldly wise, speaking by the authority of the "father of lies," have duped the gullible into believing that Jesus is a phantom, the Creator is a stream or tendency, hope is a dream, and the Book containing the sacred scriptures is a mythical collection of fairytales and is good only for its occasional Aesopian moral.

We glance back to review once more what God through the Holy Spirit and through John has told us about the "good fight of faith."

- A vision of Jesus in his sovereign majesty — chap 1
- Jesus exhorts and admonishes his loyal soldiers — chaps 2-3
- The authority and power of Almighty God — chaps 4-5
- The resurrected Lamb breaks seven seals, inaugurating a spiritual war — chap 6
- A very small remnant love truth more than life — chap 7
- Seven angel trumpeters warn of suffering and oppression — chaps 8-11
- Gloriously arrayed woman (Israel) and the great red dragon (Satan) — chap 12
- Satan and his two ugly beasts wage war on the righteous — chap 13

The authority of the august Creator and benevolent Savior has been pitted against the vulgar forces of evil under the leadership of the Devil. Outwardly

---

520 2 Pet 3:7-12

it would appear that the good and the pure have suffered a shameful defeat at the hands of Satan, but the tables are about to be turned.

The inspired writer pauses to discuss the rapture of the redeemed.

Verse 1

And I saw, and behold,
the Lamb standing on the mount Zion,
and with him a hundred and forty and four thousand,
having his name, and the name of his Father, written on their foreheads

In this vision, as John is preparing us for the terrible destruction that is waiting in the wings, he saw the warrior Lamb standing on mount Zion (a literal mountain that became, in Jewish thought, a figure of the city of David and of the temple built by David's son and of all people who "fear God and keep his commands.")

The Lamb is standing, suggesting authority, rule, interest and participation; his feet are well supported by the rocky surface of the mountain. He stands because he overcame the forces of evil and is on the threshold of utterly destroying the entire created universe.

"A hundred and forty and four thousand" stand with him for they, too, have overcome. The 144,000 is symbolic of all the saved. This number appears in chapter seven to describe the slim remnant of Jews to be saved. It is a round number, which indicates that it is not an exact number. In chapter seven the 144,000 are all Israelites but they are associated with a very large number representing the aggregate of the saved.[521] Verse three tells us that here the 144,000 represent "they that have been purchased out of the earth." They are a minority and have disciplined themselves to walk within in the confines of a narrow path. This number is repeated to show that of the masses that have lived upon the earth not many will overcome.

---

521 Rev 7.9: After these things I saw, and behold, a great multitude, which no man could number out of every nation and of all tribes and peoples and tongues, standing before the throne and before the Lamb arrayed in white robes and palms in their hands; Rev 14:3 says the hundred and forty four thousand are 'they that had been purchased from out of the earth " So, in one place it is a figure of descendants of Abraham converted to Christ and in the other place it is a figure of all the saved, Jew and Gentile. It is a remnant in either case.

It is a mighty host but comprised of a small percentage of each generation. Even a few of each age will multiply into many over a long period. Jesus said, "Many are called, but few are chosen." That is, a minority of each generation will be elevated to glory but the total of the saved from uncountable generations will be a mighty multitude. They are symbolized by a hundred and forty and four thousand indicating the exact number will not be known until the day of final judgment.

Salvation is conditional and therefore the number of redeemed is dependent upon the obedience of free-willed agents; only the ultimate judgment will reveal the total number of the saved; the outcome depends upon the obedience of the human creatures of earth. Each person on earth has the power to choose life (the blessing) or death (the curse).

"On Zion's glorious summit stood a numerous host redeemed by blood;" it is the full complement of the redeemed throughout history. They have been, like the child of the gloriously arrayed woman, caught up into the third heaven. There is not one saved person left on the earth. The godless are left with a godless earth and a godless future. They have rejected God and He now rejects them. Doom is at hand! The grim reaper has sharpened his axe and drawn his sword; the saved are within the arms of God and secure; a wall of fire encircles them.

The lawless are hopeless and helpless; they are damned, but they don't know it just yet.

Verses 2-3

And I heard a voice from heaven,
as the voice of many waters,
and as the voice of a great thunder,
and the voice which I heard was as the voice of
harpers harping with their harps
and they sing as it were a new song before the throne.
and before the four living creatures and the elders:
and no man could learn the song save the hundred and forty and four
thousand.
even they that had been purchased out of the earth.

The happy band looks to the smiling face of the Lord and in rapturous delight extols his name in songs of praise. Their hymns are loud like the roar of the sea or the sound of thunder, and also beautiful and pleasing like the gentle sound of harps.

On Zion's glorious summit stood a numerous host redeemed by blood! They hymned their King in strains divine ..."

> *May I reach*
> *That purest heaven, -- be to other souls*
> *The cup of strength in some great agony*
> *Enkindle generous ardor, feed pure love,*
> *Beget the smiles that have no cruelty,*
> *Be the sweet presence of a good diffused,*
> *And in diffusion ever more intense!*
> *So shall I join the choir invisible*
> *Whose music is the gladness of the world.*[522]

They stand with the Lamb in a perfect victory ... they have overcome and piled their trophies at Jesus feet.

Blessed is "he that overcometh."

Those whose heartstrings are struck by intense happiness often break out in joyous song. In this case only the minority of the masses that have stormed across the face of the earth have good reason to sing the happy refrains of this cheerful but unrecorded music.

Only those who have been washed in the blood of the Lamb can learn the words of this wonderful composition because only those who have come out of the conflict and tribulation of life on earth to stand unashamed in the presence of God can understand it. The fire, pain, smoke, blood and smell of war enable them to fully appreciate the song of overcoming.

Those who have fought the hard battle of a tremendous spiritual war can bring up from the depth of their emotion the proper intensity to sing this victory tune. Their voices swell as thoughts of conflict, sacrifice and suffering stroke their inner cords and bring forth a blessed harmony.

They took control of their own lives and gave themselves in a living sacrifice to the domination of a precious savior. Blessed is he that is overcoming. He,

---

522 Mary Ann Evans, aka, George Elliot; Poem: *The Choir Invisible*

day by day and hour by hour, devotes himself to overcoming one obstacle after another until his life culminates in this grand victory. And so he sings; he sings from the depth of experience and the joy of deliverance; he sings because he is standing with the Lamb and the 144,000 and looks forward to an abundant entrance into the everlasting kingdom of the Ancient of Days.

They were purchased out of the earth at the awful cost of the mangled body of the Son of God. His blood has cleansing power and they washed themselves in that blood to be free from all defilement. They heard the Savior say, "He that believeth and is baptized shall be saved"[523] and obeyed his blest commands. They knew their Redeemer said, "Except a man be born of the water and the Spirit he cannot enter the kingdom of heaven" and had consented to be plunged into the water in imitation of the death, burial and resurrection of Jesus and to be raised to walk a new life.[524]

As new creatures[525] they fought "the good fight of faith" and gained victory after victory, overcoming opposition through the whole of their lives to claim the prize and knowing "he that overcometh shall not be hurt of the second death."

Verses 4-5

These are they that were not defiled with women;
for they are virgins.
These are they that follow the Lamb whithersoever he goeth.
These were purchased from among men,
to be the firstfruits unto God and unto the Lamb.
And in their mouth was found no lie:
they are without blemish.

The prophet/apostle is not saying that marriage and its intimate bonds are unholy. The Bible approves men and women committing themselves to one another in the covenant of matrimony. God saw in the beginning of creation that it was not "good for the man to "be alone."[526] Jehovah in his

---

523 Mark 16:16
524 John 3:5; Rom 6:4
525 2 Cor 5:17
526 Gen 2:18

infinite wisdom made them "male and female,"[527] and said, "Be fruitful, and multiply, and replenish the earth, and subdue it."[528] Jesus commended marriage and said, "What therefore God hath joined together, let not man put asunder."[529] Paul compared the relationship of a husband and wife to that of Christ and his church.[530] The Song of Solomon is a beautiful ode to married bliss and love. The heroes of faith throughout the Bible were usually married and are never told to abstain from lawful intimate relations. There is too much evidence approving marriage and procreation for us to make the blunder of supposing that John is here saying that fleshly contact between a man and woman, in the sacred ties of holy matrimony, defiles the man or the woman.

The Bible is consistent in reproving sexual abuses and perversions and saying that practitioners of fornication and lasciviousness shall never look upon the face of God in peace. All such behavior is lawless; it is evil and defiles. Illicit gratification of the senses is void of moral, spiritual, and intellectual interests. It is shamefully carnal, and will not go unpunished.[531]

Idolatry features fornication and other abominations. Those who delight in sensual pleasures and unbridled passions are pagan and the Seer here points an accusing finger at them. When a society becomes so decadent that it flaunts crude bodily pleasures for commercial advantage, it is defiled; to worship the lewd and lustful is destructive of everything that is noble and pure, and this is what John condemns.

He is distinctly not saying that women are fundamentally corrupt and all association is immoral. Women have the ability to elevate society and improve public mores by the influence of their godly example, admonishment and spiritual sensitivity.

John says the host of the redeemed standing on the mountain with their chief commanding officer (a Lamb), are undefiled virgins. All of them — men, women, children, married, unmarried, and the whole company of the saved — are virgins. The fact that this mighty multitude had within its folds every type of personality makes it irresistibly plain that the inspired

---

527 Gen 1:27
528 Gen 1:28
529 Matt 19:6
530 Eph 5:22-23
531 Rev 21:8; Rom 1:20-32; Gal 5:19-21

writer is using the word "virgin" in a figurative sense; in the nature of the case, it could not be literal.

The word "virgin" is sometime used symbolically in the Bible to commend individuals or groups for purity of life. Israel (the people) are called "the virgin daughter of Zion"[532] to remind them of their high calling to be clean and pure, and to emphasize their holiness as the chosen people of God.[533]

The apostle Paul said to one church (a gathering of diverse people, including married and unmarried) "I espoused you to one husband that I might present you as a pure virgin to Christ."[534] The church is the betrothed bride of Jesus and when he comes again, he will marry the church. John speaks of that happy day in these words, "And I saw the holy city, new Jerusalem, coming down out of heaven of God, made ready as a bride adorned for her husband" [535]

A bride "made ready for her husband" is uncontaminated, washed, clean, pure and adorned.[536] The church of Christ is glorious because it has neither "spot or wrinkle or any such thing:' but is 'holy and without blemish."[537]

Symbolically the church is made up of virgins, beautified by the cleansing blood of the Lamb and holding itself in readiness when the bridegroom shall come. ''And in their [the undefiled virgins] mouth was found no lie: they [the virgin bride of Christ] are without blemish."[538]

The undefiled virgins are "they that follow the lamb whithersoever he goeth." This does not mean they merely stroll along behind Jesus, but it carries the idea of obeying him in all that he requires; he does not speak from himself, but speaks the true words of the true God;[539] therefore to receive Jesus or his appointed representatives is to receive and be received by him that sent Jesus.[540] To follow Jesus is to straitly obey him and his

532 2 Kings 19:21
533 See also Isa 1:8; 23:12; 37:22; Jer 14:17; 31:4
534 2 Cor 11:2.
535 Rev 21:2
536 Adorned implies an enhancing by something beautiful in itself "a diamond necklace adorned her neck."
537 Eph 5:27
538 Rev 14:5
539 John 12:49; 14:10
540 Mark 9:37; Luke 10:16; John 5:24, 30; 6:38; 13:20

example of respectful and determined submission to the Heavenly Father's will and works.

Jesus reminds his disciples, "We must work the works of him that sent me."[541] Those who question the importance and necessity of works should ponder these words.[542] We are to be judged and either admitted into the everlasting kingdom or rejected on the basis of our works.[543]

Jesus is the perfect example of unwavering submission to the will of God. We follow Jesus when we meticulously conform to the revealed will of the Almighty, when we deviate from that will, we are not following Jesus. The church is comprised of undefiled virgins because they "follow Jesus whithersoever he goeth."

They washed their robes in Lamb's blood when they were "buried therefore with him through baptism unto death: that like as Christ was raised from the dead through the glory of the Father so they also might walk in newness of life."[544]

Many and powerful are the sermons that could be preached from this text.

John is building up to the final judgment and in the process uses a dramatic interruptive epoch to enhance and intensify the event.

The seventh trumpet has been heard and the universe is about to be swallowed in flames and the Spirit guided apostle is preparing us for the horror of that outcome by describing the background.

Flying angels announce the utter destruction that will soon befall the earth and all of its inhabitants (the saved having been elevated to the high platform of a figurative mount Zion).

Three angels appear in succession each with a message for earthlings; the three proclamations are related. Several angels are mentioned in this context so each of these three messengers is called "another" angel.

---

541 John 9:4
542 See also James 2:14-26
543 Rom 2:6; 2 Cor 5:10; Rev 223; 20:12-13;22:12
544 Rom 6:4

Verses 6-7

And I saw another angel flying in mid heaven,
having eternal good tidings to proclaim unto them that dwell on the earth,
and unto every nation and tribe and tongue and people;
and he saith with a great voice,
Fear God, and give him glory;
for the hour of his judgment is come:
and worship him that made the heaven
and the earth and sea and fountains of waters.

The first angel and his two brother angels speak of a final judgment of the people of earth and the prelude to the collapse and melting of the universe. Each message is heavy with doom and destruction, yet the message of this first flying angel is addressed to "them that dwell on the earth." The virgins of earth have all been advanced to stand with their adored Lamb on the mountain and no longer on earth. Those left on the earth are committed sinners dedicated to decadence and corruption.

The angel crying out with a mighty voice that there is a gospel here called eternal good tidings (it offers salvation in the Lamb of God who alone has power to take away the sins of the earth). That is good news, but it falls on deaf ears. These people are too engulfed in wickedness to hear, just as were the antediluvians.

They not only will not hear but their eyes are closed and they cannot see. Their blindness is the result of unwillingness to see; they strongly prefer vice and filth and so refuse to look, or hear, or believe. Like Pharaoh down in Egypt, they have hardened their hearts and will not believe.

When the righteous were still on the earth good news was preached but the Devil's pledged followers refused to hear, see, or accept it. Now that the saints have been gathered to glory in anticipation of the righteous and ultimate judgment and only the depraved remain on earth the good message is still disregarded by these calloused, coarse, corrupt slobs.

Their stubborn ingratitude is appalling.

The flying angel makes his announcement from mid-heaven so that all may hear, seeing that the offer of salvation is to "every nation and tribe and tongue and people."

It is not too late, though the remaining time is very short, but there is this one last plea, "Fear God and give him glory; for the hour of his judgment is come; and worship the mighty maker of heaven and earth and all that is in them." That is the cry, but the fools of earth have made themselves impervious to the tender mercies and amazing grace of God.

The night will come when it will be too late to run to the open arms of God; one day the door will be shut and the lights will be off. The universal judgment is fast approaching.

Verse 8

And another, a second angel, followed, saying,
Fallen, fallen is Babylon the great,
that hath made all the nations to drink of the
wine of the wrath of her fornication

Abruptly the seer announces the fall of Babylon the Great,[545] an empire of power and moral corruption. It also represents the apex of buying and selling of commodities on a large scale.

Materialism and commercialism are impotent to save and are inevitably productive of moral decay and crude gratification of the senses.

Silver, gold and jewels are useless in that city that lies foursquare; the treasures of earth will rust and decay, the moths will eat the finest garments, and crooks will plunder the riches we are tempted to trust. All earthly stuff will fail and be lost; it has no value in a spiritual estate.[546]

Babylon represents the perishing things of earth and time; it teeters on the brink of ruin. We shall shortly read of the fall of Babylon and this angel in his announcement anticipates that fall.

Verse 9-11

And another angel, a third, followed them,
saying with a great voice,
If any man worshippeth the beast and his image,

---

545 We will comment on the identity of Babylon the Great when we discuss the seventeenth chapter where this is worked out in detail
546 Matt 6:19-20

and receiveth a mark on his forehead,
or upon his hand,
he also shall drink of the wine of the wrath of God.
which is prepared unmixed in the *cup of his anger;*
and he *shall be tormented with fire and brimstone in the presence of the holy*
angels,
and in the presence of the Lamb:
and the smoke of their torment goeth up forever and ever,
and they have no rest day and night,
they that worship the beast and his image,
and whoso receiveth the mark of his name.

A third angel immediately appears and completes the warning. Adoring and honoring Satan is marked for rejection and punishment. "If any man worshippeth (is worshipping) the beast (an agent of the dragon to whom such devotion extends), he is receiving a mark on his forehead and hand. He is a marked man. This is not something that was done to him but something he did to himself.[547]

Our tendency is to blame someone else for our sins; we blame God, our ancestors, the environment, associates, or the devil and we forget that each man "is drawn away by his own lusts and enticed."[548]

The undiluted wine of the wrath of God, poured full strength into the cup of his anger, is a symbol of the severe punishment the heedless will suffer for their hard-hearted rejection of the sacrifice of the Son of God at Calvary; it is the just recompense of reward.

Once again, the punishment of the rebellious sons and daughters of men, who bear in their bodies a God-fathered and God-given spirit, and who are therefore despicable, is etched with a pen of iron ... "he shall be tormented with fire and brimstone in the presence of the holy angels, and in the presence of the Lamb."

---

547 Some may say, "God is good and could not punish anyone in the fires of hell forever, no matter how vice-ridden." This they forget, People who reject God and his gospel bring eternal punishment on themselves and are solely responsible for this horrendous outcome. The constant plea of deity, right down to the last moment, is "O, why will you die.

548 James 1:14

For this terrible punishment to be administered before the angels and the Lamb seems barbaric, but remember these people ridiculed and laughed to scorn the lifeless body of the Son of God and the penalty includes being punished in the sight of the very beings they despised and held up for public rejection; it is no less than they deserve.

Conversely, those who appreciate the priceless and unspeakable gift of Immanuel and in undying gratitude give themselves to obey and serve God shall also receive the recompense of their reward.

Verses 12-13

Here is the patience of the saints,
they that keep the commandments of God.
and the faith of Jesus.
And I heard the voice from heaven saying.
Write, Blessed are the dead who die in the Lord from henceforth:
yea, saith the Spirit, that they may rest from their labors:
for their works follow with them.

Patience is the quality that enables the saint to wordlessly endure what he must endure and, while suffering, to be enthusiastically committed to keeping every command of the new covenant.

We "fulfill all righteousness" when we cheerfully obey the Lord even though we have heavy loads and pain. It is the willingness to take the yoke of Christ though we are weary and heavy laden.

The patience of the saints is keeping the commandments of God. It may seem inconvenient sometime to be submissive to the law of our Creator, but patience compels us to keep "the faith of Jesus:" His noble "not my will, but thine be done" made it his "meat" to "do the will of God; "we must do the works" of him that sent Jesus "while it is day, for the night comes when no man can work." Patience enables us to understand this principle and to "fear God and keep his commandments."

A voice (whose voice is not important, what is said is all important), saying, "Write, Blessed (happy, thankful) are the dead (Jesus removed the sting from death) who die in the Lord (no one ever died in the Lord who was not in the Lord before his death) from henceforth (to all eternity), thus saith the Spirit (these are not the words of man, but are the words of God), they rest from their labors (trials, sorrows, temptations, tribulations), their works follow with them (works are necessary and important)."

The works are the companion of the righteous human spirit as it soars beyond sun, moon and stars to find solace in the arms of Jesus; his works certify his standing with God and are his credentials to pass through the gate of pearl and walk down the street of gold to the throne room of God and "see him even as he is" and be like him.

This verse tells us the importance of being "in" the Lord: we are "in" Christ when our faith compels us to repent and be baptized; baptism is the crowning act that puts us "in" Christ. "As many of you as were baptized into Christ did put on Christ."[549] To be "in Christ" is to be where the Lord has placed "every" spiritual blessing."[550]

Those who continued in the faith of Jesus while enduring the rigors of the battle overcome and, in their triumph, claim a robe, a crown and a mansion.

The seventh trumpet has announced that harvest time has come.

Verses 14-16

And I saw, and behold, a white cloud;
and on the cloud I saw one sitting like unto a son of man.
having on his head a golden crown,
and in his hand a sharp sickle.
And another angel came out from the temple,
crying with a great voice to him that sat on the cloud,
Send forth thy sickle, and reap:
for the hour to reap is come;
for the harvest of the earth is ripe.
And he that sat on the cloud cast his sickle upon the earth;
and the earth was reaped.

During his earthly pilgrimage, Jesus often spoke of a judgment of condemnation and of justification that would separate the sheep from the

---

549 Gal 3:26-27; 1 Cor 12:13
550 Eph 1:3

goats.[551] He spoke of a day when his own powerful and irresistible voice would call the dead out of Hades to a resurrection of life or of death.[552] "[H]e will gather his wheat into the garner, but the chaff he will burn up with unquenchable fire."[553]

The one John saw sitting on a white cloud was "like unto a son of man," that is, he was Jesus in his glory, and all the angels with him, "sitting on the throne of his glory." His golden crown affirms his majesty and his sharp sickle affirms his judgment. The promise that "Christ ... shall appear a second time, apart from sin, to them that wait for him, unto salvation"[554] is sure. John foresees the "son of man" redeeming his promise.

The Heavenly Father gave "all judgment unto the Son; that all may honor the Son, even as they honor the Father."[555]

The universe, in John's vision, teeters on the brink of its eternal doom, but the servants of Satan do not know it. The seventh angel sounded his trumpet and judgment of all evil brings a sentence of condemnation of evil works; and by the same stroke exonerates the pure in heart that are on the verge of seeing God, being like him, and receiving the lavish rewards of the works of righteousness.

John sees a time when the harvest of the earth is fully ripe. He also foresees a time when the cup of the earth's iniquity is full and overflowing. This is the day God has appointed in which he will judge the world in righteousness by the man whom he hath ordained; whereof he hath given assurance unto all men, in that he hath raised him from the dead."[556]

The day of final judgment is not a calendar day, but is that day when the world is so utterly committed to the great red dragon that there is no possibility of reform and restoration. That will be the day Jehovah has appointed for the ultimate judgment.

Just as the flood did not come until "the thoughts of men's heart were only evil continually," and just as the defeat and eviction of the Amorite did not occur until his iniquity was full, and just as Babylon did not execute

---

551 Matt 25:31-36
552 John 5:28-29
553 Matt 3:12
554 Heb 9:27
555 John 5:22-23
556 Acts 17:31

judgment on Israel until her rebellion and sin were preponderant, so will the earth be swept away in flames of the Father's fury when humans have crossed the point of no return.

The angel who announced the irreparable fall of a worldwide society commanded the son of man to reap the harvest of earth with his sharp sickle for "the harvest of the earth is ripe." The angel "came out from the temple." Jehovah was in the temple and this angel was no doubt sent on his mission of condemnation by Yahweh (YHWH); the command he issued to the crowned Christ was not his own but was a message from the Heavenly Father.

He that sat on the cloud did not hesitate but was fully obedient; "and the earth was reaped."

Verses 17-20

Another angel came out from the temple which is in heaven,
he also having a sharp sickle.
And another angel came out from the altar,
he that hath power over fire;
and he called with a great voice to him that had the sharp sickle, saying,
Send forth thy sharp sickle,
and gather the clusters of the vine of the earth;
for her grapes are fully ripe.
And the angel cast his sickle into the earth,
and gathered the vintage of the earth,
and cast it into the winepress, the great winepress, of the wrath of God
And the winepress was trodden without the city,
and there came out blood from the winepress,
even unto the bridles of the horses,
as far as a thousand and six hundred furlongs.

Six angels are mentioned in this chapter (vv. 6, 8, 9, 15, 17 and 18). There were seven trumpeters who warned of the heaped up misery caused by the dragon and his helpers when they waged war against the Lamb. The seventh sounded his horn to announce that the end of all things material was to begin very soon, and now his six companions join him in this solemn warning.

The great and bloody slaughter is foretold in this chapter with bold and violent wordage; it is not difficult to understand; it is the description of the beginning of utmost devastation and ruin. The language is vivid because the event is so sharp and intensive.

As we read our senses quail before the apparition. It is a figurative hyperbole and it gets the point across. The sixteenth chapter helps us understand more fully the reason for the violent description of this furious laying waste of an extensive system; the long delay, which is an expression of divine compassion, is also better understood. "God is not willing that any should perish, but that all should come to repentance," but his longsuffering must not be misunderstood to mean that he is slack concerning his promise.

We look at the words and shudder … sharp sickle … fire … gathering the clusters … her grapes are fully ripe … winepress trodden … there came out blood … even unto the bridles of the horses … as far as a thousand and six hundred furlongs (187 miles).

That is the prelude announcing the fiery collapse and extinguishment of the entire universe, it falls under the weight of sin; sin is rampant because God is denied and his word is desecrated.

Revelation 15:1 to 8

Doomsday

The magnificent book of Revelation begins by a giving an intense picture of the brilliance of the one godhead and the grandeur of its only three members (Jehovah, Jesus and the Comforter).

It traces the combat between truth and mendacity and foretells the success of good and the casting down of evil.

Here is, again, a succinct summary of the spiritual battle of the ages.

- "Christ, the royal master, leads against the foe" – chapter 1
- The Captain of the army of God disciplines his warriors – chapters 2-3
- The heavenly headquarters are pictured – chapters 4-5
- The resurrected slain Lamb qualifies to break seven seals – chapter 6
- A few from all nations are recruited to follow the banners of Jesus – chapter 7 Seven trumpets reveal intense suffering and sorrow – chapters 8-13
- Preparation is made for the outpouring of the seven bowls of wrath – chapter 14

The ransomed are assembled with Jesus on symbolic mount Zion to witness the humiliation of the unmerciful tyrant of evil and his supporters. Like all cruel dictators, he is without compassion and kills his own people as well as his opponents. When sin is universal, the end of the universe is very near.

Jesus in the days of his earthly service warned that the end of the first and second heaven and the end of the earth would come suddenly ... when the world lest expected it.

> *"[B]e ye also ready; for in an hour that ye think not the Son of man cometh ... that evil servant shall say in his heart, My lord tarrieth; and shall begin to beat his fellow-servants, and shall eat and drink with the drunken; the lord of that servant shall come in a day when he expecteth not, and in an hour when he knoweth not, and shall cut him asunder, and appoint his portion with the hypocrites: there shall be the weeping and the gnashing of teeth."[557]*

The moral of the parable of the ten virgins is "Watch therefore, for ye know not the day nor the hour."[558]

> *"For yourselves know perfectly that the day of the Lord so cometh as a thief in the night. When they are saying, Peace and safety, then sudden destruction cometh upon them, as travail upon a woman with child; and they shall in no wise escape. But ye, brethren, are not in darkness, that that day should overtake you as a thief: for ye are all sons of light, and sons of the day: we are not of the night, nor of darkness."[559]*

> *"If therefore thou shalt not watch, I will come as a thief, and thou shalt not know what hour I will come upon thee."[560]*

> *"Prepare to meet thy God."[561]*

How can a mere, finite mortal prepare to meet the Mighty-Maker-of-the-earth and its wonders, of the sun, moon and stars? We are grateful that the Supreme, infinite intelligence that upholds all things by the "word of his power" graciously invites us ... "Come unto me, all ye that labor and are heavy laden, and I will give you rest."

We prepare to meet him, and come to him, by *"casting down imaginations, and every high thing that is exalted against the knowledge of God, and bringing*

---

557 Matt 24:44-51
558 Matt 25:1-13
559 1 Thess 5:2-6
560 Rev 3:3
561 Amos 4:12

every thought into captivity to the obedience of Christ; and being in readiness to avenge all disobedience, when your obedience shall be made full."[562]

John gives us an introduction to the total catastrophe of the utter overthrow and ruin of the starry host and of the world; chapter fifteen is the prelude, chapter sixteen gives some of the details.

Verse 1

And I saw another sign in heaven,
great and marvellous,
seven angels having seven plagues,
which are the last,
for in them is finished the wrath of God.

The booming voice of the Mighty Maker of all things is about to announce the full and final end of the entire universe. He made it all and has therefore the power and the privilege of ending it. Here is a running review of what brings about this divine justice:

- Through the revealed word the kingdom comes[563]
- The living church, which is the living redeemed of earth, is to preach the gospel[564]
- Churches of Christ are "golden candlesticks" in a world that lies in darkness[565]
- The unsaved of earth hate the light, but they love darkness[566]
- To align with the unsaved is to wear the mark of the beast
- World's hatred generated because the church champions truth[567]
- This cycle continues from the beginning to the termination

---

562 2 Cor 10:5-6

563 The word Jesus received from the father and taught to his first century disciples is the seed of the kingdom – see Luke 8:10-11; seed has life in it; if the seed is planted in good ground, i.e., good and honest hearts, it germinates and produces the kingdom, which is the church – see Matt 16:18-19

564 Mark 16:15-16; Matt 28:18-20

565 Rev chapters 1-3

566 John 3:19-21

567 John 8:45; 18:17; Rom 1:18; 2 Thess 2:10, 12; 2 Pet 2:2--3

The broken seals and the loud and clear trumpets tell us that the fruit of ungodliness and unrighteousness is woe, grief, regret and distress. The book of Revelation is a summation of sacred scripture, a.k.a. written revelation; it tells the bitter striving between good and evil; persecuted saints endure what they must endure, which is called in the book of Revelation "the patience of the saints."[568]

John saw another "sign" in heaven; "seven angels having seven plagues, which are the last, for in them is finished the wrath of God." This stinging statement is a clear declaration that when the saved fly away to glory the wrath of God will be finished. There is no room for a further delay or for another dispensation; the entire created, material universe comes crashing down and it happens quickly. The saints are removed from the desecrated universe, leaving only those who wear the mark of the beast and with breath-taking suddenness the wrath of God is finished. There is a full end to earth, moon, sun, planets, stars, black holes, history, space and time. The wrath of God is finished; every promise and prophecy concerning our universe is fulfilled. The dragon and his camp are scooped into judgment and the second death. They are the only earthly survivors of the great annihilation.

Verses 2-4

And I saw as it were a sea of glass mingled with fire;
and them that come off victorious from the beast,
and from his image,
and from the number of his name,
standing by the sea of glass,
having harps of God.

And they sing the song of Moses the servant of God,
and the song of the Lamb, saying,
Great and marvellous are thy works,
O Lord God, the Almighty;
righteous and true are thy ways,
thou King of the ages.

Who shall not fear,
O Lord, and glorify thy name?

---

568 Rev 1:9; 2:2, 3, 19; 3:10; 13:10; 14:12

for thou only art holy;
for all the nations shall come and worship before thee;
for thy righteous acts have been made manifest.

In this vision, all those who overcame stand rejoicing by the sea of glass (the "sea of glass" is also mentioned in the throne of God scene in chapter 4. [569] He that overcometh now exults in unbounded rapture as the promises of the seven letters are redeemed and the one hope of the children of God is realized in heavenly jubilation.

Make a joyful noise unto Jehovah, all ye lands.

Serve Jehovah with gladness: come before his presence with singing.

Know ye that Jehovah, he is God: it is he that hath made us, and we are his; we are his people, and the sheep of his pasture.

Enter into his gates with thanksgiving, and into his courts with praise: give thanks unto him, and bless his name.

For Jehovah is good; His lovingkindness endureth for ever, and his faithfulness unto all generations.[570]

The victors eat of the tree of life, are not hurt by the second death, feast on the hidden manna, have authority over the nations, are dressed in white, are pillars in the temple of God and sit with Christ in his throne;[571] they carry the white stone of admittance and exoneration, upon which is written their own new name; and they will carry it throughout all eternity.[572]

They sing in their inexpressible joy a song about Moses and the Lamb, the two great deliverers and law givers. The grand aim of Jesus is to deliver sinful man from the bondage of sin and Satan.[573]

---

569 Rev 4:6

570 Psa 100

571 Rev 2:7, 11, 17, 26; 3:5, 12, 21

572 Rev 2:17

573 "Know ye not, that to whom ye present yourselves as servants unto obedience, his servants ye are whom ye obey; whether of sin unto death, or of obedience unto righteousness?

But thanks be to God, that, whereas ye were servants of sin, ye became obedient from the heart to that form of teaching whereunto ye were delivered; and being made free from sin, ye became servants of righteousness" (Rom 6:16-18).

John reminds us of the fairness of the justice of God; as the full measure of his wrath falls upon the guilty, even they must acknowledge that He is holy and righteous. Nothing more need be said; all have learned to fear and glorify the name of the Lord.

Verses 5-8

And after these things I saw,
and the temple of the tabernacle of the testimony in heaven was opened:

and there came out from the temple the seven
angels that had the seven plagues,
arrayed with precious stone,
pure and bright,
and girt about their breasts with golden girdles.

And one of the four living creatures gave unto the seven angels
seven golden bowls full of the wrath of God,
who liveth for ever and ever.

And the temple was filled with smoke from the glory of God,
and from his power;
and none was able to enter into the temple,
till the seven plagues of the seven angels should be finished.

John also reminds us the foundation for the bowls of wrath; it comes to us in a connected series:

- The word of God is the seed of the kingdom[574];
- the kingdom is the church[575];
- the church is the saved people[576]
- by the teaching of God's powerful and living word the church comes into existence; to destroy the church (temple of God), is to incur the wrath of God and earn everlasting destruction.[577]

---

574 Luke 8:11
575 Matt 16:18-19
576 1 Pet 2:5; 1 Cor 3:16-17
577 1 Cor 3:16-17

- The church brings light (each congregation is a candlestick) to a world that lies in darkness.[578]

- The world hates the light because it loves darkness.[579]

- The rejection of the word of God is to refuse heaven's offer of mercy and forgiveness is to judge one's self "unworthy of eternal life."[580]

All of this is described in the vision of chapters twelve through fourteen where the gloriously arrayed woman (representing the church) is viciously persecuted by the red dragon and his cohorts (representing Satan and his minions).

Holiness and justice demand that those who have insulted God to his face by rejecting the "unspeakable gift" of his Son be punished. The book of Hebrews after mentioning that transgression of Moses' Law brought punishment and death says,

> *[O]f how much sorer punishment, think ye, shall he be judged worthy, who hath trodden underfoot the Son of God, and hath counted the blood of the covenant wherewith he was sanctified an unholy thing, and hath done despite unto the Spirit of grace? For we know him that said, Vengeance belongeth unto me, I will recompense. And again, The Lord shall judge his people. It is a fearful thing to fall into the hands of the living God.[581]*

People of the world do not realize what a heinous crime it is to spit in the face of Jesus by turning a deaf ear to his royal word. Such behavior is very stupid though engaged by many scholars. It is inexcusable.

Jehovah must punish, otherwise his name is sullied. Punishment of the wicked is therefore inevitable and, since the physical bodies have turned to dust, the disembodied spirit is punished; since a spirit is eternal (even a dead spirit lives – the living dead) the punishment must be without end. To reject the tender mercies of God and turn a cold-shoulder to a pleading of Christ is something the person does to himself ... not something that is done to him. God is not to blame. The hardhearted sinner can only blame

---

578 Rev 1:20
579 John 3:19-21
580 Acts 13:46
581 Heb 10:29

himself. If he would turn and obey, he would be forgiven and not be hurt of the second death.[582]

The seven angels receive seven "golden bowls full of the wrath of God." The anger of Jehovah does not overflow the bowls but it does fill them to the brim. The plague of punishment shall not be partial nor mitigated, but will be full and overpowering. God has patiently waited with outstretched arms to receive the sinners home and they looked with disdain on every manifestation of his mercy. Now the bridegroom comes, the door is shut and locked and no one else is to be admitted. It is the stroke of midnight and for the impenitent it is too late.

The scene is solemn. The door of the "temple of the tabernacle of the testimony in heaven was opened." The seven angels make an impressive entrance all dressed in regal garments as representatives of the Almighty would require. Notice they came from the place of meeting and the presence of God, indicating his authority and participation in the terrible reckoning. The books are ready to be balanced and the ends of justice and holiness are about to be served. This strikes us as grave and regretfully serious, but the day God has appointed in which he will "judge the world in righteousness" has arrived. The last trumpet has been heard. The season of forgiveness is past and the time for recompense has come.

The seven angels in all their splendor will receive the bowls of wrath and pour out their brimming contents upon the calloused followers of the devil all crusted over with sin and shame. It is an awful thing to behold. The day of God's great wrath has come, "and who is able to stand."[583]

One of the four living creatures (the guardians of the throne) gives the seven bowls of wrath to the seven angels. It is the fury of the Lord "who liveth forever and ever." Amen!

The temple was filled with smoke, indicating the presence of the Creator, Governor, Sustainer, and, now, the Executioner. The seven angels are his agents. The time has come to balance the books and it will not be denied.

The "smoke from the glory of God" reminds us of the presence of the Lord at Sinai, the cloud by which the chosen people were led in the wilderness after their deliverance, the descent of God at the dedication of Solomon's

582 Jer 27:13; 38:20; Ezek 18:31; 33:11; Prov 8:36
583 Rev 6:17

Temple, and the smoke of his being when Isaiah was consecrated to his frightful prophetic duties. This was not an idle moment. The blaze of the Heavenly Father's glory is about to be seen this one, last, final time. It is marked by grave sedateness and earnest sobriety. There is no sign of joy upon any face. It is something that must be done or the very name of God is sullied, but it gives him no pleasure. The burnished feet of Jesus will trample upon all those who had treated him, his love, his cross, his blood, and the sacrifice he offered "through the eternal spirit" with indifference.

> *none was able to enter into the temple,*
> *till the seven plagues of the seven angels should be finished.*

Wrath of God; It is done
Revelation 16:1-21

The grand scheme of God marches on. We have reviewed the first fifteen chapters of this superb writing and are enthralled by its revelation of the heart of God and alarmed by the rank evil of the devil. It is the blazing story of the ageless war between truth and falsehood and shocks us by its insistence that the vast majority of humanoids on earth persistently vote for things that are morally reprehensible and, in consequence, fill the earth with shame and sorrow. On the other hand, the valorous few that are fully committed to the path of purity and peace and whose only purpose is to bring the souls of mortals into unspeakable joy seek to fill the earth with the saving power of the word of God. So, there is confrontation and conflict.

We come now to the chapter that describes the ultimate corruption that will befall the godless sons and daughters of Adam and Eve. First, let us again look back to mark the path from the terrible sacrifice of the sinless Son of God to the moment when all earthly things are lost in the intense flames of divine judgment and condemnation.

- The opening chapter describes the might and majesty of the lone Nazarene
- The second and third chapters consist of letters Jesus wrote to seven churches
- The fourth and fifth chapters give us vision of the throne of God
- The sixth chapter tells of the breaking of the seven seals of a little book

- The seventh chapter reveals that salvation is offered to all, but few accept
- Chapters eight, nine and ten tell of the sounding of the warning trumpets
- Chapter eleven describes measuring the temple, altar and the people
- Chapter twelve tells about a woman, a dragon and a child; the formation of the kingdom
- Chapter thirteen speaks of godless government and false religion
- Chapter fourteen reports the transport of virgins to glory and the failure of materialism
- Chapter fifteen is an introduction to the bowls of wrath

You have no doubt noticed the story of the "good fight of faith" revolves around the seven seals, the seven trumpets and the seven bowls filled with the wrath of God. We are now told in blistering language of how the revelers on the "broad way" are horror stricken to witness the final judgment of justice and holiness. The seventh trumpet has sounded and the full-blown anger of God is on display.

The bowls filled with the unrelieved anger of the Almighty are poured out in either rapid succession or simultaneously upon the defenseless heads of the damned. Those who visited great misery on the innocent have that suffering boomerang on them; their joy over the suffering of the virgin-saints backfires and brings them to bitter tears and justified fears.[584]

The roaring, thunderous voice of God that has power to make the earth shake, rends the rocks into pebbles, removes the mountains and the islands out of their places is heard to the alarmed dismay of the inhabitants of the earth (there were no saved on the earth at the time of this incredible destruction because all the inhabitants of earth had been converted to the worship of Satan and his ugly dogs).

---

584 Eccl 10:8 – "He that diggeth a pit shall fall into it; and whoso breaketh through a wall, a serpent shall bite him."

Verse 1

And I heard a great voice out of the temple,
saying to the seven angels,
Go ye, and pour out the seven bowls of the wrath of God into the earth.

The majestic, powerful, irresistible voice of God makes this terrible proclamation. It is not done with joy but this sad disappointment. "The Lord is ... longsuffering to you-ward, not wishing that any should perish, but that all should come to repentance."[585] This is a lesson about the constitutional goodness of God, though he is denied, ignored and denigrated, he restrains his righteous indignation and allows men to exercise their free agency by lining up in rows to cast down goodness and burn their children in the fires of Baal. It grieved God[586] to see his human creatures turn themselves over to the devil's losing cause.

At the time of the Noachian flood there were about one and a half billion people on the earth,[587] but only 8 found safety in the ark. All the rest died in the flood waters.

Now, at the end of time, none is found to have favor in the sight of the Lord and his destructive wrath sees their boundless wickedness and commands the bowls of wrath be hurled into the earth.

The command is, "Pour out the seven bowls of the wrath of God into the earth." The seven dreadful bowls represent the finished wrath of God. Peter's first century prophecy will be fulfilled. "The Lord is not slack concerning his promise ... the day of the Lord will come as a thief; in the which the heavens shall pass away with a great noise, and the elements shall be dissolved with fervent heat, and the earth and the works that are therein shall be burned up. Seeing that these things are thus all to be dissolved, what manner of persons ought ye to be in (all) holy living and godliness, looking for and earnestly desiring the coming of the day of God, by reason of which the heavens being on fire shall be dissolved, and the elements shall

---

585 2 Pet 3:9; Luke 24:47; Mark 16:16; John 3:16
586 Gen 6:6
587 Calculated by the author on the basis of a 1,000 year timeframe when life expectancy was almost 900 years and disease was rare; to work this out month by month and generation by generation yields this surprising but reasonable number.

melt with fervent heat? But, according to his promise, we look for new heavens and a new earth, wherein dwelleth righteousness."[588]

The awesome event will be swift, unannounced, irresistible, fearful, destructive and final. When "the day of the Lord" does come the earth and all that is in it will be consumed … it will melt with "fervent heat" and there will be no mercy. The somber warnings of God have long been discounted by the inhabitants of the planet earth and now he withdraws his offer of grace. Like the five foolish virgins the wicked of the world will only be able to blame themselves and face the horrible fact that the closed door will not be opened.

For all the slaves of Satan it is now too late. Too late!

The saved are standing serene by the sea of glass.[589] The last believer on earth has closed his eyes in death, or is promoted to indestructible peace, and there is none righteous left on earth; no, not one.

Observe the pouring out of the first four bowls containing the steaming anger of an outraged and rejected God.

Verses 2

And the first went,
and poured out his bowl into the earth;
and it became a noisome and grievous sore upon
the men that had the mark of the beast,
and that worshipped his image.

The same order is followed that marked the sounding of the first four of the seven warning trumpets.

The first angel, in obedience to the command of God, poured out his bowl upon the earth and all who wore the mark of the beast and worshipped his image, that is, all humans on the earth – the totality of them – were beset with painful sores that are described as noisome, grievous, harmful, foul, loathsome, ugly, malignant, evil, horrible, stinking, disgusting, bad and poisoning.

---

588 2 Peter 3:9-13
589 Rev 15:2

The Holy Spirit in transmitting this message to John and to us uses uncommonly strong language to impress upon us the misery in which these unbelievers found themselves.

Again, worshippers of the Dragon suffer, not the saints who stand with the souls of all just men made perfect on an evergreen shore eating fruit from the tree of life and all other trees in the heavenly garden of God, whose leaves are for healing, and whose fair fruit always hangs ripe.

Verse 3

And the second poured out his bowl into the sea;
and it became blood as of a dead man;
and every living soul died,
even the things that were in the sea.

The second bowl caused the waters of the seas of earth to become coagulated blood and all marine life dies. The oceans of earth provide a large part of the human diet and if the fish are gone then humanity would be in peril of starvation. Mankind and his home are being wiped out so it does not matter that they have nothing to eat, except it expresses their vulnerability. God made it and He can destroy it. That is the lesson.

Verse 4-7

And the third poured out his bowl into the rivers
and the fountains of the waters;
and it became blood.

And I heard the angel of the waters saying,
Righteous art thou,
who art and who wast,
thou Holy One,
because thou didst thus judge:

for they poured out the blood of the saints and the prophets,
and blood hast thou given them to drink:
they are worthy.

And I heard the altar saying,
Yea, O Lord God, the Almighty,
true and righteous are thy judgments.

The third bowl is poured on fountains and sparkling rivers that provide potable water for man and beast and it is turned to blood; it is no longer drinkable and animal life cannot continue in the absence of drinking water. Again, God gave the refreshing water to man at creation and now he removes it. When land-bound rivers and lakes turn to blood man can no longer drink from the streams of water.[590]

Bear in mind that this does not happen over time but instantly because the bowls of wrath are poured out quickly.

As the consequence of the third bowl strikes the earth the angel of the waters praises God and declares that his judgment of punishment is appropriate; it is what it ought to be. As this transpires the saved, having overcome, lift up their voices, saying, "Great and marvellous are thy works, O Lord God, the Almighty; righteous and true are thy ways, thou King of the ages. Who shall not fear, O Lord, and glorify thy name? for thou only art holy; for all the nations shall come and worship before thee; for thy righteous acts have been made manifest."[591]

The angel of the waters points out that those tattooed on their foreheads with the mark of the beast and who scoff at God and his word "are worthy" to suffer the destruction of their habitat and receive the everlasting punishment that has been so long delayed. They are receiving the recompense of their reward.[592] It is not something done to them but something they did to themselves. It is the payoff of wickedness; it is reaping the corruption they, themselves, sowed.

> *Be not deceived; God is not mocked: for whatsoever a man soweth, that shall he also reap. For he that soweth unto his own flesh shall of the flesh reap corruption; but he that soweth unto the Spirit shall of the Spirit reap eternal life.*[593]

If the hot wrath of God is not finally poured out on the heads of those who deserve to be punished, then his holiness and justice are imperfect and he is not God. It is the pay they deserved for their lawlessness ... for "lawlessness is sin."[594] It is vile for a mere mortal to vainly sit in judgment

590 Psa 78:44
591 Rev 15:3-4
592 Isa 62:11
593 Gal 6:7-8
594 1 John 3:4

upon God and pronounce him bad because the just recompense of sin is paid out to those who wade through the murky mire of sin.

When a judge pronounces sentence on a criminal for some disgusting act he may condemn the judge by saying, "You did this to me." When the simple truth is that he did to himself.

The angel of the waters says of the wretched of earth at the end time, "They are worthy."

They got what they had coming to them. They earned their condemnation and their punishment is deserved.

Recall that "the souls of them that were slain for the word of God" cried out from under the altar, "How long, O Master, the holy and true, dost thou not judge and avenge our blood on them that dwell on the earth?"[595] The answer is now given. The earth, being barren of all righteousness, is destroyed. It was made to support human life and now it is ruined by the force and effect of sin and so it is utterly cast down.

Sinfulness brings its own destruction and has within it the seeds of hopelessness. Every immoral act has a repercussion in the natural realm with eternal consequences.

John Donne (1572-1631) wrote as he was meditating on his sickness:.

> "All mankind is of one author, and is one volume; when one man dies, one chapter is not torn out of the book, but translated into a better language; and every chapter must be so translated...As therefore.... this bell calls us all: but how much more me, who am brought so near the door by this sickness....No man is an island, entire of itself...any man's death diminishes me, because I am involved in mankind; and therefore never send to know for whom the bell tolls; it tolls for thee" (Meditation *XVII, 1624*).

Verses 8-9

And the fourth poured out his bowl upon the sun;
and it was given unto it to scorch men with fire.

---

595 Rev 6:10

And men were scorched with great heat:
and they blasphemed the name of God who
hath the power over these plagues;
and they repented not to give him glory.

The fourth bowl of wrath is poured out upon the sun and people on the earth are scorched with fire. In the days of Noah, shortly after the great flood, Jehovah made a promise that "while the earth remaineth, seedtime and harvest, and cold and heat, and summer and winter, and day and night shall not cease."[596] That sacred promise does not fail but is faithfully kept. As long as the earth remained, seedtime, harvest, day, night, planting and reaping would continue. The wrath of God poured out upon the sun brings an end to seasons, time and space; night, planting and reaping are no more; therefore the earth cannot and does not continue.

A preview of the ultimate end of God's creation is given in Revelation chapter six. When the Lamb broke the sixth seal "*there was a great earthquake; and the sun became black as sackcloth of hair, and the whole moon became as blood; and the stars of the heaven fell unto the earth, as a fig tree casteth her unripe figs when she is shaken of a great wind. And the heaven was removed as a scroll when it is rolled up; and every mountain and island were moved out of their places.*"[597]

The entire universe collapses as if suddenly sucked into an enormous black hole whose gravitational pull could not be denied. The starry host of heaven disappears in the blackness caused by the loss of heavenly lights. The "father of lights" has called the nocturnal illuminators into oblivion, bringing profound darkness. In the process of removing the habitation of man people still on the earth are scorched as with fire. The sun blazes up and burns out and people suffer from the unbearable heat, followed by insufferable blackness.

The terrible day of retribution continues, bringing the fierce wrath of an angry God and demonstrating that "God is not mocked" and while he does not wish "that any should perish," still, the very nature of his purity and impartial justice demands this "just recompense of reward." Sow evil, reap corruption.

---

596 Gen 8:22
597 Rev 6:12-14

The judgment scene continues:

Verses 10-11

*And the fifth poured out his bowl upon the throne of the beast;
and his kingdom was darkened;
and they gnawed their tongues for pain,*

*and they blasphemed the God of heaven because
of their pains and their sores;
and they repented not of their works.*

The foundation of the throne of the beast crumbles and the dismal darkness becomes even deeper. It is suffocating. The authority and dominion of the rank rebels disappears and the futility of serving the dragon and his beasts is apparent, and the unspeakable pain forces the champions of lawlessness to chew their tongues as if the sharp pain would cause the wounds to diminish; but, lo, it was not to be and they had to relief from their frightful disappointment and misery. Their naked nerve endings were rubbed raw and the boundless aching became inexpressible.

The unexpressed but implied thought is that even at this late stage God's mercy could be accessed and his grace might yet somehow bring relief. The evil enemies of truth could not bring themselves even in this extremity to acknowledge God and ask for the surcease of their sorrow and beg solace for their unfathomable distress. Their blindness and lostness and insensible hardness caused them to persist, untouched by either love or grief.

There was no turning back for these haters of God and despisers of his precious word; instead of logically reconsidering thy blasphemed the name of God and cursed him in the full-face of his glory, demonstrating their awful degradation and intellectual decadence. They were as bad as they could be and could not get any worse. They blamed God, excused themselves and "repented not of their works."

Verses 12-16

*And the sixth poured out his bowl upon the great river,
the river Euphrates; and the water thereof was dried up,
that the way might be made ready for the kings that come from the sunrise.*

And I saw coming out of the mouth of the dragon,
and out of the mouth of the beast,
and out of the mouth of the false prophet,
three unclean spirits,
as it were frogs:

for they are spirits of demons, working signs;
which go forth unto the kings of the whole world,
to gather them together unto the war of the great day of God, the Almighty.

(Behold, I come as a thief.
Blessed is he that watcheth,
and keepeth his garments,
lest he walk naked,
and they see his shame.)

And they gathered them together
into the place which is called in Hebrew Har-Magedon.

The sixth bowl was upon the Euphrates river, which had long protected nations on its west side from invaders from its east side. A few armies had been able to penetrate across the Euphrates, but not many. It represented a shield from exposure, injury, damage, or destruction. The sixth bowl of wrath dried up the Euphrates this wall of safety was stripped away and the people were defenseless and helpless.

There is a parallel between the sixth bowl of wrath and the sixth warning trumpet. When the sixth warning trumpet sounded "the four angels that are bound at the great river Euphrates …. were loosed;" and a great bizarre army riding bizarre horses ("I saw the horses in the vision, and them that sat on them, having breastplates as of fire and of hyacinth and of brimstone: and the heads of lions; and out of their mouths proceedeth fire and smoke and brimstone;" "The third part of men" were " killed, by the fire and the smoke and the brimstone, which proceeded out of their mouths.")[598]

"[A]nd they repented not of their murders, nor of their sorceries, nor of their fornication, nor of their thefts."[599]

---

598 Rev 9:12-19
599 Rev 9:21

When these blind and senseless rebels were immersed in the full fury of the Heavenly Father's wrath they did not have enough judgment to quit a fruitless and futile path and turn to the obedience of faith.[600] Their stiff necks made repentance impossible for them; a sinner can be so steeped in sin that he cannot decide to change.[601] His inability to decide to change makes him incapable of change, for to change one must first decide to do so. Heaped up sin has rendered him impervious to the overtures of grace. He is caught in the trap of his own making. The uplifted Christ means nothing to him. He has no sense of sorrow or shame and it is therefore impossible for him to repent. Godly sorrow works repentance: the sorrow of the world works death.[602]

The icon of demons is a frog, ugly and productive of no good thing. The three frogs come out of the mouth of the Dragon, who is Satan[603]; and who is the patron of the sea-beast and the land-beast. The three frogs represent three demons (the devil, godless government, and all false religion), a body of three blind governors leading the blind, with their uncircumcised ears and hardened hearts, to a "rendezvous with death."

John mentions specifically that the demons were "working signs." These were false signs like the sorceries of Simon of the city of Samaria[604] used to deceive the gullible. The dragon and his ugly dogs also worked what appeared to be miracles, but were not demonstrations of divine might.[605] They were deceptive works of the devil and not signs as from God. Paul warns against such "signs" when he talks of the coming of "the lawless one:"

> (even he), whose coming is according to the working of Satan with all power and signs and lying wonders, and with all deceit of unrighteousness for them that perish; because they received not the love of the truth, that they might be saved.
>
> And for this cause God sendeth them a working of error, that they should believe a lie:

---

600 Rom 1:5; 16:26
601 Heb 6:6
602 2 Cor 7:10
603 Rev 12:9
604 Acts 8:9-11
605 Rev 13:14-15; Rev 19:20

that they all might be judged who believed not the truth, but had pleasure in unrighteousness.[606]

Powerful rulers have been often deceived by the "Rasputins"[607] at their elbows and rush into unwise programs without good council from God fearing advisors.

The warning of the swift coming of the Anointed One of Jehovah, which immediately follows, may be an indication that these "signs" are the fabrications of bad magistrates whispering into the ears of corrupt government officials.

The final bowl is about to be poured out in this vision of John but, though warning flags are flying and warning trumpets have sounded, the leaders and the peoples of earth are oblivious to the inevitable destruction coming upon the universe. We are again told that Jesus will come "as a thief," but the watchful will not walk naked in shame.[608]

The gathering to Har-Megedon is at hand. The deceived earth-sovereigns follow the devil and his agents into the inescapable destruction into which the broad way leads, fulfilling the lemming myth of mass suicide (blindly following a leader to destruction). The high and mighty are sometimes also the blind and stupid, leading the ignorant masses.

Har-Megedon[609] is not a specific geographic location; it is symbolic. We are reading a book that abounds in figures and symbols and we are reading about "the good fight of faith," which is also symbolic. It is not a literal, carnal war, but deals with matters of the spirit that are unseen. It would be absurd to assign a symbolic war to a specific, literal place.

Chapter nineteen will tell us more about the unseen, spiritual battle between the invisible forces of good and the seven-headed dragon, his beasts, and their lemming-like followers. It is a spiritual war conducted in a spiritual place by disembodied spirits. It is an actual clash of good and evil, but it is not literal; therefore, "Har-Megedon" is not literal. It is vain to search for a physical mountain or valley or city or nation called "Har-Megedon." It is not a tangible region. This is why long years of research

606 2 Thess 2:9-12
607 Grigory Yefimovich 1872-1916 Russian mystic
608 Matt 24:36-51
609 This is the only time the word is used in the Bible

have not yielded information about a palpable Har-Megedon. It does not exist; geography is not a concern.

Still, the death-struggle between Satan and Jesus is real, though invisible to mortal eyes. It will determine the destiny of truth, light, life, love, hope, and the church (the people of God). It is the climatic hour of the good fight of faith. John now reports the result of the pouring out of the seventh bowl.

Verse 17

And the seventh poured out his bowl upon the air;
and there came forth a great voice out of the temple,
from the throne, saying,
It is done:

When Jesus surrendered himself a sacrifice for the sins of humanity and as he was about to command his eternal spirit to leave his lifeless, fleshly body, he said, "It is finished."

He had accomplished the work God gave him to do and was made perfect.[610] His work of offering himself for the sins of the world was finished, but what was finished at Calvary continued in his resurrection, exaltation, mediation and intercession. He has not ceased to work on behalf of this loyal followers, officiating as High Priest of their confession.[611]

Now it is different. The human drama is played out and the awful, thunderous voice from the throne of God powerfully proclaims "it is done."

The universe is no more. In the pouring out of the seven bowls full of the wrath of God everything is gone. Everything! Earth, water, sun are all destroyed and the loud voice of God announces that the universe is no more. "It is done."

Still, there is a continuation because while mundane things will cease, we shall live eternally either in perfect bliss or in deep regret. Two states continue endlessly:

---

610 Heb 5:8-9
611 Heb 2:17-18; 4 14-16; Rom 8:32-39

"Blessed are the dead who die in the Lord from henceforth: yea, saith the Spirit, that they may rest from their labors; for their works follow with them."[612]

> A man that hath set at naught Moses' law dieth without compassion on the word of two or three witnesses: of how much sorer punishment, think ye, shall he be judged worthy, who hath trodden under foot the Son of God, and hath counted the blood of the covenant wherewith he was sanctified an unholy thing, and hath done despite unto the Spirit of grace? For we know him that said, Vengeance belongeth unto me, I will recompense. And again, The Lord shall judge his people. It is a fearful thing to fall into the hands of the living God.[613]

Verses 18-21

and there were lightnings, and voices, and thunders;
and there was a great earthquake,
such as was not since there were men upon the earth,
so great an earthquake, so mighty.

And the great city was divided into three parts,
and the cities of the nations fell:
and Babylon the great was remembered in the sight of God,
to give unto her the cup of the wine of the fierceness of his wrath.
And every island fled away,
and the mountains were not found.

And great hail, every stone about the weight of a talent,
cometh down out of heaven upon men:
and men blasphemed God because of the plague of the hail;
for the plague thereof is exceeding great.

The great voice of God sealed this prophecy and certified it with demonstrations of divine power. The abundant proof was beyond measure and confirmed the fact of God and an unseen estate, but was lost on these blind, perverted foolish ones.

---

612 Rev 14:13
613 Heb 10:28-31

"The heavens" passed away "with a great noise."[614] The atmosphere of earth where birds fly, and the space between earth's atmosphere and the abode of God where the stars shine were ripped away and the noise was deafening. Earsplitting!

The destruction of the universe was attended by an earthquake surpassing all earthquakes of history, and hailstones of incredible size. All designed as more convincing proof that this was none other than the hand of God and the horn of his altar. Surely, all rational creatures, living and dead will tremble and believe.

> *".... God highly exalted him, and gave unto him the name which is above every name; that in the name of Jesus every knee should bow, of things in heaven and things on earth and things under the earth, and that every tongue should confess that Jesus Christ is Lord, to the glory of God the Father".*[615]

The great city (unnamed at this point in the vision) was split into three parts. (The next chapter will identify this city.) It was divided, conquered and brought to destruction and ruin (united we stand, divided we fall). The entire material universe evaporated. This terrible wreck is described in the next two chapters.

Across the corridors of time the voice of Jesus is heard, saying, "Work not for the food which perisheth (is perishing), but for the food which abideth (is abiding) unto eternal life, which the Son of man shall give unto you: for him the Father, even God, hath sealed."[616]

The towering mountains that seem so durable will melt in fervent heat but God's word does not, will not, cannot fail. It is everlasting and therefore cannot be destroyed. It can be resisted, refused, disobeyed, but it shall never cease. Never! Never!

It may appear to be killed but it will rise again. It may seem impotent but the all-seeing eye of the Lord God watches over it and it will never perish. It is the bread from heaven the which, if a man eat thereof shall finally make him immortal and he shall stand, clothed and unashamed in the judgment.[617]

---

614 2 Pet 3:10
615 Phil 2:8-11
616 John 6:27
617 Matt 24:35; 1 Pet 1:23; 1 John 1:17

Enormous hailstones, each one weighing about a hundred pounds, fall randomly upon the people of earth with deadly force.

> The shock and awe of the events of the last days of earth
> ought to cause the people to turn their tear-stained faces
> to God, but instead they blaspheme his holy name.

THE GREAT HARLOT
REVELATION 17:1-18

Jesus offers to scrub[618] the unrighteous; those who refuse the cleansing process are neutralized and banished; their sins separate them from God[619]. They rejected the purifying process and the consequence is compulsory removal. Christ held out to them in his nail scarred hands the priceless gift of redemption and, strange to behold, they had the arrogant boldness to turn their backs to his gracious offer.

> For many walk, of whom I told you often, and now tell you even weeping, that they are the enemies of the cross of Christ: whose end is perdition, whose god is the belly, and whose glory is in their shame, who mind earthly things.[620]

> Wherefore also God highly exalted him, and gave unto him the name which is above every name; that in the name of Jesus every knee should bow, of things in heaven and things on earth and things under the earth, and that every tongue should confess that Jesus Christ is Lord, to the glory of God the Father.[621]

The story is told. The book is finished. The door is shut. All who have been washed and made clean in the blood of the Lamb stand unashamed in the presence of the Lord of all lords and the King of all kings. The frightful end of all material things is at hand and the lovers of truth are about to be

---

618 Mal 3:2
619 Isa 59:1
620 Phil 3:18-19
621 Phil 2:9-11

promoted to a well deserved glory and stand with a mighty host ... ("just over in the glory land.")

With bare, hushed feet we reverently approach the apex of the fight of faith, knowing that "he that overcometh" shall see God and be like him.[622] That is what the Bible is all about and therefore it is what the book of Revelation is about. The picture is painted in bright hues; the finish is conveyed in the compelling imagery of poets and prophets, but is understandable and appealing, this "wonderful story of love" and holiness.

The account of the history of the world flows like this:

- God and his agents prepare for the fight of faith; the followers of the Lord are named; it is possible for us (anyone) to be in that number

- Seven seals are broken revealing the contents of a "little book" and announcing the beginning of the spiritual war between righteousness and unrighteousness

- Seven warning trumpets tell, symbolically, of the heartbreak of war; as the warning trumpets are in the process of giving notice of the consequence of disobedience we have several interludes, or sidebars, that fill in some of the details

- Seven bowls of wrath are poured out upon an unbelieving world and the consequence of evil is noted with care[623]

There follows the outpouring of the wrath of God[624] an allegory of a celebrated and attractive prostitute. Since it is an allegory, an interpreter is required.

In this study we have appealed to the Bible and ordinary sense to explain and understand what we read. The new covenant of Jesus tells us "Wherefore be ye not foolish, but understand what the will of the Lord is."[625] There

---

622 1 John 3:2

623 This amazing story is built around a series of three sevens: 7 seals, 7 trumpets, 7 bowls

624 The seven bowls of wrath utterly remove the material universe, therefore the discussion in chapters 17-18 deals with the inhabitants of earth immediately prior to the total collapse of the universe

625 Eph 5:17

are two choices: (1) understanding and (2) being foolish; there is no other alternative.

The Bible is mostly written by common men. It is not required that we have extraordinary preparation to understand the scriptures. There are some things in the Bible that only time will tell (as was the case with some of Daniel's prophecies[626]) but for the most part the teaching of God's word is plain and average people can understand it.[627] Deut 30:14: *"But the word is very nigh unto thee, in thy mouth, and in thy heart, that thou mayest do it."* Let no one beguile you into thinking that a specially prepared expert is necessary for you to know what God requires of you, except for the allegories and riddles in the Bible that are meant to challenge us and hold our attention.

Still there are some deep things in the Bible that demand serious and diligent study. The deep things of God are not in the area of commands. Commands demand obedience and you cannot obey what you do not understand. Therefore God has arranged his revelation to the human family so that we can understand its commands.

> Isn't it strange that Princes and Kings
> and Clowns that caper in sawdust rings,
> and common folks like you and me,
> are builders for eternity?
>
> By: R.L. Sharpe

The laws of God are not riddles, but are couched in clean, clear, concise language.

Yet there are allegories in the sacred scriptures that must be correctly interpreted by some being that is prepared by divine sanction to give an explanation. That is always the case with allegories. For instance, no one would understand who or what Sara and Hagar represent in Paul's allegory[628] of the two women given in the book of Galatians if the inspired writer had not given us that information.[629]

---

626 See, for example, Dan 12:9

627 Deut 30:12-13

628 Gal 4:4:21-31

629 Some, but not all, of the parables of Jesus are also allegories and must be explained (see Luke 8:9-10). Other parables given by the Lord require no such interpretation to be grasped (Matt 21:45)

Some things in the allegory of the seductive prostitute in this chapter of Revelation must be interpreted to be understood, so God sent to John an angel interpreter.[630]

There are some things in the allegory that can be understood without the need of special help but there are also some things that would never be understand in the absence of such help.

Let us turn to the chapter and study its teaching.

Verses 1-2

And there came one of the seven angels that had the seven bowls,
and spake with me, saying,
Come hither,
I will show thee the judgment of the great harlot
that sitteth upon many waters;
with whom the kings of the earth committed fornication,
and they that dwell in the earth were made drunken
with the wine of her fornication.

The interpreter-angel tells the apostle that he is about to "see" the "judgment of the great harlot."[631] In explaining this evil woman (think Jezebel) the angel says he is telling of the "judgment of the great harlot that sitteth upon many waters." Take notice of the word "waters."[632] This vulgar woman seduced earthly rulers and made many citizens of the world drunk with the deceptive, intoxicating beverage of her impurities.

The word translated "fornication" (*porneias*) is a general term meaning "all unlawful lust," including idolatry; it includes every item in the entire catalogue of sexual sins, including lasciviousness (filthy words, indecent

---

630 Rev 17:1, 7, 15

631 The KJV uses the word "whore;" the ASV and most other translation use the word "Harlot," but "prostitute" is also a good translation. She was attractive, lewd and rotten from center to circumference, a most dangerous combination; she was filthy and full of contagious diseases but made herself appear to be beautiful. No one would commit sin if he saw its true nature from the beginning

632 The angel-interpreter gives an explanation that will enlighten us about *what Mystery, Babylon the Great, the Mother of the Harlots and of the Abominations of the earth* is, but we will have to be patient for a little while for that information.

bodily movements, licentiousness, unchaste handling of males and females). Fornication covers all sexual impurities.

This ungodly woman of the streets was sin-sick from sole to crown and there was no soundness in her. Befitting her position as the cohort of the devil, she beguiled the unthinking and led them as her blind slaves into the darkness of sin, perversion and perdition. Her followers are volunteers.

Verses 3-5

And he carried me away in the Spirit into a wilderness:
and I saw a woman sitting upon a scarlet-colored beast,
full of names of blasphemy, having seven heads and ten horns.

And the woman was arrayed in purple and scarlet,
and decked with gold and precious stone and pearls,
having in her hand a golden cup full of abominations,
even the unclean things of her fornication,

and upon her forehead a name written,
MYSTERY, BABYLON THE GREAT,
THE MOTHER OF THE HARLOTS
AND OF THE ABOMINATIONS OF THE EARTH.

John's experience of being "carried away in the Spirit" is reminiscent of Jesus being "led up of the Spirit into the wilderness to be tempted of the devil." As a part of the temptation of Jesus he was shown the kingdoms of the world and their riches and was told he could have all of it if he would worship Satin. The kingdoms of the world must have passed before him in panorama. In the same way, John was carried into the wilderness to be given a comprehensive mental picture of a woman sitting upon a scarlet-colored beast, full of names of blasphemy.

The beast is especially repulsive with his red hide into which every imaginable ungodly and filthy word is tattooed. The skin of this scarlet beast was like the walls of some public restrooms where the spiritually detached display their total moral decay and abandonment of all decency. It is a rattrap for the ignorant. Senseless people are drawn to such garbage; sensible people, being sickened by it, turn away in disgust.

The woman riding on the back of the crimson beast is adorned with expensive jewelry, precious metals and luxurious robes, the pay for selling her soul to Satan. She had an outward beauty but an inward ugliness. She is deceptive beyond words, but that is to be expected since she is the pawn of the evil one. The devil, you will remember, is the "father of lies."

Lawlessness has to dress its putrid nature with artificial decorations. If the true nature of unrighteousness were advertised no one would be foolish enough to buy into it.

It is like the fisherman's hook that is covered with colorful ribbons, streamers and trinkets so the fish does not know the hook is there until it is sticking into his bleeding mouth. That is what the champion liar does in hiding the true nature of sin until the fools of earth are captured and shackled by the tricks of his trade. It is only when the sinner is tightly bound by habit and misdirection that he begins to know that wickedness is a cruel master and that he is a helpless slave. Every person who has been addicted to some sin knows how hard it is to regain his self control. Thank God that Jesus came to set the sinner free, if the sinner only has sense enough to claim his liberty by "obedience of faith."[633]

Her name is written on her forehead reveals that she is the mother of total depravity and corruption. She is a veritable stink of "death unto death,"[634] and the source of everything that is bad and repulsive.

This utterly corrupt woman is "drunk on the blood of the martyrs."

God's angel, having set the scene, now begins an explanation of the allegory.

Verse 6

And I saw the woman drunken with the blood of the saints,
and with the blood of the martyrs of Jesus.
And when I saw her, I wondered with a great wonder.

John did not understand; he was confounded, amazed and filled with immeasurable marvel. It was a state of bewilderment that called for an inspired interpretation.

---

633 Rom 1:5; 16:26; James 2:14-26
634 2 Cor 2:16

Verses 7-8

7 And the angel said unto me,
Wherefore didst thou wonder?
I will tell thee the mystery of the woman,
and of the beast that carrieth her,
which hath the seven heads and the ten horns.

8 The beast that thou sawest was,
and is not;
and is about to come up out of the abyss,
and to go into perdition.
And they that dwell on the earth shall wonder,
they whose name hath not been written in the book of life
from the foundation of the world,
when they behold the beast,
how that he was,
and is not,
and shall come.

The angel performs his office of explaining the meaning of the various items in the allegory of the prostitute. He does this over several verses, so we must be patient as we listen and learn. The woman and the beast with seventy horns will be identified in due course.

The beast on whose back the sinful woman rides is the epitome of evil and is merged gradually with another wicked power through a continuous series of intermediate forms. They are interrelated and signify the immensity of their power and the depth of their wickedness. The multiplied horns symbolize the great strength of the beast who serves the evil woman as her transport, but they are all a part of the whole system of ungodly works which they have ungodly wrought.

From the beginning of this magnificent vision Jehovah, Jesus, the Holy Spirit and John have been describing the great-war effort. Running through the whole of this awesome prophecy is the story of the "good fight of faith." It absorbs our attention, commands our respect, and reveals our destiny. A war must have at least two sides and this one clearly does. They are the evil empire of Satan and his imps and the kingdom of God with Jesus as commander-in-chief leading a bright army of virgins who have been washed and made clean by the blood of the Lamb.

John brings the army of God into view when he speaks of the broken souls that are redeemed by the Mighty Maker of the heavens and the earth and all that is in them. The saved of earth are a type of they whose name has "been written in the book of life from the foundation of the world" and are alluded to in verse eight. True, he references "they whose name" is not written in that book, but by implication cites all those whose name is written in that blessed book.

All those whose name is written in the Lamb's book of life are embraced in this comment. Who are they? Did God know them by name, face, and personality from before the creation of the universe? No, nor is such a conclusion necessary. God planned before "times eternal."[635] He is not saying that God knew each one individually, but foreknew all who would be saved by their faith and obedience. If he marked out before the birth of any of them all those who would overcome and be more than conquerors as individuals, then he would be a respecter of persons, which he emphatically is not.[636] God did, however, predetermine a plan for the saving of sinners.[637] All who obey this plan are called, saved from past sins, and added to the church, which is the kingdom of God.[638] Their names are written in a heavenly register and were known of God from before the foundations of the world. Again, it is not that God knew each one personally and individually, but appointed that all who obey the predetermined plan would thereby lay hold on eternal life.

Those who comprise one of the armies in this grand fight of faith did have their names written in the book of life; the opposing army did not have their names written in that enduring book. These are the two armies that fight to the death in this ongoing war.

John calls our attention to the resiliency of the army of the great red dragon. He comes, he is not, he comes again; this process is repeated in all human history. This is also true of the forces of the good and the pure. *"That which hath been is that which shall be; and that which hath been done*

---

635 Rom 16:25; 1 Tim 1:9; Titus 1:2

636 Deut 10:17; Acts 10:34; Rom 2:11; Eph 6:9; 1 Pet 1:17

637 The plan includes hearing the revealed word (Rom 10:17); believing (Heb 11:6; John 3:16); repentance (Luke 13:3-5; Acts 2:38); confessing Jesus as Lord (Rom 10:9-10; 1 Tim 6:12); baptism to be saved (Mark 16:16; Acts 22:16); followed by a godly, clean life (Rev 3:10). That is the plan and reveals some of the steps leading to the gates of glory.

638 Eph 1:18-23; Col 1:18-23

is that which shall be done: and there is no new thing under the sun.[639] That is, "no new thing" done by man, instead there is a monotonous repetition. Habits prevail.

Verse 9

9 Here is the mind that hath wisdom.
The seven heads are seven mountains,
on which the woman sitteth:

The mind that hath wisdom must diligently meditate to understand the figure of the great harlot. Verse one says the woman "sitteth upon many waters," and now we are told she sits on "seven heads," which "are seven mountains." It follows that the "waters" on which she sits are also "seven heads," which are "seven mountains." So the many waters, seven heads and seven mountains are different symbols describing the great harlot, which is Mystery Babylon. The interpreter angel has yet to tell us who this woman is, but she is represented by several symbols – waters, heads, and mountains.

Verse 10

10 and they are seven kings;
the five are fallen, the one is, the other is not yet come;
and when he cometh, he must continue a little while.

The seven heads, seven mountains, and the many waters are seven kings, so we have another symbol added to the list of figures that apply to Babylon the Great, Mother of Harlots. She is symbolized by waters, heads, mountains, and kings, indicating the complexity of this shameless woman. This should alert us not to be fooled by a simple explanation of who is this godless prostitute.[640]

---

639 Eccl 1:9

640 It seems strange that many commentators see this book as highly figurative, but attempt to make these kings the literal emperors of first century Rome. When they begin counting, they run into many problems. Suetonius names twelve Caesars (Julius, Augustus, Tiberius, Gaius, Claudius, Nero, Galba, Otho, Vitellius, Vespasian, Titus, and Domitian). Manipulate them as you will, there is no way to be true to history and reconcile these men to the description given in the book of Revelation. It becomes even more complicated if you take the writing

> *11 And the beast that was, and is not, is himself also an eighth,*
> *and is of the seven; and he goeth into perdition.*

To hammer this statement into a description of the rulers of Rome does violence to the text. The apostle plainly tells us that he is discussing "the beast." Who would that be? Well, "the beast" is a symbol for the totality of godless governments, philosophy, theology and also represents all lawlessness.[641] The beast would be inclusive of all of the ungodly rulers of all time and exclusive of none of them. The Holy Spirit is showing us a picture of the sum total of all ungodliness that has ever been, is now, or ever will be. The entire mix of moral corruption will go in time into perdition.

> *12 And the ten horns that thou sawest are ten kings,*
> *who have received no kingdom as yet;*
> *but they receive authority as kings, with the beast, for one hour.*

To further enhance the message and forestall a mistaken conclusion, the inspired writer talks about "ten kings, who have received no kingdom as yet. That ought to put to rest the idea that this vision is dealing exclusively with the kings of Rome, or any other one specific nation or government. Ten, like seven, often symbolizes completeness or the whole of a matter; ten multiplied by seven would carry this image to perfection.

The ten kings, representing the bad world-leaders of all time, would receive their day in the sun, with the beast, but would soon be swallowed by dust and gloom. They come and they go. Who are they? Answer: Godless rulers of all ages; ten here epitomizes all corrupt government of the entire dispensation of earth.

Verse 13

> *13 These have one mind,*
> *and they give their power and authority unto the beast.*

---

of Plutarch into account and cope with the rulers of Rome that preceded Julius (Marius, Sulla, Crassus, Pompey, Caesar [who preceded Julius], and Cicero). It is impossible to shoehorn the facts of the history of Rome into the description John gives of the allies of the dragon, who is also a beast. It is best to recognize that the apostle John is talking in a figure about evil rulers of all time and we shall see this works out marvelously in the balance of what John tells us.

641 Lawlessness is sin – 1 John 3:4; 2 Thess 2:7

Ungodly kings, presidents, parliaments, and congresses are single-minded; their one ambition is to empower the beast, representing the consolidation of all godless civil proceedings of all time. It is a broad sweep.[642]

Verse 14

14 These shall war against the Lamb,
and the Lamb shall overcome them,
for he is Lord of lords, and King of kings;
and they also shall overcome that are with him,
called and chosen and faithful.

The vision gives the outcome of the gigantic struggle between truth and falsehood, between good and bad, between purity and corruption. The dragon, beasts, prostitute, and all unbelievers are going to be defeated. Jesus and his white robed army will win. They will be "more than conquerors."

Verse 15

15 And he saith unto me,
The waters which thou sawest,
where the harlot sitteth,
are peoples, and multitudes, and nations, and tongues.

Verse one of chapter seventeen tells us MYSTERY, BABYLON THE GREAT, THE MOTHER OF HARLOTS AND OF THE ABOMINATIONS OF THE EARTH is sitting upon "many waters;" and now he gives a full explanation of "the waters which thou sawest." The waters, according to the interpreter angel, are "peoples, multitudes, nations, and tongues." Notice the plurals. Not one people, multitude, nation, and tongue, but many. It is the whole conglomeration of sordid, putrid, stinking evil of all time; the accumulation of bad government and wrongheaded religion from the first breath of Adam to the sounding of the seventh trumpet. It is a composite mass of all the sin the world has ever known or ever will know. It is every evil population center from Eden to the final judgment; it is the embodiment of everything that is ugly and

---

642 There are some good men in government, but they are few; John is not talking about them but about the evil magistrates of earth.

251

vile; every city, every ruler, every citizen of earth who is given to satanic devotion and the abomination of idolatry.

Let us recap the allegory: the interpreter angel transports John to a wilderness (where is not important ... it was a place of solitude). In this lonely setting the apostle is shown a vision of a woman riding a scarlet beast who is covered with blasphemous names; she is clothed luxuriously in purple and scarlet and adorned with gold ornaments and pearls and holds a golden cup containing the impurities of her fornication; she leads the deceived to worship things, stuff, and junk (Jehovah is ruled out) and unseen spiritual reality is ignored; on her forehead is her identification: Mystery, Babylon, mother of harlots, mother of earthly abominations; the woman is drunk with the blood of martyred saints. She is the mother-superior of all harlots. Her power is her wantonness and the appeal of pleasures and treasures. Sin and flesh dominate the fools who say there is no God.[643]

Her steed is a beast that was and is not that will ascend but be present and that came out of the abyss and is doomed to destruction and eternal damnation.[644] The beast is Satan and his cohorts. John gives an overview of history; powerful leaders rise and fall yet there is always another villain to step in the shoes of the fallen; no specific king or kingdom is intended – it is a composite of the depraved monarchs of all generations and, in keeping with this figure, he holds supreme rule of a composite of all nations, kingdoms, and peoples of the world.

The mother of harlots and the powerful of the earth combine to fight against the Lamb of God and his adherents, but the Lamb shall overcome them because he is King of kings and Lord of lords.[645]

The next chapter reiterates the fall of Mystery Babylon, the wicked woman, and all corrupt leaders, which comes about as the last tone of the seventh trumpet fades.[646] It is an allegorical presentation of "the good fight of faith," and ought to thrill the souls of the saints.

The message is that "whatsoever a man sows, that shall he also reap."

---

643 Rom 6:14-16
644 See Rev 17:8, 11
645 Rev 17:14
646 This was described in chapter sixteen

Verse 16-17

16 And the ten horns which thou sawest,
and the beast, these shall hate the harlot,
and shall make her desolate and naked,
and shall eat her flesh,
and shall burn her utterly with fire.

17 For God did put in their hearts to do his mind,
and to come to one mind,
and to give their kingdom unto the beast,
until the words of God should be accomplished.

Lawlessness carries within it the seeds of its own destruction. "Righteousness exalteth a nation; But sin is a reproach to any people."[647] There is no honor among thieves. Eventually, but too late, the customers of the great harlot will turn against her and destroy her. This was acted out in Ezekiel's allegory of Oholah and Oholibah (Israel and Judah).[648] Their own lovers turned against them and took away nose, ears, sons, daughters, stripped away their clothes and jewels. "And they shall recompense your lewdness upon you, and ye shall bear the sins of your idols; and ye shall know that I am the Lord Jehovah."[649]

Verse 18

And the woman whom thou sawest is the great city,
which reigneth over the kings of the earth.

Here is the answer we have been looking for ... the enticing prostitute, riding the back of the scarlet beast, "is the great city" (Mystery Babylon). She also symbolizes vice of every description and is the figure of not just one evil but of many. The angel interpreter tells us plainly "the woman whom thou sawest is the great city." The "great city" has to be not one certain city but all centers of crime and moral depravity throughout time. It is a composite of all the sinful towns of human history. She represents Nineveh, Tyre, Damascus, Old Babylon, Athens, Rome, Jerusalem, San Francisco, Las Vegas, London, Paris, Amsterdam, Washington D.C.,

647 Prov 14:34
648 Ezek 23:24-49
649 Ezek 23:49

Houston, and Slippery Rock. All populations centers tend to corruption and all are represented by the great prostitute (sin) riding on the back of the devil. A militant force seeking to prevent peace, good, purity and truth. She mindlessly wages war against the King of kings; she is destined to damnation.

REVELATION 18:1-23

Fall of Mystery Babylon

The book of Revelation, written by John at the appointment of Jehovah, Jesus, and the Comforter, may be summarized to this point as a history of man on earth, from beginning to end, and the fierce (sometimes violent) struggle between the truth of God and the lies of the devil.

- It begins with a strong, sharp , intense impression on our senses of the aggrandizement of Jesus and the potent, great, white throne of God – chapters 1-5

- Seven seals are broken to reveal the contents of a "little book" (the Bible) and give us a more perfect understanding of the why and wherefore of creation. The four horsemen are introduced signifying the beginning and progress of "the good fight of faith, which is a spiritual contest between good and evil, between right and wrong, between truth and falsehood. The sixth seal reveals that it will all end with the elimination of material things and the ascendency of spiritual reality – the seen versus the unseen. The seventh seal reveals the intensity and intrepidness of this real but non-carnal battle – chapters 6-7.

- Seven trumpets sound warning after warning of the afflictions and torment that will be suffered by human inhabitants of the entire world from the start of this contest to its conclusion; this is an inescapable reminder that "in the world ye have tribulation," and in this battle of Armageddon (it stretches from the inauguration of the war to the destruction of the universe). All along the writer interjects footnotes and sidebars commenting on various aspects of the fight and the participation of demons in the wrestling between the combatants. It makes us aware that there is no neutrality in this spiritual war but everyone is on one side or the other; after long delay the seventh trumpet sounds – chapters 8-11.

- Seven bowls full of the wrath of God are poured out upon the earth, bringing the entire universe to wreck and ruin – chapters 12-17.

This brings us to chapter 18 where is described the loud lamentation of all those who were wedded to the world when they saw and felt the fall of all things material; Jesus warned against laboring for the "meat that perisheth," and advised his followers to labor for the meat that endures to eternal life.

Let us contemplate the shock the misguided suffered when they saw their idols go up in smoke.

Verses 1-2

After these things I saw another angel coming down out of heaven,
having great authority;
and the earth was lightened with his glory.

And he cried with a mighty voice, saying,
Fallen, fallen is Babylon the great,
and is become a habitation of demons,
and a hold of every unclean spirit,
and a hold of every unclean and hateful bird.

The darkened earth was lighted with the splendid glory of this angelic being. The aim of this statement uttered by his mighty voice is to confirm that the universe has come to its termination, which was the inevitable result of wickedness heaped high. The destructive flood of Noah's day was a forecast of the far more devastating consequence of the pouring out of the bowls of wrath.[650] God's triumph over evil will be accomplished.

The earth and the material universe are blasted into oblivion and fit only for the habitation of unclean spirits and hateful birds of prey. The vultures

---

650 2 Pet 3:1-12

perch in their towers but there is no carrion for them to consume. All is silent. All is reduced to smoke and ashes.

Verse 3

For by the wine of the wrath of her fornication all the nations are fallen;
and the kings of the earth committed fornication with her,
and the merchants of the earth waxed rich by the power of her wantonness.

This, again, is an indictment of the fallen world's worthlessness. The overwhelming majority of the world's inhabitants turned away from their benevolent maker and in their lawlessness and drunkenness (fornication and wine) made themselves wretched.[651] They walked the broad way that leads only to destruction. John is looking by divine empowerment to the end of time and boundaries, watching as the fools of earth walk over the cliff and into a Christless eternity.

The voice of God, expressed in his certified written revelation, though loud as thunder in their ears, is ignored by those who are mesmerized by covetousness. The world has a tough time focusing on spiritual reality and obeying the Law of the Lord.

God so loved the world that he sent his son to graciously invite them to enjoy the riches of his boundless kingdom and the world killed his one-of-a-kind son. "How shall we escape, if we neglect so great a salvation? which having at the first been spoken through the Lord, was confirmed unto us by them that heard; God also bearing witness with them, both by signs and wonders, and by manifold powers, and by gifts of the Holy Spirit, according to his own will."[652] The purpose of Jesus in walking this vale of shadows and tears was to invite sinners to the immaculate feast of God rich blessings:

---

651 John speaks of all nations for all time – from start to finish. All nations throughout the earth's generations taunted the Mighty Maker. Greed caused them to toil only for meat that will not last. It is perishing meat and most of the inhabitants of the earth do not have the wit to see it, nor the courage to confess it. Revelation 18:3 is a commentary on the seven heads and 10 horns of Revelation 17:9-13, and clearly says the figure of 7 heads and 10 horns symbolizes "all nations," which agrees with Matthew 25:31-32.

652 Heb 2:3-4

Verse 4

And I heard another voice from heaven, saying,
Come forth, my people, out of her,
that ye have no fellowship with her sins,
and that ye receive not of her plagues:

The speaker is not identified, but it is obvious that he is Jesus calling the people of earth to repentance and salvation. Hear his voice: "Come unto me, all ye that labor and are heavy laden, and I will give you rest."[653] Again, "Now on the last day, the great day of the feast, Jesus stood and cried, saying, If any man thirst, let him come unto me and drink."[654] Hard hearted and sinful men, so attracted by earth's silver and gold and unwilling to prize the true riches, make themselves blind and deaf, and will not hear him and, therefore, do not obey him and consequently seal themselves to flames of destruction.

As he was on his way to Calvary, Jesus said, "O Jerusalem, Jerusalem, that killeth the prophets, and stoneth them that are sent unto her! how often would I have gathered thy children together, even as a hen gathereth her chickens under her wings, and ye would not! Behold, your house is left unto you desolate. For I say unto you, Ye shall not see me henceforth, till ye shall say, Blessed is he that cometh in the name of the Lord."[655] John is retelling the story of Jesus and his love and of how the slaves of Satan heard his offer of mercy and threw it back in his face. He is reminding us that the majority of the people on the earth will continue to defy God and refuse the gracious gifts of Christ right down to the moment when the seventh trumpet sounds and the door is shut; and it is too late.

Verse 5

for her sins have reached even unto heaven,
and God hath remembered her iniquities.

The aged apostle who had suffered much because of his loyalty to Jesus takes note of the magnitude of the iniquity of the population of the world. God so loved the world that he gave his son to die that the world might

653 Matt 11:28
654 John 7:37
655 Matt 23:37-39

have the possibility of eternal salvation, and his goodness was repaid by indifference and rejection; his unrequited love, expressed in abounding sinfulness, "reached even unto heaven" and offended the eyes of God.

Verse 6

Render unto her even as she rendered,
and double unto her the double according to her works:
in the cup which she mingled,
mingle unto her double.

The enormity of sin was monstrous and outrageous and the repayment was to double the size and weight of the world's sinful indifference. The world must now drink from the cup of the wrath of God which is prepared unmixed in the cup of his anger. The unrestricted anger of God, whose nature is love, is a terrible thing to see and a more terrible thing to bear.

Verse 7

How much soever she glorified herself,
and waxed wanton,
so much give her of torment and mourning:
for she saith in her heart,
I sit a queen, and am no widow,
and shall in no wise see mourning.

The Great Harlot was a first rate narcissist and that caused her to plunge even deeper into the flood waters of lust and extravagant sensuality. It was impossible for her to reform, seeing she had no appreciation for purity and reason. She was past the point of no return; she could not be induced to abandon her evil ways. The only thing she could understand was grief and misery and a benevolent God was compelled by her misbehavior to "give her of torment and mourning." She proudly boasted that she was invincible, ruling like royalty, and being invulnerable, incapable of being conquered, defeated, or subdued. Not helpless and defenseless like the average widow but strong and untouchable like the queen of a lionhearted king. She was confident that she would never know sorrow.

Verse 8

Therefore in one day shall her plagues come,
death, and mourning, and famine;
and she shall be utterly burned with fire;
for strong is the Lord God who judged her.

This boastful, impudent, shameless, morally unrestrained woman holds her head high and despises all others ... until her least expected retribution of punishment falls suddenly upon her. The warning signs were everywhere but she was oblivious to reason and sense and plunged full force into the atomic power of divine punishment that reckless sin inevitably brings. "Strong is the Lord God who judged her." We are reminded of the Master's admonition, "Watch therefore: for ye know not on what day your Lord cometh."

Verses 9-10

And the kings of the earth,
who committed fornication and lived wantonly with her,
shall weep and wail over her,
when they look upon the smoke of her burning,
standing afar off for the fear of her torment,
saying, Woe, woe, the great city, Babylon,
the strong city! for in one hour is thy judgment come.

"Babylon," of course, is symbolic of all evil empires. The Babylons of the world are sensual and materialistic, resulting in atheism and unbridled lawlessness, which is sinful. Babylon is wicked in every fiber of her being and sin seeps from every pore. She is sinful from top to bottom and from side to side. She gives her full attention to iniquity and "every imagination of the thoughts of his [her] heart was only evil continually."[656] She was preoccupied with the prospect of immoral adventures and ever thinking of new ways to do wrong things.

When the trumpet of all ages is heard and the destruction of the universe is set in order and prosecuted by the mighty hand of God, the godless people of the world give vent to loud lamentation and their wails of insupportable grief echo and re-echo through the corridors of a disintegrating materialistic system.

---

656 Gen 6:5

It was created good, but became one hundred percent vile, and this demanded its destruction in fervent heat. It was a matter of self-destruction or mass suicide; from a glorious beginning to a cataclysmic end.

The rapidity with which the end came is noted in the wailing and surprised observation of the devil's devotees that "in one hour is thy judgment come." These disappointed and confused supporters of the dragon, the beasts, the demons and the great harlot got as far away from the crumbling universe as possible, but there was no place for them to go. Wherever they ran the encircling wrath of the Lord God was there. His divine fury was inescapable.

Their dismay and despair was recorded in an earlier description of the final day, when John wrote: *"And the kings of the earth, and the princes, and the chief captains, and the rich, and the strong, and every bondman and freeman, hid themselves in the caves and in the rocks of the mountains; and they say to the mountains and to the rocks, Fall on us, and hide us from the face of him that sitteth on the throne, and from the wrath of the Lamb: for the great day of their wrath is come; and who is able to stand?"*[657]

Verses 11-13

And the merchants of the earth weep and mourn over her,
for no man buyeth their merchandise any more;

merchandise of gold, and silver, and precious stone,
and pearls, and fine linen, and purple, and silk, and scarlet;
and all thyine wood, and every vessel of ivory,
and every vessel made of most precious wood,
and of brass, and iron, and marble;
and cinnamon, and spice, and incense, and ointment,
and frankincense, and wine, and oil, and fine flour,
and wheat, and cattle, and sheep;
and merchandise of horses and chariots and slaves;
and souls of men.

The merchants of earth are not individually identified but are lumped together and dealt with as a whole. A particular company is not named because, as in dealing with rulers, the intent is to deal with merchants as a class and for all time. These sellers of earthly treasures are business

---

657 Rev 6:15-18

men who know how to drive a bargain and make a profit. Their eyes tell them that all of the precious things of a material world are now taken away and the merchants are broke and out of business. A salesman who cannot move his merchandise, or maybe has no merchandise to move, is out of business and without income. They were so tied to earth and uncaring of eternity that when their goods were destroyed in fire they concluded that the situation had no remedy and they were moved to tears and grief. It lasted but for a moment because they were all shortly to be called to judgment and consigned to eternal separation from God and his family and therefore from the tree and the water of life. All they could do was wring their hands and moan for they had rejected the invitation of Jesus.

Verses 14-16

And the fruits which thy soul lusted after are gone from thee,
and all things that were dainty and sumptuous are perished from thee,
and men shall find them no more at all.

The merchants of these things,
who were made rich by her,
shall stand afar off for the fear of her torment,
weeping and mourning;

saying, Woe, woe, the great city,
she that was arrayed in fine linen and purple and scarlet,
and decked with gold and precious stone and pearl!

These crafty buyers and sellers continue to lament losing their inventory and being naked and exposed. They had not learned the sinfulness of covetousness and its companion sins of greed and misrepresentation and suffered the consequence of their ignorance. These merchants had compromised themselves for gain and now understand that silver, gold, pearls, and dainties have no value in an estate that is purely spiritual. Silver and gold are nothing in the final fires but molten metal and it will turn to smoke, heat, ashes and dust. The only things that count are the enduring things of God, which are the true riches.[658]

---

658 Rev 3:17-19

Verses 17-19

for in an hour so great riches is made desolate.
And every shipmaster,
and every one that saileth any wither, and mariners,
and as many as gain their living by sea, stood afar off,

and cried out as they looked upon the smoke of her burning, saying,
What city is like the great city?

And they cast dust on their heads, and cried,
weeping and mourning, saying,
Woe, woe, the great city,
wherein all that had their ships in the sea were made rich by
reason of her costliness! for in one hour is she made desolate.

The quickness of the fall of materialism and commercialism astounded these merchants and mariners and they could hardly believe their eyes. The economic system of the earth has been destroyed and its adherents had nothing left. They had put their hope in material things and when it is stripped from them and they are without hope or purpose. To be hopeless is to be robbed and empty, having nothing to live for and without God. All their dreams are monstrous nightmares …. empty, vacant, blank, void. They had put their trust in material things and fire had reduced those things to glowing vapor. They danced with a ghost and came up with a handful of nothing but a slow mournful dirge.

Verse 20

Rejoice over her, thou heaven, and ye saints, and ye apostles, and ye prophets;
for God hath judged your judgment on her.

Mystical Babylon falls and the saints in heaven rejoice. The brokenhearted merchants and the bereft shipmasters are plunged into deep misery because they not only trusted in earthly riches but had also financed the great red dragon and the sin laced woman and were a vital part of the God-deniers and Bible haters. They had been cruel and vicious, in their opposition to the church they joined the mother of all abominations in drinking themselves drunk on the blood of the saints.

The entire godless and lawless mob had over all the centuries poured out their contempt on the children of God and had defied the heavenly father.

The wicked of all time persecuted the innocent of all ages. The headless spirits of the blessed dead who die in the Lord cry out from under the altar in heaven, saying, "How long, O Master, the holy and true, dost thou not judge and avenge our blood on them that dwell on the earth?"[659] Now, the time has come for the righteous dead to be avenged and the godless of earth to be punished.

The people of God shall have a part in the judgment of the people of the devil; as God sends the wicked away to eternal punishment, the saints shall say, "Yea, O Lord God, the Almighty, true and righteous are thy judgments."[660]

The enemies of God, their hands stained red with the blood of the martyrs, are brought face-to-face with the realization that all earthly things shall pass away and only spiritual reality shall endure. The things of God are eternal and all else is worthless illusion. So, when the recompense of reward comes down on "the kings of the earth, and the princes, and the chief captains, and the rich, and the strong, and every bondman and freeman,"[661] the pure in heart rejoice. The guilty are punished and the redeemed are rewarded. The tables are turned on the agents of evil and the saints are made forever happy and satisfied.

Verses 21

And a strong angel took up a stone as it were a great
millstone and cast it into the sea, saying,
Thus with a mighty fall shall Babylon,
the great city, be cast down,
and shall be found no more at all.

The great millstone hurled into the ocean and sinking beneath the waves signifies the irrecoverable downfall of mystery Babylon. It is poetic imagery describing the finality of the destruction of sin and its fruit.

Verses 22-23

And the voice of harpers and minstrels and flute-players
and trumpeters shall be heard no more at all in thee;

---

659 Rev 6:10
660 Rev 16:7; 1 Cor 6:2-3
661 Rev 6:15

and no craftsman, of whatsoever craft, shall be found any more at all in thee;
and the voice of a mill shall be heard no more at all in thee;

and the light of a lamp shall shine no more at all in thee;
and the voice of the bridegroom and of the bride shall be heard no
more at all in thee: for thy merchants were the princes of the earth;
for with thy sorcery were all the nations deceived.

The planet earth and all that is in it will cease. It will be, as Jeremiah said of old Babylon, "a destruction and astonishment." Every star will be put out and every moon will end. The material universe will vanish in fervent heat and all books will be brought to a final balance.

This type of language is used by Isaiah, Jeremiah, and Ezekiel to describe devastation and ruin.[662] The prophetic verbiage used here is so striking and powerful that no commentary is needed, and, in fact, would only serve to lessen the force of this colorful description of the finality and totality of the material and mortal economic system. It is pure eschatology, showing the ultimate destiny of mankind. It is a gigantic conclusion, an end beyond which there is no other end.

VERSE 24

And in her was found the blood of prophets and of saints,
and of all that have been slain upon the earth.

In mystery Babylon was found the blood of "all" that have been slain upon the earth. There is no one certain city or time of which it can truly be said that in it is the blood of all who have been murdered, which is an added reason to understand that John is writing not of a particular, specific location but of a composite of all wickedness and shame for all time.

The hand of God lays at the feet of all who reject divine law and rebel against the authority of a Supreme Being the suffocating death caused by iniquity. It is a terrible indictment but a necessary and true one. According to Thayer the word translated "slain" means "to butcher, slaughter, to put to death by violence." It is a stunning way to close this chapter.

---

662 Isa 24:8-9; Jer 7:34; 16:9; 25:10; 33:10; Ezek 26:16

Rev 19:1-21

Victory In Jesus

The book of Revelation begins with an intense picture of Jesus in his preeminence, of Jehovah on his throne, and the Spirit of Truth.[663] The entourage of the sacred Godhead is also brought into view consisting of twenty-four elders, four living creatures, and an innumerable host of heavenly messengers and servants,[664] joined by saints in Hades[665] and on earth; this mighty congress is the army of the Lord (Chapters 1-5)

Seven seals of a "little book" are broken revealing the plan of God for mankind. The first four seals open to our view four horses symbolizing the "fight of faith" (a war between good and evil, between truth and falsehood). It is, of course, a spiritual contest and not a carnal battle. The breaking of the fifth seal tells of those who were slaughtered for the word of God and the testimony of Jesus; these perfected martyrs cry, "How long, O Master, dost thou not judge and avenge our blood on them that dwell on the earth?" The breaking of the sixth seal is a forecast of the coming end of time and final judgment. The seventh seal introduces seven trumpeter angels (Chapters 6-8).

Seven trumpets sound in succession to warn of the tribulation that results from the fight over right and wrong. The sounding of each trumpet

---

663 Also known as the Holy Spirit, or Comforter
664 Good angels ministering to the Godhead
665 "Hades" is a transliterated Greek word; it means "unseen" or "the place of departed souls," whether saved or unsaved. In this sense, we all, the good and the bad, go into "Hades" at physical death; the saved and the unsaved are separated by a gulf that cannot be crossed. The righteous dead are comforted in "Hades" and the unrighteous dead suffer (See Luke 16:19-31).

reveals an aspect of the trouble and sorrow caused by disregard of the Law of God, which causes sin to multiply. There are several interludes that describe the warriors of evil and the damage they do to those who seek to show their love of God by careful obedience to his confirmed written word. Jesus said, "If you love me, you will keep my commandments" (Chapters 8-14).

Seven bowls of the wrath of God are poured out upon the sinful of the world; each bowl speaks of a particular phase of the judgment of God upon a totally sinful world. This section also has some interludes that show to the mind's eye dimensions of the war over morals and conduct and the various shades of judgment and punishment, which follow the tribulation that the warning trumpets of God announced. The vision shows us the calloused immorality of lawlessness under the figure of a great Harlot and her devotees and this leads to a discussion of the collapse of the universe (Chapters 15-18).

We now enter the last phase of this amazing book and are given a vision of the heavenly Jerusalem and the triumph of the noble band of brothers who overcame in the fight between the army of God and the army of the devil (Chapters 19-22).

First, we explore the rapturous jubilation of those who were washed and made clean in the blood of the Lamb of God and who were faithful unto death (Chapter 19).

Verses 1-3

*After these things I heard as it were a great voice of a
great multitude in heaven, saying, Hallelujah; Salvation,
and glory, and power, belong to our God:*

*for true and righteous are his judgments;
for he hath judged the great harlot,
her that corrupted the earth with her fornication,
and he hath avenged the blood of his servants at her hand.*

*And a second time they say, Hallelujah.
And her smoke goeth up forever and ever.*

The praise comes from the loud voice of a large number of unidentified people, but who obviously are the redeemed joined by celestial beings who witnessed the grace of God that "appeared bringing salvation unto all men"[666]

There is something for sinners to do to be cleansed by the powerful blood of the Lamb.

"And they overcame him because of the blood of the Lamb, and because of the word of their testimony; and they loved not their life even unto death."[667]

They overcame and received the warm welcome of God into eternal tabernacles and now exult as they taste the sweet victory that is in Jesus. They praise the name of God for "salvation" and "glory" (brightness) and "power."

This mighty multitude with powerful voices honor the one, true and living God, saying, his judgments are "true and righteous."[668] The root word for righteousness is "straightness," and means "doing right by obeying the law of the Lord." The standard for doing right is "every scripture inspired of God,"[669] which is the power that can make the man of God "perfect."

The wicked are cast down and the redeemed, having overcome, are promoted into unparalleled brightness. God is praised because it is by his wisdom and mercy that the obedient are given crowns that never fade.

The happiness is intensified as celestial beings join the redeemed of earth in a great jubilation.

Verses 4-6

And the four and twenty elders
and the four living creatures fell down
and worshipped God that sitteth on the throne, saying,
Amen; Hallelujah.

---

666 That is to say, "all men" (and all women) who in the obedience of faith submit to the commands of God to repent, be baptized and are faithful to the Lord even though threatened with physical death (Titus 2:11; Rev 2:20; 12:11).

667 Rev 12:11

668 1 Cor 6:2-3

669 2 Tim 3:16-17

And a voice came forth from the throne, saying,
Give praise to our God, all ye his servants,
ye that fear him,
the small and the great.

And I heard as it were the voice of a great multitude,
and as the voice of many waters,
and as the voice of mighty thunders, saying,
Hallelujah: for the Lord our God, the Almighty reigneth.

The war of light against darkness ends with light prevailing and darkness plunged into greater darkness. The light of truth and the darkness of falsehood cannot co-exist; they are mutually exclusive; wherever you have one the other is excluded. "God is light, and in him is no darkness at all."[670] So complicated is the human psyche that it may have light in some areas and darkness is other areas. When all is light, then the man of God is perfect in the sight of God. Such completeness can only be realized in Christ and is produced by the inerrant word of God.[671]

The New Testament speaks of the clash of light and darkness as the fight of truth and error. The persistent battle between knowledge and ignorance is the "good fight of faith."[672]

- *"[P]eople that "sat in darkness saw a great light" when Jesus began to teach*
- *It is impossible to serve God (light) and evil (darkness) at the same time*
- *When Jesus came "the light" appeared and the "darkness apprehended it not"*
- *"The light" came into the world "and men loved darkness rather than light"*
- *Jesus said, "I am the light of the world: he that followeth me shall not walk in darkness, but shall have the light of life"*
- *To walk in darkness is to walk in ignorance*

---

670 John 1:5
671 2 Tim 3:16-12; Heb 2:1-4; Rom 1:16
672 Matt 4:16; 6:23; John 3:19; 8:12; 12:35, 46; Rom 13:12; 2 Cor 4:6; Eph 5:8; 1 Pet 2:9

- *Jesus came "a light into the world;" "whosoever" believes on him shall "not walk in darkness"*

- *Paul was commissioned to "open" eyes, that Jews and Gentiles might "turn from darkness to light and from the power of Satan unto God, that they may receive remission of sins and an inheritance among them that are sanctified by faith" in Jesus*

- *"The night is far spent, and the day is at hand: let us therefore cast off the works of darkness, and let us put on the armor of light"*

- *Seeing it is God that said, Light shall shine out of darkness, who shined in our hearts, to give the light of the knowledge of the glory of God in the face of Jesus Christ*

- *"For ye were once darkness, but are now light in the Lord; walk as children of light*

- *"But ye are an elect race, a royal priesthood, a holy nation, a people for God's own possession, that ye may show forth the excellencies of him who called you out of darkness into his marvelous light"*

The fight may at times be within an individual,[673] and at other times it may be outside of the individual as he wrestles with forces of evil; the battle may be within groups such as the church or the community or the nation.

Darkness will be utterly defeated at the end of the age and the children of light will rejoice with rapture that has no parallel. This introduction to the nineteenth chapter speaks of the opening of the glory that is shared by the saved of all time. It is a happy day that never ends.

The celestial beings who are happy and at peace in the service of God join former inhabitants of the planet earth in a grand victory display. The twenty-four elders and the four living creatures fell down before God, saying, "Amen; Hallelujah." The army of the "Great I Am" vanquished the foe and stood justified and content in the presence of Jehovah, Jesus and the Holy Spirit, and saw them in their glory and was made like them.[674]

This imposing declaration of deliverance and victory is compared to the roar of many waters and loud peals of mighty thunders. All who have stood at the foot of a great waterfall and heard the waters crashing into the body of water, and all who have experienced a thunderstorm and have

---

673 1 Cor 9:27
674 1 John 3:2

been shaken by the terrible rumble of loudest thunder will appreciate this expression.

It will be awesome when the heavenly congregation praises the might of God as they bask in his brightness. That joyful sound is where the spirit directs our attention as it forcefully proclaims, *"Hallelujah: for the Lord our God, the Almighty reigneth."* The great harlot will lose her attraction and strength. Her debilitation shall be complete and the victory shout will ring through the corridors of space without end. "Blessed be Jehovah, the God of Israel, from everlasting even to everlasting. And let all the people say, Amen. Praise ye Jehovah."[675]

This jubilant, rapturous celebration of victory brings forth the invitation of Jehovah for the saved to attend the wedding of the Lamb and his bride, the church.

Verses 7-9

Let us rejoice and be exceeding glad,
and let us give the glory unto him:
for the marriage of the Lamb is come,
and his wife hath made herself ready.

And it was given unto her that she should array herself in fine linen,
bright and pure:
for the fine linen is the righteous acts of the saints.

And he saith unto me,
Write, Blessed are they that are bidden to the marriage supper of the Lamb.
And he saith unto me,
These are true words of God.

The saved are called to inexpressible, overflowing happiness. "The marriage of the lamb is come." Paul told the church of Christ at Corinth, "For I am jealous over you with a godly jealousy: for I espoused you to one husband that I might present you as a pure virgin to Christ."[676] Espousal (betrothal) is a commitment to marry. The betrothal, in many cultures, is a binding contract and can only be terminated by death or court action,

---

675 Psa 106:48
676 2 Cor 11:2

but it is not the same as marriage, which is even more restrictive than the agreement to marry. The church is called the bride of Christ because of the pledge to marry at the appointed time. At any rate, the long delay between betrothal and marriage ends with a wedding banquet. A detailed description of that feast is not given in the book of Revelation, but it will be a joyous occasion.

Marriage can be literal or figurative; it is always literal unless the context requires a figurative application. In this case, it is figurative (there is no way Jesus could "marry" the multiplied millions that the church will doubtless number when time is lost in eternity); not until then will the marriage supper of the Lamb and the church take place. It symbolizes perfect joy, a sacred covenant, and unblemished love. As we await the marriage of Jesus and his church, it is the duty of the church to keep herself pure and consecrated.

Notice that "the church makes herself ready" for the presence of the groom. She is to do something. She is to dress in fine linen, which is the lawful deeds of devotion and duty; the church is clothed in the "righteous acts of the saints." Such works glorify God

The virgin bride of Christ is dressed in good works (strict obedience to the Law of God). The church of Laodicea was counseled by the Lord to "buy" white garments. It is by her righteous acts that God is glorified and men are saved.[677]

Notice that "the church makes herself ready" for the presence of the groom. She dresses in fine linen, bright and pure, the lawful deeds of devotion and duty; the church is clothed in the "righteous acts of the saints." We are judged by the Law of God and our works,[678] and it is by conformity to the word of God that the church covers the "shame of her nakedness."[679]

The marriage of Jesus and the church will be an occasion of unspeakable gladness; the church in tribulation, affliction and persecution is to take heart and rejoice because of the promised joy. In the dark days of earthly woe the blessed bride of Christ rejoices.[680] She lifts the clear eyes of faith to the throne of the universe and to him who sits thereon and is unafraid and unashamed.

---

677 Matt 5:16
678 Rev 20:12
679 Rev 16:15
680 Rom 5:1-2

The Spirit through the pen of John sets down this clarion affirmation, "*These are true words of God,*" therefore "be faithful unto death." The saved have nothing to dread. In Christ we overcome, leading to final victory, upheld by the power of the Creator's own words. The "true words of God" give the saints a confidence that cannot be shaken and in all their trials they smile through their tears and look forward in the fullness of faith to that grand day when they sit down with the groom and seal their marriage contract.

Verse 10

And I fell down before his feet to worship him.
And he saith unto me, See thou do it not:
I am a fellow-servant with thee and with thy
brethren that hold the testimony of Jesus:
worship God;
for the testimony of Jesus is the spirit of prophecy.

John was so overcome by the tremendous events the visions had unfolded before his eyes and the teaching that had sounded in his ears, that he forgot himself and fell before the angel to worship him.

The heavenly messenger of God rebuked his behavior and commanded the apostle not to worship men or even the angels of Jehovah, but to worship God. We can and should give honor to whom honor is due among mortals, but not worship. It is unseemly to bow before men or angels but our actions and words that indicate superiority and praise must be reserved for God and for him only. To worship God is to put him first; to put God first is to worship him, declaring him to be the supreme good.[681] Jesus said we are to worship and serve the Lord God and him only.[682] To worship God includes putting him before all else; to serve him is worship.

It is astounding and should thrill us to know that we are fellow-workers with seraphim, cherubim, archangels and all of God's messengers, prophets and apostles, as we go about our labor in the vineyard of the Lord. Paul often told the brethren of the first century they were his co-laborers. Think of the wonder of the amazing fact that common folks, like you and me, are workers for eternity and stand shoulder to shoulder with all of God children in heaven and on earth. This concept is too weighty for our finite minds but

681 Matt 22:37; Mark 10:18
682 Matt 4 10

if some glimmer of it gets through to our spirit we should be impelled to put all that we have and are and our very lives also on the altar of heaven.[683]

Jesus is the burden of all prophecy. From Adam to John, the son of Zebedee, all the prophets point to Jesus. As we ponder the Old Testament we are overawed at the constant testimony of every act and word as pointing to the Nazarene who is elevated, admired and worshipped. Jesus is great beyond measure.

Now John is ready to show us the magnificent Christ in his power and glory.

Verses 11-13

And I saw the heaven opened;
and behold, a white horse,
and he that sat thereon called Faithful and True;
and in righteousness he doth judge and make war.

And his eyes are a flame of fire,
and upon his head are many diadems;
and he hath a name written which no one knoweth but he himself.

And he is arrayed in a garment sprinkled with blood:
and his name is called The Word of God.

To the wondering eyes of John there appeared from the open gates of heaven a white horse and its rider,[684] called "faithful and true," and his name is "The Word of God."

In the beginning was the Word,
and the Word was with God, and the Word was God.
The same was in the beginning with God.
All things were made through him;
and without him was not anything made that hath been made.
In him was life;
and the life was the light of men.
And the light shineth in the darkness;
and the darkness apprehended it not.[685]

---

683 Rom 12:1
684 Rev 6:2
685 John 1:1-5

The blood on his garments is not his own blood but the blood of his enemies. He comes from the awful war between God and the devil. The battles lines were drawn, the battle fought and the victory won. He sits his horse like a conqueror and his flaming eyes testify to his perfect knowledge. The many diadems symbolize triumphs and testify to the power of the living and active word of God.

He was a part of the First Great Cause and as the maker of all things has a perfect right to bring all things down. The unbridled anger of God is terrible to behold. The surpassing sin of Adam's descendents is an unwillingness to listen, learn and be thankful.

Jesus is word, light, life and hope. Without him earthy beings are nothing, but with him they are everything.

It is heart-rending to know that darkness rejected the light of heaven; light came "and the darkness apprehended it not" (shame on the darkness). The fault is in the beholder, not in the light. Be therefore careful how you look and hear and read; redeem "the time, because the days are evil."[686]

Verses 14-15

And the armies which are in heaven followed him upon white horses,
clothed in fine linen, white and pure.

And out of his mouth proceedeth a sharp sword,
that with it he should smite the nations:
and he shall rule them with a rod of iron:
and he treadeth the winepress of the fierceness
of the wrath of God, the Almighty.

Christ is King over all kings and is Lord over all lords; he, together with his Father and the Comforter, is supreme. The Godhead is without parallel, highest in rank, degree, quality, and enduring in war and labor. Besides them, there is none other. The glory-clad armies of heaven followed him.

Isaiah was given visions of God in his splendor and of Jesus in his power to redeem. With a few bold strokes he was able to describe the grandeur of Messiah and his victory over all foes. About 600 years before Christ was born in Bethlehem Isaiah said of him:

---

686 Eph 5:16

Who is this that cometh from Edom, with dyed garments from Bozrah? this that is glorious in his apparel, marching in the greatness of his strength? I that speak in righteousness, mighty to save.

Wherefore art thou red in thine apparel, and thy garments like him that treadeth in the winevat?

I have trodden the winepress alone; and of the peoples there was no man with me: yea, I trod them in mine anger, and trampled them in my wrath; and their lifeblood is sprinkled upon my garments, and I have stained all my raiment.[687]

This vivid description applies to other judgments of God, but culminates in his ultimate judgment that brings an end to tangible things of earth; it is the ultimate fulfillment of this forceful prophecy.

We look upon it with wonder and amazement but also with confidence and joy. Jesus made several mysterious appearances in the Old Testament and all of them give credibility of his redeeming function; He is "glorious in his apparel" and marches "in the greatness of his strength and announces that he is "mighty to save."

Salvation is what the kingdom of God, the Bible, and the church is about. To strike forgiveness and salvation out of the scheme is to render it impotent. The strength of the gospel message is the power of Jesus to save. We bow our heads, cast down our eyes, and confess with Paul, "I am not ashamed of the gospel: for it is the power of God unto salvation to everyone that believeth; to the Jew first, and also to the Greek."[688] If you get that, you get what Jesus is about and if you miss that, you miss the purpose of God.

With salvation's sweet song in your heart, you grasp the message of the book of Revelation and of the entire Bible. To understand the outcome of the "good fight of faith" is to understand the mystery of your life and the purpose of your existence.

Verse 16

And he hath on his garment and on his thigh a name written, KING OF KINGS, AND LORD OF LORDS.

---

687 Isa 63:1-3
688 Rom 1:16

The transcendent beauty and power of the sinless son of Jehovah and the incredibly wonderful gift of salvation he brings to the human race defies full comprehension. It is more than our poor human minds can fully understand; far above all that we can think or dream of; "Thanks be to God for his unspeakable gift."[689]

The Spirit is now ready to reveal through John the destruction of the dragon, the two beasts and of all who follow them. A momentous event.

Verses 17-18

And I saw an angel standing in the sun;
and he cried with a loud voice,
saying to all the birds that fly in mid heaven,
Come and be gathered together unto the great supper of God;

that ye may eat the flesh of kings,
and the flesh of captains,
and the flesh of mighty men,
and the flesh of horses and of them that sit thereon,
and the flesh of all men,
both free and bond,
and small and great.

An angel standing in the sun demands close attention. He heralds a message from eternity that reemphasizes the casting down of demons and punishment of earthly beings that have chosen to follow debasing things that insult the "Father of spirits." A disobedient and unworthy son is a shame to his father. Man's preference for darkness over light is not a small and passing thing with the God who gave him his spirit. The fact that the voice was loud underscores the importance of the message. Even the hard of hearing will hear this message.

Everyone who falls into the category of God deniers and defamers is in a barren wasteland, facing an exciting horror.

The birds flying in mid heaven are invited to feast on the decaying remains of those slain by the sword of righteousness. This is, of course, figurative and symbolizes those who suffer the second death. They are presented as dead soldiers, small and great, who fell in the field of battle, and suffered the

---

689 2 Cor 9:15

ignominy of being unburied. They include the high and mighty as well as the small and weak. God is not mocked, all who have made the terrible choice of following the dragon whose red hide is inscribed with every foul and filthy thing that can be imagined are the pile of carcasses comprising those who were forced, too late, to bow before Prince Immanuel and confess his name.[690]

The fact that these mid-heaven-flying-birds are summonsed to consume the corpses of those who were killed in the battle of Har Magedon shows them to be vultures and not song birds. The godless, rapacious dead are the putrefying flesh upon whom buzzards feed. It is disgusting and ugly, but helps us understand the "horror of a great darkness."

The powerful and the puny shall suffer this fate if they do not put God first in their lives. The entire spectrum of unbelieving creatures will be included, and being weak and pitiful will not make an exemption.

It is the inescapable wrath of God.

The deep humiliation and disgrace of being found fighting against God is etched in this portrait of the destiny of the unrighteous. The only way to be sure that we will stand is to turn to him who is "the way, the truth, and the life." No one comes to the heavenly Father but by Him. If we prove our love of Jesus by keeping his commands in life, we shall be unashamed when we stand before him in judgment.

This short passage is filled with red-letter warnings.

Verses 19-21

And I saw the beast,
and the kings of the earth,
and their armies,
gathered together to make war against him that sat upon the horse,
and against his army.

And the beast was taken,
and with him the false prophet that wrought the signs in his sight,
wherewith he deceived them that had received the mark of the beast
and them that worshipped his image:
they two were cast alive into the lake of fire that burneth with brimstone:

---

690 Phil 2:10-11

and the rest were killed with the sword of him that sat upon the horse,
even the sword which came forth out of his mouth:
and all the birds were filled with their flesh.

"The beast," in this passage, is the dragon otherwise known as Satan; he fights against the "Word of God" on his white horse, which is the role of the dragon. He is assisted by two other hideous beasts, but he is the leader. He is the wicked red dragon who is also a beast.

The evil one is ever concerned about destroying the full force of God's mercy and he can only do this by inveighing against the new covenant. He is supported by all who disrespect the Bible as absolute truth. Some do this wittingly and others unwittingly, but all who attempt to dilute the teaching of inspired scripture fall into this category.

The documentary hypothesis and all its ramifications are the present day curse that wrongs the Godhead and mankind by planting the seed of doubt and unbelief. The more informed in this camp demonstrate a basic and shameful dishonesty. Their fundamental lack of character permits them to stumble into promoting fraud and deceit. This is evident in their double-dealing behavior and unwillingness to openly, frankly and fairly answer questions and discuss issues. Were they aboveboard they would lose a following and generate opposition. So they hide behind a wall of secret maneuvering and shameful deceptions. They are not honest. The fate of the red dragon and his two agents is to be cast headlong into a lake of fire that is burning with brimstone. Not a pretty sight but one that is well deserved. They have no honor and have earned their punishment.

All the other followers of this dastardly, evil angel (Satan) are to be killed by the sword of the Christ of God and eaten by vultures. Their shame is magnified.

In the closing three chapters we are told of the glorious, eternal future of those who overcome.

The Thousand Year Reign
Rev 20:1-15

In earlier chapters, we have learned of the demands and disappointments of contending for the one faith, but also of the satisfaction of holding to God's unchanging hand and the comfort of the downy under-feathers of the Lord's mighty wings, so that even when we are battered and bruised we know the comfort of the bright hope before us.

We must never allow ourselves to become discouraged as we fight for the right and against the wrong; there is a danger of allowing our zeal for righteousness to ooze out of our fingertips and make us weary in well doing.

The Holy Spirit through the apostle John tells us of the tumult and the strife that is certain to come to those who love the Lord and soldier on in his army; there is a millennium of trials and tribulations that end at the beautiful gates of heaven when we are welcomed by the approving smile of Jesus.

- A quick sweep of human history as outlined in the book of Revelation begins with the majesty of Jesus (chapter 1) as he teaches the "hands of his church to war" and its "fingers to fight;"[691] the saints contend for complete obedience to the law of God (chapters 2-3);

- the glory and beauty of the throne of God and the marvel of his grace as he provides the gift of his unique son for the sins of the world; the breaking of the seven seals and the consequent

---

691 Psa 144:1

struggle between the good and the bad, sometimes called "the good fight of faith" (chapters 4-6);

- mercy and the possibility of forgiveness and salvation is extended to all humans (chapter 7);

- the sounding of the seven trumpets and the misery of the necessary fight between truth and error, including the work and nature of the church, the vicious opposition of Satan and his cohorts, the deceptiveness and corruption of evil, (chapters 8-15);

- culminated in the outpouring of the seven bowls of the wrath of God (chapter 16);

- the fall of materialism and covetousness and the casting down of every thought and imagination that is contrary to godliness (chapters 17-18);

- the victory of Jesus over all wickedness, the marriage of the Lamb, the bridegroom, and the church, the bride; and throwing the devil and his adherents into the depths of their richly deserved punishment (chapter 19).

That brings us to the threshold of the peace and joy that will be inherited by all those who overcome in the war between light and darkness. Chapter twenty is the beginning place for this description of the brightness and satisfaction of all those who walk in the footsteps of Prince Immanuel, which lead to the good and abundant life in its most attractive sense.

The chapter begins with a strong affirmation of the long fight between purity and filth; the writer looks back to view again the ground that has been covered.

Verses 1-3

And I saw an angel coming down out of heaven,
having the key of the abyss and a great chain in his hand.

And he laid hold on the dragon, the old serpent,
which is the Devil and Satan,
and bound him for a thousand years,

and cast him into the abyss,
and shut it,
and sealed it over him,
that he should deceive the nations no more,
until the thousand years should be finished:
after this he must be loosed for a little time.

The mission of this unidentified angel was to throw the Devil into the bottomless pit and seal it over him. God's revealed word has power to bind Satan. When the evil one tempted Jesus his arguments were made impotent by quotations from divine revelation.[692] Three times the Devil threw his fiery darts at Jesus and three times Jesus defended the honor of God by saying "It is written …"

The shield of faith was sufficient to protect against the best weapons the devil could use.

The written word of God is sufficient to cast down "imaginations and every high thing that exalts itself against the knowledge of God"[693] and cause Satan to flounder in sheer impotency. God made it possible for humans to bind Satan by giving them his written word. It is also possible for mortals not to use this mighty weapon and by their neglect of God eternal word to make themselves the dupes of the Devil, as every religious liberal does. Satan's influence waxes and wanes according to whether the sword of God's eternal word[694] is used or is allowed to rust. God gave us this powerful tool, but does not force us to accept it or use it.

We are told that Satan was bound for a thousand years, or a millennium. It is necessary to a correct understanding of this portion of the book of Revelation to know what the thousand years is. The Bible explains itself; it does not leave us in the dark, but is a "lamp" to our feet and a "light" to our path.[695]

The writer of the book of Revelation, John, also wrote one of the four gospels, and gives us a good commentary on the two deaths and the two resurrections. There is a first and second resurrection and a first and second

---

692 Matt 4:1-11
693 1 Cor 10:5
694 Eph 6:17
695 Psa 119:105

283

death[696]; understanding the millennium is contingent upon understanding the two resurrections and the two deaths.[697]

We shall walk through John's inspired statement one step at a time to have an understanding of the two deaths and the two resurrections, which will give us a basis to grasp the meaning of the millennium mentioned in the book of Revelation.

John 5:25

Verily, verily, I say unto you,
The hour cometh,
and now is,
when the dead shall hear the voice of the Son of God;
and they that hear shall live.

Jesus' "verily, verily" would call special attention to what he was about to say; it is equivalent to saying, "Pay attention," or "Listen closely." He then says two things:

- The hour is coming
- and (the hour) now is

Jesus preached a message of salvation and freedom from sin. He began his public teaching ministry at about the age of 30 immediately following his baptism and temptation. From the moment he came up out of the water of baptism his life took on a new focus, and he pursued with consecrated vigor his work of proclaiming the good news of reformation, redemption and reward. The kingdom of heaven was at hand.

For the next forty-eight months he gave himself to teaching the reality of a spiritual empire and the possibility of being a citizen in that marvelous community. Each step he took and each day he lived brought him closer to the moment he would lay down his life for the sins of the world. So, he said, "The hour is coming."

---

696 If there is a "first" resurrection there must be a second resurrection; if there is a second death there must be a first death

697 I am indebted to J. Marcellus Kik, a Presbyterian preacher, for calling attention to the relationship between Rev 20:1-6 and John 5:24-29 in his book *Eschatology of Victory*.

Amazingly, he adds, "and now is." That is, he was already teaching about serving God and saving man, but no one could receive the actual gift of washing away sins until Jesus closed this chapter of his earthly pilgrimage on the cross when he said, "It is finished," and made his blood available to all who would be saved; our sins are washed away in the blood of the Lamb.[698]

The hour is coming (it was only one breath away) and not only that but it now is. Jesus forgave sins in anticipation during his four year service of teaching the things of God, he therefore adds, in the certain expectation of the Lamb of God taking away the sins of the world, it "now is."

What grand and glorious things were on the near threshold? Jesus does not leave us uninformed on this vital point, but goes on to say, "the dead shall hear the voice of the Son of God and they that hear shall live."

- The dead will hear ...
- the hearing will live

"The dead" cannot reference physical death because there was no general resurrection of the physically dead during the personal ministry of Jesus nor has there been such a resurrection since he finished his work of providing on the cross the possibility of absolute forgiveness and eternal happiness; it has not happened. Therefore the word "death" in this verse must refer to something else.

The Bible speaks not only of a physical death but also of a spiritual death; a person can be spiritually dead but physically alive. Some in the first century were said to be "dead" while living.[699] The living dead ... dead in the spirit but alive in the flesh.

A dead physical body does not hear, yet Jesus said the hour is near and now is when the dead shall hear and they that hear shall live. This cannot in the nature of things be said of the physically dead, but must refer to those who are spiritually dead, but physically alive.

---

698 Rev 7:14
699 1 Tim 5:6

The New Testament tells us of some who were "dead in trespasses and sin."[700] "We know that we have passed out of death into life, because we love the brethren. He that loveth not abideth in death."[701]

Death is separation. If we transgress the Law of God, we are separated from God.[702] Spiritual death is the inescapable result of sin because it separates us from God, who is life. Physical death is the separation of the spirit from the body; when spirit leaves the body of flesh, soul goes with it and the body is dead; it is lifeless flesh because the life departed from the body when the spirit and soul departed.

The spirit dies when sin enters (not physical death but spiritual death). Jesus says, in the verse we are studying, that the dead (in sin) may be made spiritually alive again. "The Spirit of the Lord is upon me, Because he anointed me to preach good tidings to the poor: He hath sent me to proclaim release to the captives, And recovering of sight to the blind, To set at liberty them that are bruised,"[703]

When a sinner hears "the voice of the Son of God," saying, "He that believeth and is baptized shall be saved; but he that disbelieveth shall be condemned,"[704] and "in the obedience of faith"[705] is ""buried therefore with him through baptism unto death: that like as Christ was raised from the dead through the glory of the Father, so we also might walk in newness of life."[706] We are resurrected from the burial of baptism to a new life.

In the process of salvation the sinner, dead in his trespasses and sins, is buried in the water of baptism and raised from that burial to a new life. It is a burial and a resurrection. This is the first death and the first resurrection; Jesus himself so identifies it.

To recap and summarize:

- The hour comes
- And now is

---

700 Eph 2:1, 5; Rom 8:10; Luke 15:32; 1 John 3:14
701 1 John 3:14
702 Isa 59:2
703 Luke 4:18
704 Mark 16:16
705 Rom 1:5; 16:26
706 Rom 6:4

- When the dead in sin
- Hear the voice of the Son of God
- And are buried in baptism and raised to a new life[707]

Now, the next step in our study of John 5:25-28

John 5:26-27

For as the Father hath life in himself,
even so gave he to the Son also to have life in himself:

and he gave him authority to execute judgment,
because he is a son of man.

These two verses tell us the authority by which Jesus spoke and that certify him as the "lamb of God who taketh away the sins of the world." We can be washed and made clean in the blood of the lamb because that lamb is the Son of God. The heavenly father is life, light, and love and these same virtues abide in the Son.

This brings us to a third step in understanding this passage:

John 5:28-29

Marvel not at this:
for the hour cometh,
in which all that are in the tombs shall hear his voice,
and shall come forth;
they that have done good,
unto the resurrection of life;
and they that have done evil,
unto the resurrection of judgment.

Jesus knew his claims were mind-boggling so he cautioned his listeners not to be perplexed by his extravagant claim of being the source of salvation because it was about to be exceeded by his next utterance.

The Christ of Jehovah now asserts in the face of possible contradiction a more elaborate power of invoking a general resurrection of all the dead by

707 Col 2:12; Rom 6:4

the sole power of his word. Just as God in the beginning of time spoke the universe into existence so does Jesus claim the astounding power of being able to resurrect all the dead by his potent command.

He says, "The hour cometh," but does not add (as in his previous assertion), "and now is." There was another time to come that was not near at hand. He makes the absolute statement that at some future time he would invoke creative might to cause a general resurrection of all the dead. Inhabitants of hades would hear his voice and come from the unseen world to stand before him and be judged.[708]

This includes every soul of man that once "lived, and moved, and had its being" but was no longer in the flesh, but in the spirit was waiting the time of resurrection.

The powerful voice of the amazing son of God would call them out of an unseen world and Jesus would "render unto each according to his works." He is declaring that it was within his authority to raise and judge the dead; they that lived godly in this present world would receive life; and the evil doers would receive judgment.

That is a terrifying thought for the lawless but a glorious hope for the righteous.

In just a few words Jesus, in unclouded and lofty tranquility, presents himself the indisputable arbiter of all humans. He does not speak of a few but of "all" that are in hades, the good and the bad, and insists they are accountable to him. The believing receive life, the unbelieving receive death. Since death is separation, when the faithless are sent away from God, they suffer a "second death," from which there is no recovery.

To recap and summarize:

- Do not be surprised
- The hour comes at some future, unknown time
- When Jesus will resurrect all the human dead
- The good will be raised to life everlasting
- The bad will suffer the second death, which is endless separation from God

---

708 Matt 25:31-46

The interval between the times Jesus preached a gospel of redemption and the time of his second coming is the millennium, also called "the thousand years." It is the cycle between the first preaching of the good news of salvation and the day God sends his Son a "second time, apart from sin, to them that wait for him, unto salvation."[709]

To prove this we cite a second time the opening verses of Revelation chapter twenty:

Verses 1-3

And I saw an angel coming down out of heaven,
having the key of the abyss and a great chain in his hand.

And he laid hold on the dragon, the old serpent,
which is the Devil and Satan,
and bound him for a thousand years,

and cast him into the abyss,
and shut it,
and sealed it over him,
that he should deceive the nations no more,
until the thousand years should be finished:
after this he must be loosed for a little time.

The angel came down and with the chain of divine revelation bound Satan for a thousand years; "the old serpent, which is the Devil" was cast into the bottomless pit and its lid was locked "until the thousand years should be finished." Toward the end of all ages, the chief adversary of mankind will be "loosed for a little time."

We are not told who this angel was but the Old Testament speaks of a mystery being who appears at strategic times in history

- Melchizedek who was greater than Abraham and received tithes and offerings from the patriarch
- the angel that guided the freed slaves in the wilderness
- the angel that confronted Balaam

---

709 Heb 9:28

- the angel with the drawn sword encountered by Joshua at the beginning of the conquest of Canaan
- the angel that ascended in the flame of the sacrifice of the parents of Samson

The identity of this mystery angel may have been revealed when Paul wrote, "For I would not, brethren, have you ignorant, that our fathers were all under the cloud, and all passed through the sea; and were all baptized unto Moses in the cloud and in the sea; and did all eat the same spiritual food; and did all drink the same spiritual drink: for they drank of a spiritual rock that followed them: and *the rock was Christ.*"[710]

Christ descended from the majestic throne room of God to bring the word of God to sinful man.[711] The word of God is the chain that binds Satan. To the extent it is taught, believed and followed, Satan is bound; to the extent it is denigrated or denied, the Devil is released, active and destructive. The proposition turns on whether people of the earth believe the message from God.

Mortals have no way to have an accurate and universal appraisal of how many true believers there are in the world at any given time; God alone has the ability to measure this matter and he is governed in his action and reaction by that information.

Satan was bound but toward the end of the Christian age he is to be released for a little while. This merely means that as time goes on evil will gain the ascendancy and when the situation is in full flower, the end comes. This has ever been the case.

Note the following:

- When the thoughts of men's heart were *only evil continually,* God sent a flood to destroy everything in which there was the breath of life, except for those who were on the ark with Noah[712]
- When the iniquity of the Amorite was full, God allowed the nation of Israel to invade and destroy them[713]

---

710 1 Cor 10:1-4
711 John 6:38-63
712 Gen 6:1-22
713 Gen 15:16

- When Israel was past the point of no return in the abomination of idolatry, the Babylonian army destroyed them
- When Israel was beyond recall and demonstrated her unworthiness by rejecting the unique son of God, the Romans destroyed Jerusalem

It is therefore plausible that the day God has "appointed in which he will judge the world in righteousness" is not a calendar day, but that day in which humans on earth have passed the Rubicon and are beyond the point of no return. It is the day in which Jesus will appear "a second time, apart from sin, unto them that wait for him, unto salvation."[714] Since the time of complete human departure from God is contingent upon human action and since man is a free-moral agent, it cannot be absolutely foreknown; yet God knows the day;[715] He knows it as dependent upon the behavior of his human creature.

This brings us to the next two verses:

Verses 4-5

And I saw thrones,
and they sat upon them,
and judgment was given unto them:
and I saw the souls of them that had been beheaded for the testimony of Jesus,
and for the word of God,
and such as worshipped not the beast,
neither his image,
and received not the mark upon their forehead and upon their hand;
and they lived, and reigned with Christ a thousand years.

The rest of the dead lived not until the thousand years should be finished.
This is the first resurrection.

John, speaking as he was moved by the Holy Spirit, says emphatically that the sainted martyrs of the first century "lived and reigned with Christ a thousand years." All of the saved, who are also saints, are made to be unto God "a kingdom and priests; and they reign upon earth."[716]

---

714 Heb 9:28
715 Matt 24:36
716 Rev 5:10

John, then, unambiguously declares "*This is the first resurrection.*"

We have identified that "first resurrection" as being the time between the cross and the second coming. *That is the thousand years.* It is the day of grace in which the Almighty offers to penitent believers the opportunity of being born again "of the water and of the spirit" into his eternal kingdom.[717] This is not guess nor speculation but a plain statement of fact, and is beyond debate. It cannot be successfully refuted.

"Thousand" is used in the prophetic imagery of inspired scripture to mean a large but uncertain number. The exact number is contingent on variable factors and therefore cannot be absolute. Here are a few examples:

- Keeps covenant with those that love and obey him to a "thousand generations."[718] The precise number is sure to be large but its exact size is determined by human behavior, which is uncertain; that is, to them that love him and keep his commands; the "thousand generations" is hyperbole

- "One shall chase a thousand" ... this has never happened, but it is used by prophets to emphasize the importance of having the favor and support of deity in times of war.[719] This another hyperbole.

- Job said not one man "of a thousand" can answer God's examination; and there is not "an interpreter, one among a thousand, to show man what is right for him"[720]

- David refers to "cattle upon a thousand hills," meaning a large but not precise number

- "one day is with the Lord as a thousand years, and a thousand years as one day"[721]

In these verses the word "thousand" is used symbolically; it is also used figuratively (for reasons already given) in Revelation 20:4 and merely means a huge but imprecise number. It is a hyperbole. This millennium is that period in history that men often refer to as "the Christian dispensation;" the period between the first and second comings of Christ.

---

717 John 3:5
718 Deut 7:9; 1 Chron 16:15; Psa 105:8"
719 Deut 32:30; Joshua 23:10; Isaiah 30:17
720 Job 9:3; 33:23
721 2 Pet 3:8

John says, "This is the first resurrection," and that ought to settle the matter.

"The rest of the dead" that "lived not until the thousand years should be finished" are made in the sight of God "a kingdom and priests; and they reign upon the earth."[722]

A confirmation of this view of the millennium is in the next verse:

Verse 6

Blessed and holy is he that hath part in the first resurrection:
over these the second death hath no power;
but they shall be priests of God and of Christ,
and shall reign with him a thousand years.

"Blessed" (happy, supremely blest, fortunate, well off) "is he that hath a part in the first resurrection," that is, he that is regenerated by the obedience of faith and enters the kingdom of God by birth "of water and the spirit." He may face tribulation and persecution but he is the chosen of Jehovah (an adopted child) and is promised an "abundant entrance" into the heavenly phase of God's unending kingdom.

He is jubilant even in the midst of sorrows, "knowing that tribulation worketh stedfastness; and stedfastness, approvedness; and approvedness, hope: and hope putteth not to shame; because the love of God hath been shed abroad in our hearts through the Holy Spirit which was given unto us."[723]

"Blessed is he that readeth, and they that hear the words of the prophecy, and keep the things that are written therein: for the time is at hand."[724]

The prophecy turns to the end of the thousand year (Christian age) reign of Christ and his brothers, some of whom are martyrs and others rule "on the earth" during this last dispensation. When Jesus ascended on high, he "led captivity captive and gave gifts unto men."[725] He comes again to assemble the nations of all ages and judge the world.[726]

722 Rev 5:10
723 Rom 5:3-5
724 Rev 1:3
725 Eph 4:8
726 Matt 25:31-46; John 5:25-29

John discusses briefly the closing hours of the created universe.

Verses 7-9

And when the thousand years are finished,
Satan shall be loosed out of his prison,

and shall come forth to deceive the nations
which are in the four corners of the earth,
Gog and Magog,
to gather them together to the war:
the number of whom is as the sand of the sea.

And they went up over the breadth of the earth,
and compassed the camp of the saints about,
and the beloved city:
and fire came down out of heaven,
and devoured them.

At the end of the long but undetermined epoch, described symbolically as "the thousand years" Satan shall be loosed. Unbelief will wash over the earth like a supernatural tidal wave of fire and carry the mass of men into perdition.

Jesus raised the question "when the Son of man cometh, shall he find faith on the earth?"[727] He does not answer this question, but the implication is clear. Apostasy, which is departure from God by unbelief, will be popular and believers will be few, if any, when Jesus comes to call the dead out of the unseen world to be judged.

Satan deceives the nations into thinking they can successfully oppose and overcome the three supreme beings that make up the true Deity; instead, they reap a harvest of eternal damnation.

Satan summons the stiff-necked, hard-hearted, blind and deaf nations of earth to flex their muscles and attempt to cast God down but are themselves cast into the burning sulfur river that will never cease to flow. They are rocked with eternal damnation, which is the second death and from which there is no resurrection.

---

727 Luke 18:8

The Dragon (Satan, serpent, devil) calls Gog (the princes of earth) and Magog (the nations "in the four quarters of the earth"), representing all earthly rulers and all earthly nations, to gather their weapons of mass destruction and march against the omnipotent Lion of God.[728]

Satan, Gog and Magog do not realize they are hopelessly outgunned. It is, of course, not a battle of gun and sword, but a fight of truth versus error. Unbelief (the lies of Satan) may appear to win, but are unconditionally defeated. Truth will out and he that overcometh shall not be hurt of the second death.

Satan is loosed, as he was in the first century, but it is only "for a little season." It is his last gasp. As the victory of resurrection overcame the apparent defeat of the cross, so shall the last push of the devil be smashed by the all-conquering Christ.[729] The righteous stand with him and are "more than conquerors."[730]

Wickedness grows apace but is stopped suddenly and decisively. The good in every generation lament the increase of evil. Still, Satan is bound as long as a small remnant of the righteous – law keepers – remain and fight for freedom; it is not a carnal struggle but is a moral contest. It is no easy thing to stand up for Jesus in a perverted world; the beast against which we fight is red in tooth and claw and uses every unfair device to destroy ethical behavior. Spiritual wars can provoke savage inquisitions. The ambition of the serpent is to castrate truth, for truth is his deadly enemy. The devil is "the father of lies" and has no stomach for truth.[731]

In view of the unabashed villainy of the great red dragon the church must be forceful in resisting his lies. A timid church is sure to fail. Boldness must be our watchword.[732] Discipline must be exercised and heresy must not be tolerated if the church is "a city on a hill that cannot be hidden."

Satan thought he had won the war and his lies had overcome God's truth, but failed to take into account the fire from heaven. When the populace of earth is wholly given to the lawlessness of sin then shall the end come and

---

728 Rev 5:5
729 Rev 6:2
730 Rom 8:37
731 John 8:44-47
732 Acts 4:13, 29, 31; 9:27; 13:46; 14:3; 19:8; 28:31; Phil 1:20

the fire from heaven will consume both the rebels and the universe.[733] The evil of earth cannot defend against God's hammer blows. Keep in mind the spiritual nature of this war.

Verse 10

And the devil that deceived them was cast into the lake of fire and brimstone,
where are also the beast and the false prophet;
and they shall be tormented day and night forever and ever.

The Bible records the biography of the devil as follows:

- Rebellion in heaven – Jude 6-7

- Christ overcame the Devil and cast him out – Rev 12:9-11

- Deceived Eve and she enticed Adam – Gen 3:1-6

- Lies and murders recorded in human history – John 8:44

- Controlled most of the world most of the time – John 14:30; 2 Cor 4:4; Eph 2:1-2

- Bound by the victorious Christ – Rev 20:3

- Loosed for a little season – Rev 20 3, 7

- The final doom of the devil – Rev 20:10

The entire college of evil is to be eternally committed to misery where the "worm dieth not and the fire is not quenched."[734] "[T]*hey shall be tormented day and night forever and ever.*" He that has eyes to see and ears to hear understands from this that the punishment of the ungodly knows no end.

Verse 11

And I saw a great white throne,
and him that sat upon it,
from whose face the earth and the heaven fled away;
and there was found no place for them.

The "great white throne" symbolizes the supreme excellence and power of God. It is greater than all the thrones of earth for all time combined. In

733 2 Thess 1:7-9; Rev 16:1-21
734 Mark 9:44

that awesome day when Jesus comes in his glory and before him all the nations shall be assembled "that in the name of Jesus every knee should bow, of things in heaven and things on earth and things under the earth, and that every tongue should confess that Jesus Christ is Lord, to the glory of God the Father."[735]

There was no place remaining for "earth and the (1ˢᵗ) heaven" because they were annihilated,[736] but not so for the lawless human inhabitants of earth – a place was found for them in the sulphuric-river … "where the worm dieth not and the fire is not quenched."

Now comes the universal judgment:

Verses 12-13

And I saw the dead,
the great and the small,
standing before the throne;
and books were opened:
and another book was opened,
which is the book of life:
and the dead were judged out of the things which were written in the books,
according to their works.

And the sea gave up the dead that were in it;
and death and Hades gave up the dead that were in them:
and they were judged every man according to their works.

Many tremble at the thought of judgment, even the wicked demons shudder[737] at the thought of being called to account.

Some say they do not want a religion based on fear, but that depends on the object of the fear. If it is a benevolent father who is longsuffering and filled with loving-kindness, and whom it is a joy to obey, there is no cause for dread, unless, of course, that gracious Being has been dishonored by being disobeyed. Jesus used the thought of judgment to rouse men to fear.[738]

---

735 Phil 2:10-11
736 Psa 102:25-26; 2 Pet 3:8-13
737 James 2:19
738 Luke 12:5

The loud and persistent voice of inspiration tells us to "fear God and keep his commandments.[739]

If we fear God, we have nothing else to fear.[740]

The accountability of creatures and the judgment of God is prominent in the New Testament. It is found in many of the parables of Jesus:

- Rich man and Lazarus (which probably is not a parable)
- Unrighteous steward
- Parable of the pounds
- Parable of the talents
- The wheat and tares
- The wicked servant
- The marriage of the King's son
- The ten virgins

It is clear that Jesus viewed the world under the aspect of judgment and eternity. If final judgment were removed from the gospels, what would be left?

- Not Jesus' saving work; redemption is concerned with the high issues of life and death
- Not ethical teaching because morality is based on the judgment[741] and on human accountability to a higher power

The final judgment is graphically described. The message is brief but very plain and includes these elements:

- Jesus is seated on the great white throne
- The Father and the Spirit are conjoined with Jesus
- All nations are gathered;[742] the teaming masses are assembled
- They come from the sea, death, and Hades

---

739 Deut 5:29; 6:2; 8:6;13:4; 1 Sam 12:14; 2 Kings 17:34, 37; Psa 111:10; Eccl 12:13
740 Luke 12:32; Psa 23; Rom 8:31
741 Matt 5:29-30; 18:8-9
742 Matt 25:31-33; 16:27; Rom 14:10; 2 Cor 5:10; 2 Tim 4:1; Heb 9:27

- Books were opened, including the Lamb's book of life
- The dead were judged according to the things written in the books, according to their works

The books that were opened need to be identified and this is especially true if our own individual judgment is to be based on what is written in those books. One of these books is the "book of life," as we are told in verses twelve and fifteen. This book is mentioned several times in the Bible and refers to the roster of the saved written by the authority of God.

Moses refers to this book when he pleads for Israel[743]; it is also mentioned in the book of Daniel in connection with judgment[744]; Paul mentions some whose names were written in the book of life[745]; and it is mentioned six times in the book of Revelation[746].

Reading these references confirm that this refers to a book kept in heaven in which is written the names of the saved; the unsaved are omitted from that sacred register. If your name is written there then your crown of life is assured; if your name is not written there you will not be allowed to enter heaven. According to Moses plea for the nation of Israel[747], a name that is written in the book of life may be removed. We must so live that our name is not stricken from that divine catalog of the redeemed.

The other book mentioned must be the Law of God; the moral law was written originally on the human heart, in the Old Testament it was given primarily for the benefit of the Jews and was written as with pen and ink, and in the New Testament it was written on various materials and with a writing instrument, but is to be "implanted" into the heart of the saved.[748]

The written word is more permanent and more difficult to misunderstand or misrepresent. It can be mistreated, of course, but there is always a standard by which the correctness of the writing can be gauged.

---

743 Ex 32:32-33;
744 Dan 7:10
745 Phil 4:3
746 Rev 3:5; 13:8; 17:18; Rev 20:12, 15; 21:27
747 Ex 32:32-33
748 James 1:21

Jesus taught that heaven and earth can pass away (Revelation 19 records the passing of heaven and earth) but says "my words shall not pass away."[749]

At any rate, the promise is that God's written law shall not perish but will endure to the judgment and be the standard to measure human conduct. Peter tells us, "the word of the Lord abideth forever."[750] Jesus said, "He that rejecteth me, and receiveth not my sayings, hath one that judgeth him: the word that I spake, the same shall judge him in the last day."[751]

The passage also stresses the importance of works; all will be judged at the last by the word of God and the works of the person. This judgment scene mentions works twice and tells us emphatically that we shall be judged "according to our works."[752] Though often denied it is nevertheless true that the works of man play an important and necessary role in the salvation process.

- Without works faith is dead[753]
- We must do the works of him that sent Jesus[754]
- Their works follow those who die in the Lord[755]
- The obedience of faith is works[756]
- Faith produces works and works perfect faith[757]
- Faith is a work[758]

At the last, we will be judged by the word and by our works.

John now records the time when this was done. We will be judged by the words of the new covenant and it therefore behooves us to know, understand, and keep that contract.

---

749 Mark 13:31
750 1 Pet 1:25
751 John 12:48
752 Rev 20:12, 15
753 James 2:17
754 John 9:4
755 Rev 14:13
756 Rom 1:5; 16:26
757 James 2:22
758 John 6:29

This brings us to the end of the interlude recorded in Revelation 20, and we now turn to the tremendous close of this book as John guides us into an understanding of the beauty and wonder of the everlasting reward of the faithful and true.

The Beauty of the New Jerusalem
Revelation 21:1-27

We have traveled through the ages from the time of the inauguration of Jesus as the King of God on earth to the ultimate promotion of the saints. The primary exaltation of this noble band of believers occurred when their faith was perfected by repentance, confession and baptism.[759] "Having been buried with him (Jesus) through baptism," they were "raised with him," and all their sins were washed away.[760] At that moment their names were written in the lamb's book of life, which is a promotion from slavery in sin to freedom in Christ; this preferment comes from knowing and obeying truth.[761]

- We have seen through the eyes and by the words of a prophet of God the excellent name of God …
- broken seals …
- sounding trumpets …
- bowls of the hot wrath of God …
- vanity of materialism …
- Hallelujah chorus …
- and a recap of the good fight of faith.

Now we step to the door of eternity and by the light of the glory that gilds Jordan's wave we behold the new heaven and the new earth, which fulfills all spiritual prophecy and redeems every promise of God. It is the delight

759 Jas 2:14-26; Acts 2:38; Rom 10:9-10; Acts 22:16
760 Col 2:12-13
761 John 8:32; 14:6; 1 Pet 1:22-23

of the ages. All the saved are there, their hearts beat high, and their feet are jubilant.

In retrospect we remember the saints enlisted in the Lord's army for the duration of the good fight of faith. That war (sometimes called the battle of Har-Magedon) did not abate until the conquering Christ atomized the world and carried its evil rulers to the justice of perdition. The conflict between truth and error displayed all the horrid abominations of war; and brought to reality the rapture of the saved.

The final triumphant victory of truth is absolutely certain.

We will read and make a few short comments on the introduction to chapter 21.

VERSE 1

And I saw a new heaven and a new earth:
for the first heaven and the first earth are passed away;
and the sea is no more.

The expression "new heaven and a new earth" is used to mean a fresh start. We sometime speak of turning a page to mean a restructured order of things and that is the sense of this phrase. Isaiah spoke of a new heaven and earth to describe renewed Israel after the Babylonian captivity. The idea is simply a radical change of pace. It connotes extreme revision. Isaiah's use of the expression was an affirmation that there would be a destruction of the old order and the creation of a reformed nation; he explains the meaning when he quotes Jehovah as saying, "I create new heavens and a new earth; and the former things shall not be remembered, nor come into mind."[762]

"The sea" separated people who were of the same mind and loved each other, John the apostle was kept from his beloved brethren at Ephesus by the sea. Isaiah says of the troubled sea "it cannot rest, and its waters cast up mire and dirt."[763] The painful separation and churning evil will be no more and this is certified by the non-existence of the sea in God's new and final arrangement.

---

762 Isa 65:17; see also Isa 66:22
763 Isa 57:20

Verse 2

And I saw the holy city, new Jerusalem,
coming down out of heaven of God,
made ready as a bride adorned for her husband.

The "new" Jerusalem is not a renovated old Jerusalem; it descended out of heaven from God and was not earth born, or merely the old Jerusalem repaired and repainted. This figurative description of the symbolic city that descended from God is given after this earth and the heavens of the universe have been melted into nothingness by flames of fire. There is nothing to clean up and rebuild because material things no longer exist.[764] The city described by the Spirit through the human instrument, John, makes us aware of the glory and splendor of the heavenly reward of the righteous dead; nothing is more brilliant, resplendent and gorgeous. The city "not made with hands" is "not of this creation."[765]

John's inspired pen adds another figurative element and compares the wondrous "new" Jerusalem with "a bride adorned for her husband. We have earlier seen this used to indicate the souls of the just made perfect (all of them), which is the church. The expression "new Jerusalem" is found only three times in the Bible.[766] It comes down out of heaven from God.

The church of Christ is the saved of all ages and is the figurative bride of Christ. The wedding takes place at the return of the bridegroom. The bride (church) is washed and made clean in the blood of the Lamb of God, and she is adorned by the truth she shields, proclaims and explains; the slaves of Christ beautify the gospel by being true to it as the confirmed word of God.[767].

The prepared bride is "adorned for her husband."[768] She is exceedingly beautiful. The bride (church) of Christ is dressed in a robe as bright and white as a clear noonday summer sun. "

"[F]or the marriage of the Lamb is come, and his wife hath made herself ready: arrayed in fine linen, bright and pure: for the fine linen is the

---

764 2 Pet 3:8-11; Rev 16
765 Heb 9:11
766 Once in Revelation 3 (verse 12) and twice in Revelation 21 (verses 2 and 10)
767 Titus 2:10 – servants were to adorn the gospel by being pure in word and deed
768 See Isa 49:18; 61:10

righteous acts of the saints."[769] The bride of Christ makes herself ready to receive him when he comes by keeping herself untainted in teaching and practice.[770] Pure doctrine makes a pure church.

Verse 3

And I heard a great voice out of the throne saying,
Behold, the tabernacle of God is with men,
and he shall dwell with them,
and they shall be his peoples,
and God himself shall be with them,
and be their God:

The voice John heard was high, large, loud, and mighty, a majestic and penetrating sound, and it was making the grand announcement that the mighty God will meet with the saved to be their God and they shall be his people. This speaks of a closeness and companionship unequaled in human history. This communion between the Great I Am and the ransomed is closer and more gratifying than the meetings on the mount between Jehovah and Moses because this communion is uninterrupted and complete. It is eternal. The purified of earth shall be with God to enjoy the comfort and shelter of his tabernacle unendingly. Think of being with the highest of the high, basking in his glory, benefiting from his wisdom, looking upon his face in an unchanging embrace that never ends.

"We know that, if he shall be manifested, we shall be like him; for we shall see him even as he is." Moses saw God's after-glory; the saved shall see his resplendent full-glory."

Verses 4-7

and he shall wipe away every tear from their eyes;
and death shall be no more;
neither shall there be mourning, nor crying, nor pain, any more:
the first things are passed away.
And he that sitteth on the throne said,
Behold, I make all things new.
And he saith, Write: for these words are faithful and true.

---

769 Rev 19:7-8
770 2 Cor 11:2

And he said unto me, They are come to pass.
I am the Alpha and the Omega, the beginning and the end.
I will give unto him that is athirst of the fountain of the water of life freely.
He that overcometh shall inherit these things;
and I will be his God, and he shall be my son.

The deep-down satisfaction of being with God, sheltered in the arms of Jesus and laying down our weary heads upon his breast, is wondrously inexpressible. It is too big to be framed in human language, an eloquent monument of God's redeeming love. And it lasts eternally in the unfading power of perfect peace that passes understanding.

While in the flesh and on the earth our eyes are often dimmed by unwelcome tears wrung from us by surprise, disappointment, heart-wrenching change, and the separation caused by the death of those who are dearest on earth to us; things that hurt too much for us to dwell on or talk about. The dull and somber sadness brought on us by unbearable burdens needs the solace that only the majestic First Cause can impart. The finger of God, in that miraculous heavenly fellowship with deity, shall wipe away our tears and dry our eyes and soothe our broken hearts.

He that sits upon the highest throne whispers sweet assurance and by his grace and power he mends our souls with the assurance, "Behold, all things are made new." Think of that … for all new creatures in Christ all things made new; not patched, washed and pressed, but new.

"These words are faithful and true." They shall not fail, but will come to pass! We have the promise of he who is the beginning and the end on that. It is a refuge to which we can confidently flee and find shelter. It is the cleft in the Rock of Ages where we can hide ourselves from the abrasions of life on earth.

Overcome! Overcome and you will inherit these things and be refreshed by the water of life and never be thirsty again.

The Alpha and the Omega gives his solemn word that if we overcome he will be our God and we shall be his sons. There is no word beyond this word. "What more could he say than to you he has said, you who unto Jesus for refuge have fled?"

The agents of iniquity have a dreadful future as described by John's inspired pen:

Verse 8

But for the fearful,
and unbelieving,
and abominable,
and murderers,
and fornicators,
and sorcerers,
and idolaters,
and all liars,
their part shall be in the lake that burneth with fire and brimstone;
which is the second death.

The contrast between the crown of the victors in Christ and those who wallow in the vices of earth is shocking, and takes away our breath. Such conduct is enough to make us shudder. The solaced souls of those who have been purchased by the blood of the Lamb is magnificent and indestructible.

The English Standard Version translates the list "the cowardly, the faithless, the detestable, murderers, the sexually immoral, sorcerers, idolaters, and all liars,"

And it translates their portion as "the lake that burns with fire and sulfur, which is the second death."

"Sorcerers" could be translated all who are addicted to illegal drugs and revel in the corruption it produces; "idolaters" could be rendered "covetous," which is the greedy grasping at the disappearing skirts of material stuff; it robs its victims of all happiness.

Their part shall "be in the lake that burns with fire and sulfur, which is the second death."

Death is separation and the second death is to be everlastingly severed from God and his fellowship. Contrast that with the joyous communion with God the souls of the just made perfect enjoy and you will be impressed with the greatness of the loss of the damned and the joy of the redeemed.

Verse 9

And there came one of the seven angels who had the seven bowls,
who were laden with the seven last plagues;
and he spake with me, saying,
Come hither, I will show thee the bride, the wife of the Lamb.

One of the seven angels that carried the bowls of wrath offered to show John "the bride, the wife of the lamb," which is the church, which is the people, which is the saved. They are here once again called the bride of Christ; "the wife of the Lamb." On earth they were the espoused virgin of Jesus. Now the time had come for the bridegroom to take his bride into the inner chambers of God and let her see his brightness and experience a transformation unequalled in human history.

We are approaching the grand finale of human metamorphosis. They are soon to see the Father on his throne and hear him say, "Welcome home, ye weary pilgrims, welcome home."

First, let us look with John on the bride of Christ, the wife of the Lamb.

Verses 10-21

And he carried me away in the Spirit to a mountain great and high,
and showed me the holy city Jerusalem,
coming down out of heaven from God,
having the glory of God:
her light was like unto a stone most precious,
as it were a jasper stone, clear as crystal:
having a wall great and high;
having twelve gates,
and at the gates twelve angels;
and names written thereon,
which are the names of the twelve tribes of the children of Israel:
on the east were three gates;
and on the north three gates;
and on the south three gates;
and on the west three gates.
And the wall of the city had twelve foundations,
and on them twelve names of the twelve apostles of the Lamb.

And he that spake with me had for a measure
a golden reed to measure the city,
and the gates thereof, and the wall thereof.
And the city lieth foursquare,
and the length thereof is as great as the breadth:
and he measured the city with the reed, twelve thousand furlongs:
the length and the breadth and the height thereof are equal.
And he measured the wall thereof,
a hundred and forty and four cubits,
according to the measure of a man, that is, of an angel.
And the building of the wall thereof was jasper:
and the city was pure gold, like unto pure glass.
The foundations of the wall of the city were adorned with all
manner of precious stones. The first foundation was jasper;
the second, sapphire;
the third, chalcedony;
the fourth, emerald;
the fifth, sardonyx;
the sixth, sardius;
the seventh, chrysolite;
the eighth, beryl;
the ninth, topaz;
the tenth, chrysoprase;
the eleventh, jacinth;
the twelfth, amethyst.
And the twelve gates were twelve pearls;
each one of the several gates was of one pearl:
and the street of the city was pure gold, as it were transparent glass.

To read this passage of sacred scripture slowly, deliberately, thoughtfully and prayerfully fills one with a sublime sense of veneration, and wonder. It is awesome. He that overcomes has the right to think of himself as a part of this holy city Jerusalem because it is the church purchased at the awful cost of the blood of the unique son of God. Now it is glorified as all of God children are beatified.

This is the bride, the wife of the Lamb.

The wall of the city is great and high; it has twelve gates and each gate is one huge pearl; angels stand guard at every gate; its gates are inscribed with the names of the twelve tribes of the children of Israel; its successful conquest of evil guarantees the absolute security of absolute safety (the enemies of God are in the lake of fire); its wall has twelve foundations and on the foundations is inscribed the names of the twelve apostles of the Lamb;[771] its foundations are adorned with twelve gems of the great beauty of perfection; its street is pure gold;[772]

This description of the New Jerusalem, the wife of the Lamb, takes your breath away. It is too excellent and magnificent for words. To look upon it is dazzling and deeply impresses the observer with its brilliance. It is, of course, symbolic; the shining city is too wonderful to be pictured in words and so God makes us aware of its superlative beauty by using the most impressive jewels and costly metals known to man to describe it. Imagine a gate made of one pearl bearing the names of Old Testament worthies and a foundation made up of twelve layers of the most glorious jewels our human experience can yield. It is unbelievably gorgeous. It makes Solomon's temple pale by comparison.

Verse 22

And I saw no temple therein:
for the Lord God the Almighty, and the Lamb, are the temple thereof.

The tabernacle and temple of the Jews was a meeting place with God. God is everywhere but dwells somewhere with greater emphasis than in tabernacle or temple. In the New Testament the temple of God is the church but in the ultimate arrangement the church and God are immediately present. Those who overcome are "pillars" in the temple of the Lord.[773]

There are no temples in heaven because Jehovah and Jesus are its only temple. When we are always in the immediate presence of God that serves as the only temple we need. In this life the children of God can talk to God at any moment of the day or night. All they need do is incline their heads and pray. In that glorious future estate we can see God anytime we want to see him. All we will need to do is look. The fellowship of the third heaven

771 Eph 2:20
772 Glass is purified ground up rock when it is refined and all blemishes removed it becomes crystal; the street of the city is pure gold, as pure as the most exquisite crystal.
773 Rev 3:12

is so perfect that we will need no artificial support to worship and serve; all we need do is fall upon our faces and adore the object of our affection.

Verse 23

And the city hath no need of the sun,
neither of the moon, to shine upon it:
for the glory of God did lighten it, and the lamp thereof is the Lamb.

The brilliance of God outshines the sun, moon and all the stars. It bathes the shining city of heaven in uninterrupted light. Since that is the case, there is no night there. Jesus is life that is light but the majority of earthly people love darkness rather than light and close their eyes very tight and refuse to let the light in.[774] Believers in Jesus are the light of an unredeemed world[775] but that light is hampered by hardhearted unbelief. In heaven it will be different and the light that is God shines with a more perfect brightness than it could in a world of stiff-necked scoffers. In the eternal city the light is undiminished by rejection and doubt and therefore shines with a light that is unapproachable by mortals. We will not be mortal in the portals of the New Jerusalem where the light of God blazes uninterrupted. There will be no night there.

Verses 24-27

And the nations shall walk amidst the light thereof:
and the kings of the earth bring their glory into it.
And the gates thereof shall in no wise be shut by day
(for there shall be no night there):
and they shall bring the glory and the honor of the nations into it:
and there shall in no wise enter into it anything unclean,
or he that maketh an abomination and a lie:
but only they that are written in the Lamb's book of life.

Everything that is contrary to God and righteousness shall be shut out of heaven and everything that is good shall be included in that radiant city of God. Whatever glory earthly kings have will be stripped from them and reassigned to the corridors of the eternal city. Its open gates affirm

---

774 John 1:4-5
775 Matt 5:14

the absence of threats and terror and the presence of peace and spiritual prosperity. It will be calm and rich. The vulgar and the filthy are excluded and only they whose names are in the register of the Lord will pass through its open gates to walk its golden street and eat the healing leaves of the trees lining the banks of the river of life. The fruit of the trees always hangs ripe and is ceaselessly enjoyed by the saved. "There shall in no wise enter into it anything that is unclean."

This appraisal of the shining city of God is continued in the nest chapter, the closing chapter of the book of God.

Revelation 22:1-21

Epilogue

We come now to the concluding section that rounds out the design, not just of the book of Revelation, but of the entire Bible. The curtain of revelation is about to fall and this is the last view we get as the communication of divine truth is finished and will be no more until Jesus comes. It is the "once for all delivered faith"[776] and has been ever since Jude penned those inspired words.

We have in our completed Bible the final words of the Almighty; revelation is finished. That is only fair since all the generations from the cross to the final judgment will have access to the full revelation and an equal opportunity of knowing the mind of God and doing his will. "Thy kingdom come, thy will be done on earth as it is in heaven."

Before we take up this closing statement let us refresh our memory ... the book of God's word begins with creation and flows through the time of rampant sin that was so universal that only one man found favor in the sight of the Lord; that wicked world had to be washed away in a great universal flood. Then comes the march of the earliest patriarchs ... Abraham, Isaac, Jacob, Joseph, Moses, Joshua, the Judges, Saul, David, Solomon, and all the kings and prophets of Israel and of Judah; which brings us to the Babylonian captivity of the Jews and their dispersion throughout the world; next comes four hundred years of silence from the throne of God; the silence is broken when, in the fullness of time, God sent forth his son and we are told of his life, teaching, service, tragic death, glorious resurrection and triumphant ascension (he that descended also

---

776 Jude 3

ascended); after the cross Jesus sits upon the throne of God and is High Priest for his loyal followers; the great war called "the good fight of faith" rages through the centuries until we come to the end of the world and the entire universe disappears in the flaming fire of the hot wrath of an outraged God; the climax is when every child of God is gathered to his people. This is where the book of Revelation takes us and then, once more, God falls silent and there is no further word from his throne until that coming great day of victory for all who know, love and obey the absolute truth of God's undying revelation.

By the light of the word picture John painted for us as he was instructed by the angels and moved by the Holy Spirit we stand in anticipation of the end of time and think of the eternity that is infinity; we turn our faces toward God and in our mind's eye can see the fabulous city of the Lord God towering over us. Here is the scene John revealed in the previous chapter:

The shining city of God has a wall about it that is 350 feet high, which is more than the length of a football field. Think of standing at the ground level of that great wall and looking up 350 feet to its top. The wall surrounds the city and is made of pure jasper; and sparkles like a diamond reflecting the intensity of sunlight as it mirrors the glory of God. The city is a cube, its height, width, and length being equal. On each of its four sides are three gates that are never closed. Each gate is made of one giant lustrous pearl, most impressive to see. The foundations of the gate and the city are visible. They are twelve in number and there is the implication that each foundation is about 300 feet thick. Each row is made of a different precious gem. One layer would be solid ruby and another emerald and another sapphire and another amber and another diamond and so on -- twelve bands of the most beautiful gems imaginable. On either side of the golden street of that city of stately grandeur the river of life flows in uninterrupted splendor and along its banks are large beautiful trees with health in their leaves and nutrition in the sweet juicy fruit that is always available and always ripe. The golden avenue leads to the throne of God in its splendor. The city is 375 miles in every direction. Think of it … 375 miles high … 375 miles wide … 375 miles long; it is foursquare. Its enormous size speaks to us of its comfort and of the fact that the number of the saved in glory will be very large (a limited number from each generations but an untold number of generations). The twelve gates have written on them the names of the twelve sons of Jacob and the twelve foundations have written on them the names of the twelve apostles of the Lamb.

To read the description is to recognize the author is speaking to us in the figures and symbols of poetry and prophecy. It is not literal but it will be as marvelously beautiful to spirit eyes as a mighty city made after the order described would be to mortal eyes. It is truly awesome – overwhelmingly mind boggling and stunning.

How beautiful heaven must be.

As the cross of Christ draws us to him so does this descriptive account of the glory-city of God inspire us to yearn to walk its street, taste its fruit, drink its life-giving water and rejoice in its graceful loveliness.

And to think we will have as companions Jehovah, Jesus, the Holy Spirit, the souls of the just made perfect, including all those we have loved "long sense and lost awhile." Won't it be wonderful there?

We now give attention to the final chapter of the Bible and of revelation. It begins:

Verses 1-2

And he showed me a river of water of life, bright as crystal,
proceeding out of the throne of God and of the Lamb,
in the midst of the street thereof.

And on this side of the river and on that was the tree of life,
bearing twelve manner of fruits,
yielding its fruit every month:
and the leaves of the tree were for the healing of the nations.

The author (God) continues a description of the charm and appeal of the New Jerusalem, which is the bride of Jesus, which is the church. The water of life is inexhaustibly available; it is sparkling, pure, cool and animating. The only source for this life giving water is the "throne of God and of the Lamb." There are no health issues in the great city of God because there is no disease, but the leaves of the tree of life heal the nations in the sense of giving to those who enjoy the leaves energy and super power.[777] The

---

777 God is never sick yet he is at times is stirred to vigorous, intense activity and this is health

river of the water of life brings calm, joy, abundance; all the happiness of heaven originates with God, who freely gives with abundant liberality. The treasure house of God overflows with gifts and all its wealth is available to the residents of glory. The leaves of the tree are for the healing of the people (nations). The jubilant joy of heaven is limitless and unbounded rapture. The ecstasy of ultimate salvation is the constant, overflowing, companionship with God.

"My God and I go in the fields together … we walk and talk … we clasp our hands, our voices ring with laughter, my God and I walk through the meadow's hue."

The writer again mentions the absence of evil in the purity of the New Jerusalem. No wickedness can exist in the virgin[778] bride of Jesus. The abundant blessings of the city of God foreclose the entrance of the bad and the ugly. To admit the practitioners of iniquity and lawlessness into the holy city of God would be to defile its purity and destroy its peace. God is too holy to have his presence sullied by vain and vulgar things.

Verses 3-5

And there shall be no curse any more:
and the throne of God and of the Lamb shall be therein:
and his servants shall serve him;
and they shall see his face;
and his name shall be on their foreheads.
And there shall be night no more;
and they need no light of lamp, neither light of sun;
for the Lord God shall give them light:
and they shall reign forever and ever.

The curse of Eden, the curse of sin, the curse of war shall be wholly eliminated – in fact, no curse of any kind shall be in the bride of Jesus, which is the New Jerusalem; not only shall there be "no curse any more" but the punishment caused by the curse shall be no more. All will be serene and tranquil. God's will is done, God's blessings are enjoyed as God's kingdom shines in its solitary splendor. Happy are those who enter its

---

778 Virgin in the sense of being free from the guilt of sin, having been washed and made clean in the blood of the Lamb.

gates and enjoy its blessings; in that majestic land there will be "no tears, nor sorrow, nor death, nor crying, nor pain, nor curse."

The throne of God represents his high rank and incredible power.

It would be expected in this environment that all of God's children would obey him implicitly, joyfully, consistently, and receive for their faithful service the bliss of paradise.

The communion between God and his children will have a smooth continuity.

The just made perfect shall look on the face of God and be like him[779] "When by his grace I shall look on his face that will be glory ... be glory ... for me."

The name of God written on the foreheads of the happy citizens of heaven announces they are the heritage of God ... his property ... they belong to him and he belongs to them. Each inherits the other.

No sun or lamp is needed for the brightness of God and the lamp of the Lamb is the light of that golden, foursquare city, where there is "peace, perfect peace."

The mighty host of all the saved, of every order, blend with the Godhead to reign forever and ever. The limitations of time and sense yield at the last to boundless eternity of timelessness.

Jesus certifies the message:

Verses 6-7

And he said unto me,
These words are faithful and true:
and the Lord, the God of the spirits of the prophets,
sent his angels to show unto his servants the things
which must shortly come to pass.

And behold, I come quickly.
Blessed is he that keepeth the words of the prophecy of this book.

---

779 1 John 3:2

Jesus pronounces his blessing upon this closing book of the Bible and by implication upon the entire Bible. It is God's word, though written by selected humans, and is indestructible, living, active, sharp and piercing.

"The grass withereth, and the flower falleth: But the word of the Lord abideth for ever. And this is the word of good tidings which was preached unto you."[780]

"Heaven and earth shall pass away, but my words shall not pass away."[781]

God is the spirit of the prophets – all of them. Therefore every recorded word of the prophets are included in this certification mark of Jesus. He puts the impress of his royal ring upon it.

All these things, Jesus said, "must shortly come to pass;" and he adds "Behold, I come quickly." This must not be misconstrued to mean that the events foretold in the book of Revelation will happen immediately and that Jesus would return straightway for final judgment, for that is not true of the events or of the return.

To better understand this promise and warning, we need to drive down a stake that we are absolutely sure pegs a basic truth about when Jesus "appears a second time, apart from sin, to them that wait for him, unto salvation." [782]

- Jesus also said to the dwellers on earth "watch ye therefore, for in an hour that ye think not the son of man cometh."[783]

- Again the Savior said, "But of that day and hour knoweth no one, not even the angels of heaven, neither the Son, but the Father only."[784]

- Paul, the apostle, said, "For yourselves know perfectly that the day of the Lord so cometh as a thief in the night."[785]

- Peter wrote, "But the day of the Lord will come as a thief; in the which the heavens shall pass away with a great noise, and

780 1 Peter 1:24-25
781 Matt 24:35
782 Heb 9:28
783 Matt 24:40
784 Matt 24:36
785 1 Thess 5:2

the elements shall be dissolved with fervent heat, and the earth and the works that are therein shall be burned up."[786]

That nails it down. Other scripture could be cited, but this is sufficient to convince any fair-minded, Bible-believing person that at the time of the final return of Jesus to the vicinity of the earth, we shall see him[787] and be caught up in the clouds to meet him.[788] He will come when we least expect it; no one on earth knows the hour or the day; he will come as a thief in the night (that is, unannounced and unexpected).

Anyone who tries to give a specific day for the final coming of Jesus is whistling in the dark; he does not know whereof he speaks and his words are nonsensical.

We know that he is coming, but we do not know when … only the Heavenly Father has that information for "he (the Father) hath appointed a day in which he will judge the world in righteousness by the man whom he hath ordained; whereof he hath given assurance unto all men, in that he hath raised him from the dead."[789]

As we have previously pointed out, the "day" God has appointed for the return of his Son (Jesus) is not a certain day on the calendar, but "the day" in which the iniquity of the world is so intolerable that there is no possibility for reformation and it must be destroyed. That will be the day of his coming and that day is conditioned upon human behavior, and human behavior is controlled by the free-will of humans and so the specific day is not and cannot be known. It is the day humans have sold their souls to Satan, and are so crusted over with sin that it is impossible for them to repent that existence on earth must be terminated. Its Creator becomes its Terminator.

It follows that when Jesus said of his return to earth unto judgment that it would happen "shortly" and "quickly" he is talking about the suddenness and swiftness of earth's destruction and the dispatch in which the entire system will be obliterated, and is not talking about a specific day, time, year. No one on earth has that information. Some say that inspired men knew the second coming of Jesus would dawn in their lifetime. But it is

---

786 2 Peter 3:10
787 Rev 1:7
788 1 Thess 4:16-17
789 Acts 17:31

evident the day cannot be unknown and yet inspired first- century writers knew it would happen directly, or straightway (in their lifetime); that would be tantamount to knowing the day and defeat the purpose of the warning.

John pronounced that person happy who keeps the words of God and is delivered from the loss and grief the unprepared shall suffer when Jesus suddenly returns and quickly destroys the universe.

Verses 8-9

And I John am he that heard and saw these things.
And when I heard and saw,
I fell down to worship before the feet of the
angel that showed me these things.

And he saith unto me,
See thou do it not:
I am a fellow-servant with thee and with thy brethren the prophets,
and with them that keep the words of this book: worship God.

John testifies that what he has written is true and the exceptional nature of all that John had seen and heard caused him to fall upon his face before the angel who had been sent to show the apostle the things that are written in the book of Revelation. John intended to worship the messenger from the throne of God, but is forbidden to do it; "see thou do it not" is the command of the angel. This had happened once before[790] but John was apparently so overawed by the power, beauty, and brightness of the Heavenly Jerusalem and the thought of eternal fellowship with the Mighty Maker of all things that he forgot the previous lesson and had to learn it again.

The angel explains to John that, while they are on different levels, before God they are nevertheless fellow-workers in God's everlasting scheme of salvation. John was overpowered by it all.- so great, so grand, so dazzling, so wonderful. The blinding brightness of that marvelous city of God was more than John could stand ... and so he fell on his face and offered misdirected worship. He offered to the angel what properly belongs only to God – the utter devotion of a pure heart.

---

790 Rev 19:10

Verse 10

And he saith unto me,
Seal not up the words of the prophecy of this book;
for the time is at hand.

Jesus broke the seals of the little book he received from the throne of God and made the good news of salvation plain to see and understandable. Now John is told not to seal the words of the closing book of the Bible. The entire Bible is now unsealed. You can understand and need no human priest or scholar to enable you to know the message and meaning of the undying book of God. Read it as a sincere soul seeking to understand. Knock and it shall be opened to you; seek and you shall find; ask and you shall receive.[791] The book of revelation is unsealed and each one of us is invited to believe and to obey the Law of God; "if you will to do his will, you shall know" ... yes, you shall know."[792]

"For" (that is, here is why ... the reason is assigned) "the time is at hand."

The author of the Bible (God) does not reveal what is conditional and uncontrolled. "The Lord is not slack concerning his promise, as some count slackness; but is longsuffering to you-ward, not wishing that any should perish, but that all should come to repentance."[793] The promise made to Abraham;[794] and remembered by Peter;[795] is to every person in the entire world and will continue to be fulfilled while the world stands. It will not stand forever. It shall pass away.[796] Jesus is standing at the door[797] and at any moment could walk through the door signaling the end of time. He has been standing at the door ever since the destruction of Jerusalem in A. D.. 70 (over 2,000 years) and will continue to stand there until the thunderous voice of Almighty God pronounces the words "It is done"[798] and the trumpet of all ages peals out its warning and divine dismantlement brings the universe back to chaos and non-existence.

---

791 Matt 7:7; Luke 11:9
792 John 7:17
793 2 Peter 3:9
794 Gen 22:18; 26:4
795 Acts 2:39
796 Matt 24:35
797 Matt 24:33
798 Rev 16:10

It could happen at any moment and that is what the angel means when he says, "the time is at hand."

Therefore "watch ye."

Verse 11

He that is unrighteous, let him do unrighteousness still:
and he that is filthy, let him be made filthy still:
and he that is righteous, let him do righteousness still:
and he that is holy, let him be made holy still.

As long as the final trumpet of judgment is silent, men may change ... they may repent and come to God in obedience and walk with him in faith, but when the heaven around the earth is filled with the penetrating sound of that last trumpet there is no further opportunity to change. The door is closed and will not be opened again. In the parable of the ten virgins, Jesus concluded the teaching by saying, "And while they went away to buy, the bridegroom came; and they that were ready went in with him to the marriage feast: and the door was shut. Afterward came also the other virgins, saying, Lord, Lord, open to us. But he answered and said, Verily I say unto you, I know you not. Watch therefore, for ye know not the day nor the hour."[799]

The warning of the Lord is that at his second coming the time for repentance and confession is over ... the unrighteous and the filthy must be forever unrighteous and filthy and the righteous and the holy shall be eternally righteous and holy.

Unrighteousness is lawlessness and righteous is carefully keeping the law. Honoring the law of God is honoring God, or doing right according to the unsealed Law of God.

Verse 12

Behold, I come quickly;
and my reward is with me,
to render to each man according as his work is.

---

799 Matt 25:10-13

The warning flags have been flying ever since the holy of holies was defiled by the rude boots of Roman legionnaires and will continue to fly until all of the inhabitants of earth are startled by the ear-splitting blast of the trumpet of God, and hear his awesome voice.

Jesus brings with him his reward ... the word rendered reward (*misthos* Young's NT:3408) means, according to Young and Thayer, "a primary word; pay for services (literally or figuratively), good or bad: hire, reward, wages." Let all those who think works have nothing to do with salvation prayerfully ponder this passage. The word for "render" in this verse means "pay." The "pay" Jesus brings with him is "according as" each one's "work is."

Verses 13-14

I am the Alpha and the Omega,
the first and the last,
the beginning and the end.

Blessed are they that wash their robes,
that they may have the right to come to the tree of life,
and may enter in by the gates into the city.

Jesus is everything good and wholesome and wonderful. He is "the first and the last, the beginning and the end." He stands before us in the last chapter of the last book in the Bible with his hands outstretched and words of welcome on his lips for all those who have washed their robes in the blood of the Lamb to make them clean.

The gospel of salvation begins with a baby born in Bethlehem; and a host of angels announced to dumbfounded shepherds watching over their flocks that a king is born.

> *"And there were shepherds in the same country abiding in the field, and keeping watch by night over their flock. And an angel of the Lord stood by them, and the glory of the Lord shone round about them: and they were sore afraid. And the angel said unto them, Be not afraid; for behold, I bring you good tidings of great joy which shall be to all the people: for there is born to you this day in the city of David a Saviour, who is Christ the Lord."* [800]

---

800 Luke 2:8-11

Adding to the wonder "suddenly there was with the angel a multitude of the heavenly host praising God, and saying,

Glory to God in the highest,
And on earth peace among men in whom he is well pleased."

Jesus grew up in comparative obscurity and, when he was about 30, he went to John the baptist to be baptized of him in the river Jordan; when Jesus came up out of the water the Holy Spirit descended out of heaven in the form of a dove and coming upon Jesus; and a voice out of heaven said, "This my beloved son, in whom I am well pleased."[801]

John the forerunner of Jesus pointed him out and said of him, "Behold the Lamb of God, that taketh away the sin of the world!"[802]

Jesus was meek, gentle and kind and went about "doing good and healing all who were oppressed of the devil."[803] "Preaching good tidings of peace by Jesus Christ (He is Lord of all.)"[804]

At the end of a four year ministry Jesus came to Jerusalem, meek, and riding upon an ass and a colt the foal of an ass," signifying that he came to "cut off the chariot from Ephraim, and the horse from Jerusalem; and the battle bow shall be cut off; and he shall speak peace unto the nations: and his dominion shall be from sea to sea, and from the River to the ends of the earth."[805]

The tide of public opinion turned against him and evil men reviled him, spat upon him, struck him with their fists and sneered at the blindfolded Jesus, "Prophesy unto us, thou Christ, who was it that struck thee?" [806]

"He was led as a sheep to the slaughter; And as a lamb before his shearer is dumb, So he openeth not his mouth: In his humiliation his judgment was taken away: His generation who shall declare? For his life is taken from the earth."[807]

---

801 Matt 3:17
802 John 1:29, 36
803 Acts 10:36, 38
804 Acts 10:36
805 Zech 9:10
806 Luke 22:64
807 Acts 8:32-33

He died upon a cross to take away the sins of the world by his innocent blood.

At the end of the ages He will come again riding, not upon a lowly donkey but upon a magnificent warhorse at the head of an army of angels and an uncountable host of those who washed their robes in his blood and, though they were as scarlet, he made them white as snow. His name is "the word of God" and he is "King of kings and Lord of lords."

He stands before the golden foursquare city of God – the New (Heavenly) Jerusalem and its flashing brilliant beauty dazzles the eye of all who see it. God is its only temple; there is no sun, moon, or stars because the glory of God is its light and the Lamb of God is its lamp.

The Alpha and the Omega, the first and the last, the beginning and the end – the Lamb of God – says to them: *Blessed are they that wash their robes, that they may have the right to come to the tree of life, and may enter in by the gates into the city.*

Every foul and filthy thing is excluded from this eternal city of God so its goodness and purity may never be marred.

Verse 15

"Without are the dogs,
and the sorcerers,
and the fornicators,
and the murderers,
and the idolaters,
and every one that loveth and maketh a lie.

The beauty of the golden, sparkling, glittering city of God shall never be corrupt, or unclean, or impure; the ungodly and all unbelievers (in their rebellious disobedience) shall be shut out and will not be given access to the open gates of heaven. In that amazing city there is nothing untoward, coarse, morally crude, offensive, lewd or profane. Its unmarred beauty shall ever delight the eye of the beholder.

Verse 16

I Jesus have sent mine angel to testify unto you these things for the churches.
I am the root and the offspring of David,
the bright, the morning star.

Jesus adds his testimony to that of Jehovah, the Spirit, and the angels and he guarantees the truthfulness of all that is written in the Bible from the time Moses picked up his pen to the time John laid his pen down. Jesus is all he ever claimed to be or that his apostles, saints, and angels have said of him. Hallelujah!

Verse 17

And the Spirit and the bride say, Come.
And he that heareth, let him say, Come.
And he that is athirst, let him come:
he that will, let him take the water of life freely.

Speaking from the throne of God and of the Lamb the gracious invitation is extended, "Come unto me, all ye that labor and are heavy laden, and I will give you rest. Take my yoke upon you, and learn of me; for I am meek and lowly in heart: and ye shall find rest unto your souls."[808] And now is added the voice of the Spirit and the bride. The Spirit here must be the Spirit of Truth and he joins the Father and the Son in inviting hungry, thirsty, struggling sinners to come while there is yet time to the pleading Lamb and in faith to wash away their sins in baptism.[809] The voice of the bride of the Lamb – the church – is also lifted up to make a lovely melody of harmony with the voice of Jehovah, Jesus, and the Spirit in urging the lost to seek salvation.

The book closes with a solemn warning:

Verses 18-19

I testify unto every man that heareth the words of the prophecy of this book,
if any man shall add unto them,
God shall add unto him the plagues which are written in this book:

---

808 Matt 11:28-29
809 Mark 16:16; Acts 22:16

and if any man shall take away from the words of the book of this prophecy,
God shall take away his part from the tree of life,
and out of the holy city, which are written in this book.

The word of God and of the Lamb as revealed, protected and published by the Spirit of Truth, through the agency of humans, is sacred. To take from it, add to it, and alter it in any way is to incur the wrath of God and inherit the plagues that are written in the book.

Verse 20

He who testifieth these things saith,
Yea: I come quickly.
Amen: come, Lord Jesus.

Jesus comes suddenly, not in the sense of immediately, but in the sense of when least expected and the results of his coming will be swift.

The children of God on earth in the first century often prayed, "Come quickly, Lord Jesus." When we think of the incredible riches of the heaven of God and its loveliness, we, too, will say, "Come quickly, Lord Jesus." We pray for his soon coming. When we think of the toils of the road we must travel on earth and contrast that with the sublimity and soothing solace of heaven, we long to be there and instinctively say, Yea, come soon and let us taste more fully the power of the age to come.

Verse 21

The grace of the Lord Jesus be with the saints. Amen.